THE WORLD WONDER'D

WHAT REALLY HAPPENED OFF SAMAR

ROBERT LUNDGREN

𝒩IMBLE BOOKS LLC

NIMBLE BOOKS LLC

PUBLISHING INFORMATION

Nimble Books LLC

1521 Martha Avenue

Ann Arbor, MI, USA 48103

http://www.NimbleBooks.com

wfz@nimblebooks.com

+1.734-330-2593

Copyright 2014 Robert Lundgren

Printed in the United States of America

ISBN-13: 9781608880461

♾ The paper used in print versions of this publication meets the minimum requirements of the American National Standard for Information Sciences—Permanence of Paper for Printed Library Materials, ANSI Z39.48-1992. The paper is acid-free and lignin-free.

CONTENTS

Publishing Information..ii

List of Abbreviations...v

Aircraft Terminology...vii

Note on Sources viii

Acknowledgments ix

Introduction..1

Chapter 1. Surprise Encounter: 0645-0715 9

Chapter 2. The Run to the East: 0645-0715 43

Chapter 3. *Johnston* and *Hoel* Counterattack: 0715-0745 69

Chapter 4. Yamato Forced North: 0745-0815 101

Chapter 5. Gambier Bay's Plight: 0815-0845...131

Chapter 6. The Decision: 0845-0945 157

Chapter 7. The Divine Wind: 0945-Midnight 199

Chapter 8. Withdrawal: 26 October..241

Bibliography..259

Index..267

LIST OF ABBREVIATIONS

1YB - Kurita's 2nd Fleet

AA - Anti-aircraft

AP – Armor-piercing

ASP - Anti-submarine Patrol

CAP - Combat Air Patrol

Capt. - Captain

Cdr. - Commander

C.I.C. - Combat Information Center

C.O. - Commanding Officer

CVE - Escort Carrier

DE - Destroyer Escort

FS - Funnel Smoke

HC – High-capacity

(jg) - Junior Grade

LCI - Landing Craft, Infantry

Lt. - Lieutenant

OTC - Officer in Tactical Command

SAP - Semi-armor-piercing

TBS - Talk Between ships

TF - Task Force

TG - Task Group

TU - Task Unit

VC - Composite Squadron

VF - Fighter Squadron

VT - Torpedo Squadron

XO - Executive Officer (second in command)

AIRCRAFT TERMINOLOGY

American Aircraft:

B-24 Liberator - United States Army heavy bomber

F4F Wildcat - United States Navy fighter

F6F Hellcat - United States Navy fighter

FM-2 Wildcat - United States Navy fighter

SB2C Helldiver - United States Navy dive bomber

SBD Dauntless - United States Navy dive bomber

TBM Avenger - United States Navy torpedo bomber

TBM-1C Avenger - United States Navy torpedo bomber

Japanese Aircraft:

Betty - G4M1, Japanese medium bomber

Jake - E13A1, Japanese Navy floatplane

Jill - B6N1, Japanese Navy torpedo bomber

Judy - D4Y1, Japanese Navy dive bomber

Kate - B5N2, Japanese Navy torpedo bomber

Lily - Ki-48-II, Japanese Army medium bomber

Nick - KI-45, Japanese Army fighter

Oscar - KI-431A, Japanese Army fighter

Tony - KI-100-1, Japanese Army fighter

Val - D3A1, Japanese Navy dive bomber

Zeke - A6M2, Japanese Navy fighter, "Zero"

NIMBLE BOOKS LLC

NOTE ON SOURCES

The text of this account relies predominantly on official reports by the American and Japanese participants. These materials, along with the photographic originals, are held at the National Archives in College Park, MD. See the footnotes for specific citations as well as the supporting published sources.

ACKNOWLEDGMENTS

This book is dedicated to my late aunt, Ruth Ewing, who worked for BuShips during World War II. When I was ten years old, she gave me Walter Lord's book on the Battle of Midway, *Incredible Victory*. It caught my imagination and inspired my love of history and the U.S. Navy. She was very important in my life, and I promised her if this book ever became a reality, I would dedicate it to her. The World War II participants are almost gone; now it will be up to their descendants to remember their sacrifices and teach future generations.

Many other people helped make this book possible. My co-worker, Jeih-San Liow, Ph.D. Physicist for the Molecular Imaging Branch at the National Institute of Health in Bethesda, Maryland, took the time to teach me how to read the Japanese documents and reviewed my work. Without his help, the details derived from Japanese records would have been impossible for me to understand. Yoshifumi Urade, a professional translator from Tokyo, also helped. I am grateful to both men.

James Grace, author of *The Naval Battle of Guadalcanal: Night Action, 13 November 1942* (Naval Institute Press, 1999), provided peer review. Tony DiGiulian reviewed and helped edit three other articles that I wrote and placed them on his web site NavWeaps.com: www.NavWeaps.com. Thanks are extended to Vlad Petnicki and his web site on *Yamato*, www.battleshipyamato.com. He gave invaluable input and has been a great supporter of the project. I can't overlook the support of Richard Worth, author of *Fleets of World War II* (Nimble Books, 2014). My deepest appreciation and special thanks go to Nathan Okun, who works for NAVSEA and who has taught me more about physics, ballistics, and armor than anyone else. He had to be extremely patient with a student who knew nothing before we met. Byron Como of Baton Rouge, Louisiana also contributed to this work and his efforts are extremely appreciated. Brian D. Gray of Tell City, Indiana contributed to this book and I would like to thank him for his input. Of course there is also my family—my wife Dawn, daughter Cara, and son William—who stood with me as I put together this project over a period of ten years. I owe you my appreciation.

NIMBLE BOOKS LLC

INTRODUCTION

Figure 1: Vice Admiral Takeo Kurita

At 1714, 24 October 1944, Vice Admiral Takeo Kurita turned his fleet east and headed toward San Bernardino Strait to resume his mission. He would then pass down the east coast of the island of Samar on his way to Leyte Gulf where U.S. forces had established a beachhead to re-take the Philippine Islands. Japan's SHO plan already had fallen into disarray. Vice Admiral Ozawa's carrier force, intended to be detected by the Americans on 23 October to lure the U.S. Third Fleet north and away from the central Philippines, had been discovered only at 1540 the next day; this left over 250 U.S. carrier aircraft free to concentrate on Kurita's Second Fleet. They sank one of his battleships, *Musashi*. Several other ships including his flagship *Yamato* also suffered damage, and the heavy cruiser *Myoko* was forced to withdraw after a torpedo hit. This, added to the torpedoing of three heavy cruisers on 23 October in Palawan Passage, had reduced his heavy cruiser strength by 40%. To transit San Bernardino Strait his fleet would have to form a single column that would stretch thirteen miles, surely suicidal while under the threat of additional U.S. air attack, so he had turned west at 1600 until the air attacks had ceased. When his staff informed him that they had not heard from Admiral Toyoda in response to Kurita's message explaining his temporary withdraw he replied, "That's okay, let's go."[1] This maneuver may have saved his fleet, but it also broke any coordination with Vice Admiral Nishimura's and Vice Admiral Shima's task forces in attempting to break into Leyte Gulf from the south through Surigao Strait. This coordination was critical for the double penetration strategy to be effective. As the sun set, the men of Kurita's Second Fleet sailed toward their destiny, not knowing what to expect.

At the same time, on board the U.S. battleship *New Jersey*, Vice Admiral William F. Halsey reviewed the day's results from his strikes against Kurita's fleet. He was about to make the most important decision in his career. Three Japanese task forces (identified by the Americans simply as the Southern, Central, and Northern forces) were approaching Leyte Gulf simultaneously. Which of these enemy forces represented the greatest threat to the invasion, and how should he distribute his own forces to stop them? He had issued a preliminary order for concentrating his battleships into a single force, TF 34, capable of meeting Kurita in a gun duel; however, developments led him toward a different plan. In Halsey's own words,

> "Although the Center Force [Kurita's Second Fleet] continued to move forward, the Commander Third Fleet decided that this enemy force must be blindly obeying an Imperial command to do or die, but with battle efficiency greatly impaired by torpedo hits, bomb hits, top side damage, fires, and casualties. From long experience with the Japs, their blind adherence to plan, and their inability to readjust disturbed plans, the Commander Third Fleet had long ago adopted a policy of attacking first. The Southern [Nishimura's and Shima's task groups] and Center Forces had been under heavy and persistent air attack while proceeding through inland waters in daylight. Jap doggedness was admitted, and Commander Third Fleet recognized the possibility that Center Force might plod through San Bernardino Straits and on to attack Leyte forces, a la Guadalcanal, but Commander Third Fleet was convinced that the Center Force was so heavily damaged that it could not win a decision, while the possible maximum strength of the Northern Force as reported by CTF 38 constituted a fresh and powerful threat. It was decided that earliest possible attack on the powerful Northern [Ozawa's carrier] Force was essential for breaking up the enemy plan and retaining the initiative."[2]

---

[1] Ito, Masanori. *The End of the Japanese Navy*, W. W. Norton & Company, 1956, p 132.

[2] CTU 38 Action Report.

Figure 2: Vice Admiral William F. Halsey

He sent a message to Vice Admiral Thomas Kinkaid that all three groups of Third Fleet would attack the Northern Force at 2024. He felt this communication was sufficient to let Kinkaid know that the Third Fleet was no longer guarding San Bernardino Strait and that the Seventh Fleet had to adjust to the new tactical plan. At 2032, he ordered Vice Admiral Marc Mitscher to attack the Northern Force with all of the Third Fleet.[3]

Vice Admiral Thomas Kinkaid was in command of Seventh Fleet with the responsibility of direct support for General Douglas MacArthur's troops. Kinkaid sent out his battle plan at 1443, issued his orders to the Seventh Fleet, then informed Halsey, Nimitz, and Admiral King in Washington, D.C., of his decisions. His orders were as follows: "Prepare for night engagement. Enemy forces estimated two battleships, four heavy cruisers, four light cruisers, ten destroyers reported under attack by our carrier planes in eastern Sulu Sea 24 October. Enemy may arrive at Leyte Gulf tonight. Make all

---

[3] Ibid.

preparations for night engagement TG 77.3 assigned to CTG 77.2 as reinforcement. Station maximum number of PT boats lower Surigao Strait to remain south of 10° North during darkness."[4]

Figure 3: Vice Admiral Theodore S. Wilkinson, Vice Admiral Thomas C. Kinkaid, and Rear Admiral Daniel E. Barbey discuss their plans for KING II on 20 October 1944.

At 1512 on 24 October he had received Vice Admiral Halsey's preparatory battle order to form TF 34 around the U.S. fast battleships. He didn't notice that this was a preparatory order and assumed Halsey had formed TF 34 with the intent to guard San Bernardino Strait. Since Kinkaid believed that TF 34 had already been formed as a fourth group, when he received Halsey's message that three groups were going north under Halsey's command at 2024, he assumed that TF 34 was to remain and guard his northern flank. Kinkaid waited on his flagship *Wasatch* for the Japanese Southern Force to commit to battle. The conditions were now set that would lead to the Battle off Samar in which both sides would be caught by surprise.

This book presents a completely new analysis for the Battle off Samar using the primary documentation from both sides. Damage reports receive special attention as they leave a ballistic fingerprint regarding projectile size and the direction of the firing ship. Only three Japanese battleships fired dye-loaded projectiles, and the mixture of colors observed by the Americans will be

---

[4] CTU 77 Action Report.

4

fully explained. Review of the documents shows that the battle has never been recounted accurately and that prevalent myths—for example, that *Yamato* played no significant role in the battle—can be corrected.

Ship track charts for all six Japanese columns, every U.S. escort, and the U.S. carriers are provided, broken down into one-minute intervals. In this way every ship and its location can be seen in relation to all other ships at any given moment. The primary documentation provides bearings, ranges, salvos fired—clues literally pointing to the intended targets.

Photos from the National Archives have been placed within the book at the appropriate points, allowing the reader to witness the battle. In fact, all still photos came originally from film cameras; after the war, this film was cut up into still frames. However, since the photos were originally shot as film, it is possible to put them back in order as they were taken. Many photos within the book are shown in series so the reader can see before, during, and after certain events that were documented within the written reports.

ORDER OF BATTLE

Vice Admiral Thomas C. Kinkaid's Seventh Fleet included 738 ships, mostly amphibious warfare units, but the Bombardment and Fire Support Groups under Rear Admiral Jesse B. Oldendorf consisted of six battleships, four heavy cruisers, four light cruisers, and twenty-nine destroyers. Kinkaid's carrier groups operated under the command of Rear Admiral Thomas L. Sprague. Often referred to as "taffies," they bore the brunt of the fighting for the U.S. at Samar:

Task Unit 77.4.1 (Taffy 1): Rear Admiral Thomas Sprague

Escort carriers *Sangamon, Suwannee, Santee, Petrof Bay*

Destroyers *McCord, Hazelwood, Trathen, Richard S. Bull, Eversole, Richard M. Rowell, Coolbaugh*

Task Unit 77.4.2 (Taffy 2): Rear Admiral Felix B. Stump

Escort carriers *Natoma Bay, Manila Bay, Marcus Island, Savo, Ommaney Bay, Kadashan Bay*

Destroyers *Haggard, Hailey, Franks*

Destroyer escorts *Oberrender, Abercrombie, Richard W. Suesens, Walter C. Wann, Le Ray Wilson*

Task Unit 77.4.3 (Taffy 3): Rear Admiral Clifton A. F. Sprague[5]

Escort carriers *Fanshaw Bay, Kalinin Bay, White Plains, St. Lo, Kitkun Bay, Gambier Bay*

---

[5] Clifton Sprague and Thomas Sprague were not related, although both attended the U.S. Naval Academy and graduated in the same year.

Destroyers *Hoel, Heermann, Johnston*

Destroyer escorts *Dennis, Samuel B. Roberts, John C. Butler, Raymond*

Halsey placed his flag on board the battleship *New Jersey*. Third Fleet had its main combat strength in the four task groups of Task Force 38 (nominally under the tactical command of Vice Admiral Marc Mitscher).

Task Group 38.1: Vice Admiral John S. McCain

Three fleet carriers

Two light carriers

Four heavy cruisers

Two anti-aircraft light cruisers

Fourteen destroyers

Task Group 38.2: Rear Admiral Gerald F. Bogan

One fleet carrier

Two light carriers

Two battleships

Three light cruisers

Sixteen destroyers

Task Group 38.3: Rear Admiral Frederick C. Sherman

Two fleet carriers

Two light carriers

Four battleships

Three light cruisers

One anti-aircraft light cruiser

Seventeen destroyers

Task Group 38.4: Rear Admiral Ralph E. Davison

Two fleet carriers

Two light carriers

One heavy cruiser

One light cruiser

Eleven destroyers

Halsey detached TG 38.1 to head to Ulithi to refuel and rearm, so this group was not immediately available.

The multi-pronged Japanese attack force included a southern component under Vice Admirals Shoji Nishimura and Kiyohide Shima totaling two battleships, three heavy cruisers, one light cruiser, and eight destroyers; Vice Admiral Jisaburo Ozawa's northern force of four aircraft carriers, two hybrid battleships, two light cruisers, and eight destroyers; and in the center, Admiral Kurita's Second Fleet:

Battleship Division 1: *Yamato, Nagato*

Battleship Division 3: *Kongo, Haruna*

Cruiser Division 4 and 5: heavy cruisers *Chokai, Haguro*

Cruiser Division 7: heavy cruisers *Suzuya, Kumano, Tone, Chikuma*

Second Squadron: light cruiser *Noshiro*, destroyers *Shimakaze, Hayashimo, Akishimo, Kishinami, Okinami, Naganami, Fujinami, Hamanami*

Tenth Squadron: light cruiser *Yahagi*, destroyers *Kiyoshimo, Nowaki, Urakaze, Isokaze, Hamakaze, Yukikaze.*

The Japanese also had significant land-based air power, including Vice Admiral Takijiro Onishi's 110 planes and Vice Admiral Shigeru Fukudome's 250, all based at Luzon. Onishi's desperation for a weapon to stop the U.S. armada led him to organize the first kamikaze unit of the war. He approached Fukudome and requested he adopt such tactics as well, but Fukudome refused. Only thirteen pilots were slated for this kamikaze attack, but they would play an important role in the Battle off Samar, and their success would alter Japanese naval strategy for the remainder of the war.

NIMBLE BOOKS LLC

CHAPTER 1. SURPRISE ENCOUNTER: 0645-0715

ON BOARD THE *YAMATO*

Kurita had received a message from Nishimura late in the afternoon of 24 October that stated, "Our force will storm the center of the eastern shore of Leyte Gulf at 0400 on 25 October." Coordination with Nishimura and Shima was now impossible. Kurita's staff had revised their schedule and dispatched a message to all other forces at 2145. It read, "Main Force of First Diversion Attack Force plan to pass through San Bernardino Strait at 0100 on 25 October, proceed southward down east coast of Samar and arrive at Leyte Gulf at 1100 on 25 October. Third Section will break into Leyte Gulf as scheduled and then join forces with Main Force about ten miles northeast of Suluan Island at 0900 on 25 October."[6]

Then at 2213, he sent an additional message to reassure Combined Fleet Headquarters of his intent:"We were subjected to repeated enemy carrier-based plane attack all day long on the 24th resulting in considerable damage to us. Powerful enemy task forces to the east and to the north of Legaspi are exceedingly active. Main Force of First Diversion Attack Force, chancing annihilation, is determined to break through to Tacloban anchorage [on Leyte] to destroy the enemy. The air force is ordered to carry out full strength attack against task forces."[7]

Rear Admiral Nobuei Morishita was the captain of the *Yamato*, and it was his duty to keep the *Yamato* safe. He received reports for damage suffered by his ship during the day of 24 October. One medium-sized bomb hit her at frame 70 on the port beam. The blast blew out the side shell between frames 54-78 creating a hole 46 feet long by 16 feet wide between the tween and lower deck just above the waterline. Consequently, twenty heavy-fuel oil tanks were flooded, and 710 tons of water flooded void tanks. Another medium-sized bomb struck the forecastle deck at frame 33, made a 1.2-foot hole, passed through the upper deck making a 1.5-foot hole, continued to the tween deck where it made a 3-foot hole, and exploded below the waterline. The bomb blew two holes in the outer shell, one 3 feet by 6 feet and the other 6 feet by 12 feet on the port side. An officer's bedroom on the upper deck was moderately damaged, the dental operating room on tween deck was

---

[6] The air attacks suffered on 24 October broke the time table set between the Japanese Central and Southern forces. A coordinated attack was vital if the strategy as envisioned was to succeed. The double penetration strategy was based on Julian Corbett's philosophy of division. Kurita had hoped that the majority of U.S. forces would be lured north by 23 October and what remained would concentrate on his larger force leaving Nishimura to penetrate the Gulf with little opposition. None of this had occurred, and now U.S. forces could focus on the southern pincer, and Kurita was not in position to help. Corbett, Julian S. *Some Principles of Maritime Strategy*, pp 131, 134. Bates, Richard W. *The Battle for Leyte Gulf, 20 October to 23 October Strategic and Tactical Analysis, Vol. III*, Naval War College, 1957, p 160.

[7] Combined Fleet Headquarters Detailed Action Report.

seriously damaged, and the forward windlass room was flooded. Warehouse compartment number seven was flooded, and the ship took on 3,000 tons of water. In addition, the hull indicated a variation in heel of 2°- 3° to port and in trim of 10 feet down by the bow. Maximum speed fell from twenty-seven to twenty-six knots. Minor damage from fragments was found in the boat garage; the Warrant Officer Room at port side frames 19-21 suffered fragment damage. The 7th and 5th AA guns were disabled, there were nine broken communication circuits, and the left catapult had an electrical wire broken. Twenty-four aerial wires were down, and the port side boat hoist was unusable.[8]

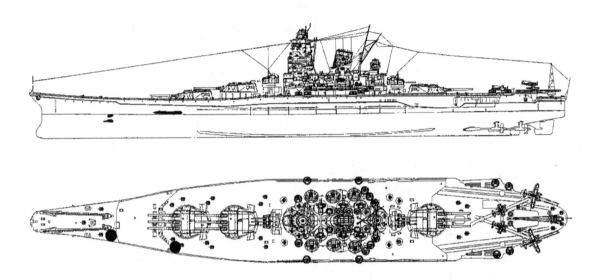

Figure 4. The *Yamato's* battle damage October 24.

Kurita also received damage reports for the rest of his fleet. Rear Admiral Yuji Kobe, commanding the battleship *Nagato*, reported two bomb hits amidships. The first bomb struck the boat deck just aft of the main pagoda superstructure, penetrated this deck, and exploded next to the port side No. 4 casemate gun. Ready ammunition for casemate guns No. 2, No. 4, and No. 6 exploded within the No. 2 crew compartment and disabled all three casemate guns on the forecastle deck. The air intake to No.1 boiler room was damaged, which forced the No. 1 boiler room to shut down and reduced her top speed to twenty-two knots. Due to the secondary explosions, fire spread to the deck below, disabling the No. 4 casemate gun on the upper deck level as well. Fragments disabled the starboard side Type 91 director for her starboard 5-inch guns.

The second bomb entered the ship's galley through the sky window, detonated in the rear of the command communications room, and killed two officers and twelve men, with six more seriously

---

[8] *Yamato* Detailed Action Report.

injured. The machine shop, laundry room, and passageway were destroyed. In total, three officers and thirty men were killed, another three officers and thirty-three men wounded. She regained use of her No. 1 boiler room later that evening and her top speed returned to twenty-five knots. Near-miss bombs had opened approximately seven hundred fragment holes in her hull between frames 24 and 25. These were plugged by the crew over the next forty-eight hours.[9]

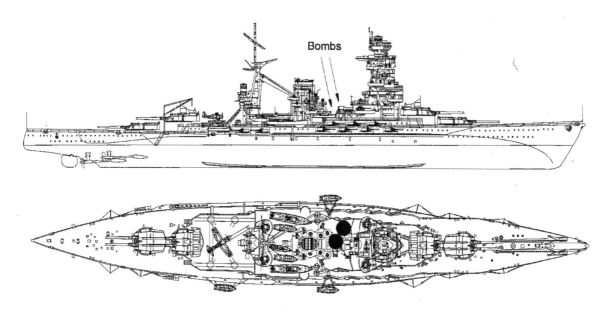

Figure 5. The *Nagato's* battle damage October 24.

The *Kongo*, *Haruna*, *Haguro*, *Noshiro*, and *Yahagi* didn't suffer any direct hits, only near misses and strafing attacks that caused minor damage. There were significant casualties to the AA crews on the *Yahagi*. The heavy cruiser *Tone* suffered three bomb hits on 24 October. The first hit the captain's sea cabin, and the second hit the forward 5-inch gun shell supply room on the starboard side. This started a fire that was rapidly extinguished. The third bomb penetrated to the middle deck above the No. 2 boiler room but failed to detonate.

As the *Yamato* neared San Bernardino Strait, the time had come to find out if Vice Admiral Ozawa had successfully lured the U.S. armada north. Vice Admiral Kurita's staff and crew were not optimistic; they fully expected to have to fight their way out. Some felt the greatest threat would come from submarines, while others anticipated a surface battle. The night was clear, and Kurita could determine the fleet's position visually while it traversed the narrow passage. Part of the crew rested while other crew members manned battle stations in multiple shifts, and heavy fatigue affected every man. Lookouts scanned the horizon while her search radar continued to seek out

[9] *Nagato* Detailed Action Report.

targets, but no contacts were ever made. At 0037 on 25 October the *Yamato* sailed past the southern tip of Luzon and into the Philippine Sea with not a single American ship in sight.[10] Did Ozawa succeed, or were the Americans waiting for daylight?

Vice Admiral Ugaki expressed his fear in his diary. "But what I feared was that the enemy which detected our movements continuously tonight would concentrate their air attacks upon us at a point over one hundred miles off the coast after dawn came. Unless we get enough cooperation from our base air forces, we can do nothing about it, and all of our fighting strength will be reduced to nothing at the end." Therefore, it was Ugaki who recommended a night search pattern once the fleet exited San Bernardino Strait.[11]

Kurita directed his fleet to the east until 0300 and then turned southeast towards Leyte Gulf. He deployed his forces in a night search formation that covered a thirteen-mile front of six columns. He was blind with no usable information on the location or size of the American navy's disposition. He spread out and hoped he could make contact, but found nothing in the area.

When Kurita's fleet had left Brunei on 22 October he had forty-four aircraft distributed amongst his ships. Kurita's seaplanes were placed under the command of the 901st air group at San Jose at the southern end of Mindoro. Twelve aircraft were transferred each day to San Jose beginning 22 October, and five were destroyed when the battleship *Musashi* was lost. As dawn approached on 25 October, all that remained were *Yamato*'s No. 1 and No. 2 planes plus the *Nagato*'s No. 1 plane, which had been transferred to the *Yamato* before the fleet had sailed from Brunei. Kurita depended on intelligence from land-based aircraft and so far had received little information.

In fact the only intelligence report on U.S. shipping was provided by a scout plane from Vice Admiral Nishimura's fleet to the south received at 1400 on 24 October. The plane reported that there were four battleships, two cruisers, and two destroyers to the north of the bay, and four destroyers and some torpedo boats near Surigao Strait. There were eighty transports off the landing area. In addition there were twelve carriers and ten destroyers in position forty miles southeast of Leyte. This report would be the only intelligence that either Nishimura or Kurita would receive about U.S. ships located at Leyte Gulf for the entire battle.

He had not heard from Vice Admiral Ozawa, and this was due to the fact that Ozawa's flagship the carrier *Zuikaku* had a bad radio transmitter. Ozawa had been sending messages totally unaware that they were not being received. He had not received any reassurance from the First or Second Air Fleets but without their support his fleet remained particularly vulnerable to air attacks. After Kurita's ordeal in what would become known as the Battle of Sibuyan Sea on 24 October, it was the

---

[10] *Yamato* Detailed Action Report.

[11] Ugaki, Matome. *Fading Victory: The Diary of Admiral Matome Ugaki 1941-1945.* University of Pittsburgh Press, 1991, p 491.

ability of U.S. forces to strike through the air that weighed most heavily on Kurita and his staff, for his fleet had no ability to counter such an attack. U.S. forces never had to engage in a surface battle but could whittle away at his force from over the horizon, outranging him indefinitely until his force was crippled.

As time passed, Kurita waited for word from Nishimura reporting any success of the southern pincer. He had received a message at 0230 on 25 October that Nishimura was entering Surigao Strait and at 0335 he had sighted three enemy ships. Nothing had been heard after this for over two hours. On the *Yamato's* bridge, the staff remained hopeful that good news would arrive soon. Then at 0532 a message from Vice Admiral Shima notified them that both the battleships *Fuso* and the *Yamashiro* had been destroyed, the heavy cruiser *Mogami* was afire, and he was retiring. His gamble to achieve a double penetration into Leyte Gulf had failed. Kurita didn't believe the U.S. fleet had been lured away. Instead, he suspected the Americans had pulled back to entrap his fleet after daylight.

ON BOARD THE *WASATCH*

Since before 0200, Vice Admiral Kinkaid's focus remained on developments to the south as he heard reports of the Japanese approach to Surigao Strait, and later, the successful actions of Oldendorf's battle force. All seemed well until Kinkaid realized he had never received confirmation from Halsey regarding TF 34. At 0412, he sent dispatch No. 241912 to Halsey, "Is TF 34 guarding San Bernardino Strait?" Events were winding down in Surigao Strait. Rear Admiral Oldendorf sent Kinkaid a message at 0420 that suggested he ready air attacks to engage Japanese units heading south and prevent their escape.

Figure 6: The Battle of Surigao Strait as photographed from the battleship *Pennsylvania*.

ON BOARD THE *SANGAMON*

Rear Admiral Thomas Sprague, in command of Taffy 1, in accordance to the directions of Vice Admiral Kinkaid, launched a strike against the remnants of the enemy fleet in Surigao Strait. This strike consisted of eleven torpedo bombers escorted by seventeen fighters with 500-lb SAP bombs at 0545.

He had directed Rear Admiral Felix Stump of Taffy 2 to search Surigao Strait and Mindanao Sea from sunrise until 0900, through a sector from 340° to 030° for 135 miles from Suluan Island as a point of origin. At the same time, TG 77.4 was directed to keep strike groups loaded with torpedoes and SAP bombs.[12]

ON BOARD THE *FANSHAW BAY*

Morning on 25 October began in a routine fashion aboard the *Fanshaw Bay*. At 0525, Rear Admiral Clifton Sprague had the task force set at condition 1, material condition A, for morning alert. Eight fighter planes had been launched for local fighter patrol at 0540, and one torpedo bomber was launched to observe target area over Leyte Gulf. At 0545, the task force changed course to 350° true and began zigzagging in accordance with plan 25 USF-10(A).[13] Seven more fighters were launched at 0615 to report to Commander Support Aircraft Central Philippines for strike assignment. By 0637, everything changed. CIC reported intercepting Japanese voice conversations on Inter Fighter Director net, 37.6 megacycles, strength 5, and modulation 5. Could this be an attempt at jamming? The Japanese had used this method in an attempt to disrupt communications in the past. No Japanese ships could be that close, could they?[14]

ON BOARD THE *LEXINGTON*

Vice Admiral Marc Mitscher's last report of the Japanese Northern force's location was at 0235. The pilot reported that this Japanese force was approximately 130 miles to the northeast of Luzon; this was an error, and the distance was approximately 250 miles between Third Fleet and Ozawa's carriers. The pilot did give their correct course of 150°. At 0240 on 25 October, TF 34 was formed with six modern U.S. battleships, seven heavy cruisers, and seventeen destroyers under the command of Vice Admiral Willis Lee. This task force was placed ten miles ahead of the carrier groups. At 0430, Mitscher ordered the first strikes loaded, prepared to launch at dawn in the event the Japanese maintained their course overnight. It didn't happen. The Japanese had turned to the

---

[12] CTU 77.4 Action Report.

[13] 25 USF-10(A) is an example of special instructions the U.S. Navy had developed entitled PAC-10. This allowed different task force commanders to join at sea on short notice for concerted action against the enemy without exchanging a mass of special instructions.

[14] *Fanshaw Bay* Action Report.

north instead of continuing south. Mitscher launched search planes at 0540 to determine where the Northern Force had gone. He didn't wait for the Japanese fleet to be found; he launched the first strike by 0600. It would be ready to strike when search planes located the enemy.[15]

At 0710 on 25 October, Mitscher received a contact report locating the Japanese northern force. It was 145 miles distant, but because his first strike was already up in the air these aircraft were only seventy to ninety miles to the south when the contact report was received. The search planes maintained contact and radioed in the Japanese position, vectoring in the first strike so that they would reach their target within an hour. Immediately the Third Fleet readied a second strike now that the quarry had been found. The Third Fleet's course was adjusted to close, but a simultaneous attack by surface forces and carrier aircraft was now impossible. Air power had to strike first and cripple as many Japanese ships as they could, which would allow the battleships to catch them in a way similar to an operation that Admiral Spruance had completed off Truk in February. This time the *New Jersey* would seek out four carriers and two battleships whereas at Truk only a single light cruiser and two destroyers as her primary targets.[16]

ON BOARD THE *YAMATO*

Daylight approached, and Kurita ordered his fleet to regroup and form a circle pattern. They expected air attacks similar to those received on 24 October to resume. The sun rose at 0614 and revealed a grey overcast day. The wind from the east-northeast at approximately eight knots produced slight, low swells. Occasional rain squalls lowered the ceiling to 1,000 feet, and surface visibility was approximately 41,648 yards.

At 0623, the *Yamato*'s search radar detected enemy planes bearing 130°, distance twenty-seven miles. Kurita ordered a change in course at 0640 to 170° true. His fleet was eighty miles from his objective, the Island of Suluan which marked the northern entrance to Leyte Gulf. The six search columns had closed ranks, but the circle pattern hadn't been established. The Fifth Cruiser Squadron (the *Haguro* and the *Chokai*) was on the fleet's far left flank. The *Yahagi* with the Tenth Destroyer Division made up the next column westward. The Third Battleship Division (the *Kongo* and the *Haruna*) made up the next column followed by the Seventh Cruiser Squadron (the *Kumano, Suzuya, Chikuma*, and the *Tone*). These four columns were on the flagship's port side. The First Battleship Division was now the *Yamato* and the *Nagato*, making up the fifth column. The *Noshiro* with the Second Destroyer Division, the sixth column, were the only ships to the *Yamato*'s starboard side.

---

[15] CTU 38, Action Report.

[16] CTU 38.3 Action Report and the *Lexington* Action Report.

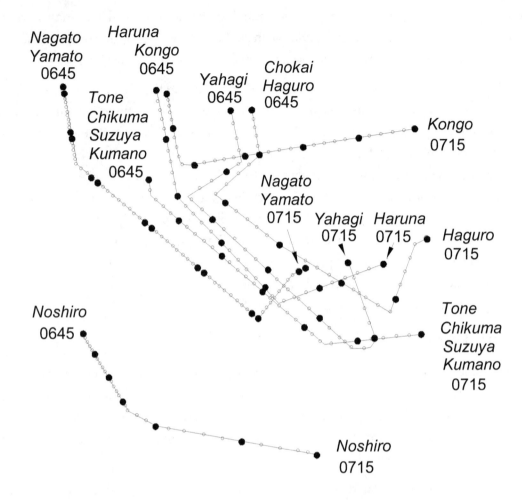

Figure 7: Track chart plotted directly from Japanese Detailed Action Reports for the *Haguro, Yahagi, Kongo, Haruna, Yamato, Nagato, Suzuya, Tone,* and *Noshiro*. In the Yamato's action report, the *Yahagi* was to the extreme port side not the *Haguro*. Both columns maneuvered at the beginning of the battle almost identically, and the plotted courses match range and bearings to targets later in the battle. Based on the distances and bearings provided in the individual action reports, this disposition appears more accurate.

At 0645, the *Yamato*'s lookouts sighted seven ship masts bearing 115°, distance 40,552 yards. Seconds later, two Grumman-type torpedo bombers were sighted approaching the force. Orders were issued to immediately stand by for maximum battle speed. The *Yamato*'s AA guns opened fire on the two American planes at 0646, but checked fire a minute later. By 0650, it was determined that the sighted masts were those of an enemy task force. Lookouts reported three carriers, three cruisers, and two destroyers.[17]

---

[17] *Yamato* Detailed Action Report.

As the Americans were discovered, Kurita's staff attempted to identify which group they had encountered, using intelligence based on POW interrogation from US pilots captured after their attack on Formosa on 11-15 October 1944. The Japanese report stated,

> *"The first group: four carriers, three cruisers, and eleven to twelve destroyers. The second group: four carriers, two battleships (Iowa class and New Jersey class), five cruisers, and sixteen destroyers. The third group: four carriers, five battleships (two South Dakota class, one Iowa class, two North Carolina class), two cruisers, and thirteen destroyers. The fourth group: three to four carriers, one or two battleships (one South Dakota class and one North Carolina class), two or three cruisers, and twelve to fifteen destroyers. Total strength: sixteen carriers, eight to nine battleships, twelve to thirteen cruisers, forty-five destroyers. In addition, there were five replacement carriers to the above in TF 38 and the following eight battleships which are directly attached to the Third Fleet: Colorado, Tennessee, California, Nevada, New Mexico, Pennsylvania, Texas, and Arkansas."[18]*

This information in hindsight fundamentally described Third Fleet's formations, and this is what Kurita's staff believed represented the U.S. Fleet in its entirety. He had no intelligence that the U.S. Navy had split into the Third and Seventh Fleets and still believed the U.S. command structure maintained a unified command under Vice Admiral Halsey. This information was also an admission by Admiral Toyoda that the reported success of sinking several U.S. carriers during the Battle of Formosa had been false.

What Kurita and his staff did not know is the U.S. had begun in June to create additional carrier groups centered on escort carriers. The five replacement carriers may be a reference to these, but the information Kurita was provided did not specify class or type. His staff had no photos or intelligence of the escort carrier, and from a distance they believed they had run into one of the Third Fleet's carrier battle groups, confirming their perception that the U.S. fleet had not been diverted north. This further confirmed in the minds of his staff that the U.S. carriers had pulled back and had planned to wage a war of attrition during the day by attacking with their aircraft and reducing the effectiveness of his surface ships. Once crippled the Americans would surround and then annihilate his force. Running into one of these carrier groups had just been a matter of pure luck.

Kurita recorded his assessment of the situation at the opening of the battle, "The enemy was encountered at a time when neither he nor we expected it. Employing every trick known to him, the enemy would try to put distance between him and us, so that he could carry out a one-sided air action against us. So that we could take advantage of this heaven-sent opportunity, we should take

---

[18] Bates, *Leyte Gulf*, pp 170-172.

after the enemy in pursuit formation and at top speed. We planned first to cripple the carriers' ability to have planes take off and land, and then to mow down the entire task force."[19]

Rear Admiral Koyanagi, Kurita's chief of staff, gave more details about the mood on the *Yamato*'s bridge at that moment in a postwar interview. "This was indeed a miracle. Think of a surface fleet coming up on an enemy carrier group. Nothing is more vulnerable than an aircraft carrier in a surface engagement, so the enemy lost no time in retiring. In a pursuit the only essential is to close the gap as rapidly as possible and concentrate fire upon the enemy. Kurita didn't therefore adopt the usual deployment procedures but instantly ordered General Attack. This order instructed each ship captain to give chase and conduct his engagement independently with speed of action as the primary concern."[20]

Kurita didn't have the wind or weather to his advantage, and the Americans quickly seized it. Kurita's only ability to stop the carriers from launching their planes was to damage their flight decks quickly. The only weapon immediately available would be the main batteries of the battleships and heavy cruisers because the light cruisers and destroyers had to close considerable distance before they could engage. Instead of a direct charge at the Americans by individual ships, the six columns initially got in each other's way, so each squadron stayed together with the exception of the *Kongo* and the *Haruna*. Ugaki commented on this point, "We had always thought about how to cope with such an occasion as this, but each unit seemed very slow in starting actions due to uncertainty about the enemy condition."[21]

PILOTS OF VC-20, THE *KADASHAW BAY*

At 0546, the *Kadashaw Bay* of Taffy 2 launched Ensign Hans Jensen of VC-20 on a routine ASP (anti-submarine patrol) for the northwest sector. At 0555, Jensen and his radioman D. G. Lehman noted blips on their radar screen thirty-five miles away and decided to investigate although this took him away from his assigned sector. As he came through the low clouds at 0645, he encountered the Japanese fleet and immediately reported four battleships, eight heavy cruisers, and a number of destroyers twenty-five miles from Taffy 3 with a speed of twenty knots. Anti-aircraft fire greeted his arrival, and he climbed up into the clouds.

He saw the Japanese fleet open fire on Taffy 3. He picked out what he believed to be a *Mogami*-class cruiser and turned his plane over into a dive at 2,500 feet, then released his three depth charges at 1,200 feet. His turret gunner K. M. Soter strafed the decks as the depth charges exploded off the ship's starboard quarter throwing water over the decks. Anti-aircraft fire was intense, and several

[19] Combined Fleet Headquarters Detailed Action Report.

[20] Evans, David C. (ed.) *The Japanese Navy in World War II*. Naval Institute Press, 1969, pp 355-384.

[21] Ugaki, *Fading Victory*, p 492.

bursts shook his plane violently as he reached the cloud layer to recover from his attack. He couldn't see any damage to his target.[22]

PILOTS OF VC-65, THE *ST. LO*

At 0530, the *St. Lo* launched two TBM-1C aircraft under command of Lt. Warden and Lt. (jg) Calan for ASP for the Leyte area and four TBM-1C aircraft including Ensign Brooks, Lt. Van Brunt, Lt. MacBride, and Lt. Fields for local ASP over Taffy 3.

Brooks was flying sector 4, 270° to 000° true, when he emerged from the clouds at 0647 to find the Japanese fleet below him. He immediately made a contact report to Taffy 3 that the enemy was twenty or thirty miles from his own task force. Brooks circled and sent amplifying reports that the enemy course was 120°, speed 12/15 knots and consisted of four battleships, four heavy cruisers, two light cruisers, and ten or twelve destroyers. The Japanese ships opened fire on him, so Brooks climbed to 9,000 feet and looked to drop his depth charges on a target. At approximately 0700, he made a glide-bombing attack on what he believed to be a heavy cruiser and released his three depth charges at 5,000 feet. His depth charges landed alongside the cruiser, but no damage was observed. He saw no other planes in the area at the time of his attack.[23]

ON BOARD THE *FANSHAW BAY*

For Clifton Sprague, the situation became clear when, at 0640, his lookouts spotted anti-aircraft fire bearing 300°, distance twenty miles; and then a minute later, CIC reported unidentified surface craft bearing 292°, distance nineteen miles. He ordered TU 77.4.3 to change course to 220° true.[24]

Clifton Sprague later recalled, "A half-hour after sunrise—0645, to be exact—I received a radio message from one of our planes on local anti-submarine patrol, and I remember that I was very much annoyed. In plain language, the message ran something like this:

"'Enemy surface force of 4 battleships, 7 cruisers, and 11 destroyers sighted 20 miles northwest of your task group and closing in on you at 30 knots.'

"'Now, there's some screwy young aviator reporting part of our own forces,' was the disgusted thought that ran through my mind; 'undoubtedly he's just spotted some of Admiral Halsey's fast battleships.'

"'Air Plot, tell him to check his identification,' I yelled into the squawk box.

---

[22] Composite Squadron VC-20, the *Kadashan Bay*, Ensign Hans Jensen.

[23] Composite Squadron VC-65, *St. Lo*, Ensign William C. Brooks. The ship he dropped his depth charges on may have been the *Kongo*, which reported being attacked by aircraft at 0700.

[24] *Fanshaw Bay* Action Report.

"While I waited for a reply, I went back to worrying about the schedule of strikes and patrols we had to send Commander Support Aircraft that day. It would keep my deck crews on the jump until sundown, just fueling, arming, and launching the regular combat air patrols, antisubmarine patrols, and photo, search, and support missions—let alone the special strikes he was sure to ask for. Each day got tougher than the one before, and this was our eighth on Philippine air support for my task group of 6 baby flattops, 3 destroyers, and 4 destroyer escorts operating that morning to the north of the southern tip of Samar Island.

"About 100 miles to the south and west of us, as a ship would cruise, the shore was black with thousands of men establishing a beach-head on Leyte, and their ships were thick in the harbor. Forty miles to the west of us, where the morning light was just beginning to penetrate, stood the vague, gray outlines of the Samar Mountains, now blacked out all over the northwest by the inky clouds of a heavy squall.

"This was the picture…at 0648 on October 25 (1944) as I got my reply from the pilot who had sent that contact report. 'Identification of enemy force confirmed,' he radioed. 'Ships have pagoda masts.'

"Pagoda masts! Well, that was the clincher for me, and I knew I was on the spot. But if there still remained the slightest doubt that this was an enemy fleet, it was dissolved a moment later when a thick pattern of anti-aircraft puffs speckled the sky above the squall to the northwest, making it hot for the flier who had smelled them out. And as it turned out, he was giving them hell too! Pushing over into the flak of the whole Japanese fleet, this plucky lad, Ensign William C. Brooks, USNR, of Pasadena, California, dive-bombed a cruiser with his antisubmarine loading—two measly depth charges. I blush to recall any unkind thoughts I ever had about him."[25]

ON BOARD THE *YAMATO*

By 0652, Kurita informed the rest of his fleet that the enemy carriers were launching planes. The *Yamato* increased speed to twenty-six knots. Lookouts reported a minute later that the enemy aircraft carriers had turned to port. Kurita ordered a course change to 130° to pursue.[26]

The Americans initially were on a course of 220° when sighted by *Yamato* but turned to the east and by 0650 had settled on a new course of 090° true. At 0650, the Fifth Cruiser squadron led by the *Haguro* and the *Yahagi* with the Tenth Destroyer Squadron turned to a new course of 230° true. They maintained this course for four minutes and then turned back onto a course of 130°, but the result was they cut in front of the Third Battleship Division. The *Kongo* was forced to turn to the east to avoid any possible collision and for the remainder of the battle acted independently. These

---

[25] Sprague, Clifton. "They Had Us on the Ropes." *American Magazine*, April 1945.

[26] *Yamato* Detailed Action Report.

maneuvers broke up the Third Battleship Division as the *Haruna* maintained her position close to the *Yamato*. The principle of cohesion was not in evidence. Without clear direction, the individual commanders hesitated and mimicked the movements of the *Yamato,* and formed a loose battle line of several different columns.[27]

Tradition and protocol remained important within the Imperial Japanese Navy, and while the ships prepared for battle they waited for their flagship to give them permission to open fire. The *Yamato* was the flagship and had the honor of the very first salvo. At 0659, Kurita gave the order, "Ready for surface battle"; the *Yamato* opened fire from her forward 6.1-inch guns, quickly followed by both forward main battery turrets. The range was an estimated distance of 34,524 yards. The first salvo for the main battery was loaded with Type 3 AA shells because Kurita believed the fleet would come under air attack before they reached Leyte Gulf. The 6.1-inch/55-caliber gun's maximum range was 31,784 yards but due to tradition *Yamato* opened fire despite the range. At 0700, after this first salvo, Kurita gave the order to the rest of his fleet, "Transmit order to battleship and cruiser divisions to open fire and attack." Efforts to switch ammunition from Type 3 projectiles to Type 1 AP were then begun. The *Yamato*'s Type 1 projectiles had no dye color, so her shell splashes appeared white.[28]

ON BOARD THE *NAGATO*

Rear Admiral Kobe in command of the battleship *Nagato* gave orders to prepare for surface battle, to engage the carriers to port with both main and secondary weapons and to hoist the battle flags at 0654. At 0700, he ordered speed increased to twenty-five knots. The *Nagato*'s Type 1 AP projectiles were loaded with pink dye that was described as a brilliant pink color which stood out the best for the dye-loaded projectiles.[29]

ON BOARD THE *HARUNA*

At 0655, Rear Admiral Shigenaga on board the *Haruna* received the message, "Order from the *Kongo*, our target is carrier group bearing 120° use gunnery method B."[30] Shigenaga issued an order to open fire from main guns tracking target on point bearing 308° at 0701, but the time when her

---

[27] Opening maneuvers were taken from individual action reports for the *Haguro, Yahagi, Kongo, Haruna, Yamato, Nagato, Suzuya, Tone,* and *Noshiro.*

[28] *Yamato* Detailed Action Report. Kaigun Hôjutsu-shi [The History of Naval Gunnery]. Kaigun Hôjutsu-shi Kankôkai, 1975 list the colors used by the Japanese Battleships.

[29] *Nagato* Detailed Action Report. Only Japanese battleship-caliber shells and specifically the Type 1 AP projectiles were fitted with dye loads. The 8-inch and 6.1-inch Type 91 AP projectiles never had dye loads. Only three ships at Samar had dye-loaded projectiles: *Nagato, Kongo,* and *Haruna.* The Japanese Type 91 battleship-caliber shells which had no dye load were replaced with the Type 1 projectile shortly before the war began in 1941. Bureau of Ordnance OP 1667, Japanese Explosive Ordnance.

[30] Gunnery method B was instructions to fire half salvos vs. full salvos.

first shells were fired wasn't directly recorded.[31] She fired from her forward turrets only. Her Type 1 AP projectiles were loaded with yellow dye; however, it was a greenish-yellow so that her shell splashes were described as either yellow or green.[32]

ON BOARD THE *KONGO*

By 0659, the *Kongo* received the signal from the *Yamato* to open fire. Rear Admiral Shimazaki gave permission to open fire with the main battery at 0700. Her Type 1 AP projectiles were dye-loaded, and her color was red, but it was a blood red and it was viewed as red, purple, or even blue. On the flat, blue water, the red dye created a purple color. At 0701, she targeted two aircraft to port; her gunners continued to engage the aircraft.[33]

ON BOARD THE *WHITE PLAINS*

Captain C. J. Sullivan on board the *White Plains* received reports from his lookouts at 0659, "The enemy force was observed bearing 289°, distance 31,300 yards. Splashes were observed approximately 4,000 yards astern,[34] and followed immediately by a salvo of heavy caliber shells falling approximately 300 yards on the starboard bow. The *Samuel B. Roberts* reported splashes off her stern."[35]

---

[31] Based on the evidence from film and photos, it appears the *Haruna* and the *Kongo* did not open fire until 0705 when splashes began to fall around the *Fanshaw Bay*, whose crewmen recorded their dye colors of red and yellow. The *White Plains* recorded only pink and no color splashes, which corresponded to the *Nagato* and the *Yamato*.

[32] *Haruna* Detailed Action Report. This will be confirmed by the destroyers of Taffy 2 which describe the shell splash color as yellowish green or greenish yellow. The *Haruna* was the only Japanese ship to fire on these destroyers. This is caused by the use of a primary color as the dye load. Seen through blue water the dye will look green.

[33] *Kongo* Detailed Action Report.

[34] These splashes were the 6.1-inch projectiles from the *Yamato*'s secondary battery falling short.

[35] White Plains Action Report.

Figure 8: This photo shows the *White Plains* as seen from the *Kalinin Bay* at 0659 with the *Yamato's* first salvo. Three small splashes are astern of the carrier to the port side, followed by two large splashes off her starboard bow. The number of planes on the *Kalinin Bay's* flight deck and on the *White Plains* shows this to be at the very beginning of the action. Neither carrier was emitting smoke, which almost all the U.S. ships produced within minutes of the first salvos fired.

Once the salvo landed, "Observers on deck reported that while under enemy shell fire, and shortly after the first salvo, three or four shell bursts nearby and about 400 feet in the air showering sparkling silver colored particles in a downward cone. These particles settled quickly in the water and there was little percussion with the burst. It is possible these were radar marking shells for spotting but their exact nature is not known."[36]

---

[36] Ibid.

Figure 9: As the bow splashes faded, a white streak appeared overhead. The Yamato fired Type 3 AA shells with possibly four exploding mid-air. Note the foul weather on this overcast morning.

Captain Sullivan continued, "With fighters turning up and waiting for the ship to turn into the wind, two enemy shells burst a mile to two miles from the ship in the direction of the enemy attracting attention. These bursts were mentioned in particular because of the singular appearance and because it is believed they were only two of their kind sighted during the action. Those who saw them do not fully agree but they state that they were not positive whether they burst on the surface or in mid-air. It is believed they burst from 200 to 500 feet above the surface. The result was a silvery shower of small particles which fell quite rapidly to the surface. About twenty seconds were consumed during the fall. The light from these showers was reflected—not due to incandescence. Lastly, there was almost no smoke visible from the burst. All which lead to the belief that the shells were to assist radar spotting or perhaps to counter our radar, though the latter seems improbable."[37]

---

[37] *Ibid.* Japanese Type 3 AA projectiles had been used to bombard Guadalcanal in 1942 as well as being fired on U.S. ships in the November Naval Battle of Guadalcanal, yet none of the U.S. action reports properly identified this type of Japanese projectile.

Figure 10: The *Yamato's* second salvo landed and made the cameraman jump at 0700. The *Johnston* can be seen to the left, and she has not begun to emit smoke. The *Yamato* was the only battleship that could fire a six-gun salvo from her forward turrets, and none of the other battleships or heavy cruisers had opened fire when this salvo landed.

ON BOARD THE *YAMATO*

At 0700, the *Yamato's* forward main-battery turrets fired their second salvo. She observed a straddle on her target. Kurita ordered Ugaki to take command of the First Battleship Division. From this point forward Ugaki directed the movements and gunfire for the battleship division. Kurita sent a message at 0700 back to General Headquarters informing headquarters that the *Yamato* had opened fire, and he was engaged in action against an enemy task force that included six aircraft carriers. He wanted to believe that the earlier reports of Nishimura's destruction were false, and at 0702 he sent a message to have Nishimura join the main fleet.[38]

ON BOARD THE *NAGATO*

At 0701, Kobe gave the order to "Commence firing at carrier from main guns bearing 063°, distance 35,948 yards" and noted the *Yamato* was firing at the same target. The *Nagato's* two forward main turrets fired, and her lookouts evaluated the first four-shell salvo as a straddle.[39]

---

[38] *Yamato* Detailed Action Report.

[39] *Nagato* Detailed Action Report.

Figure 11: A second view of the *Yamato's* second salvo. The cameraman tried to bring the *White Plains* back to the center of his view. There was no warning as the shells traveled faster than the speed of sound. The shells smashed into the sea like six lightning bolts, and the splash rose to its full height instantly. It took almost thirty seconds for the splash to disappear on the film, not just dropping but fading from view as the hovering water vapor dispersed.

Figure 12: A third view of the *Yamato's* second salvo. The shell splashes begin to fade.

ON BOARD THE *WHITE PLAINS*

On board the *White Plains* Captain Sullivan reported at 0700, "Straddled by a salvo estimated to be three 14-inch or greater caliber shells. At 0700, all power failed in communications as a result of near miss by battleship salvo, silencing all receivers and rendering transmitters useless. Same salvo buckled leg of radio table canting two receivers. The TBY radio was set up on the bridge replacing the TBS. Then at 0702, another straddle, several splashes were observed."[40]

Figure 13: A fourth view of the *Yamato's* second salvo. The splashes are almost gone.

ON BOARD THE *YAMATO*

At 0704, the *Yamato* fired her third main-battery salvo from her forward turrets; it was observed to straddle a carrier and set her on fire. Kurita remarked in his post-war interrogation, "The second or third salvo of the *Yamato* was followed by a very great explosion from the middle of the smoke. I do not know what ship."[41] Ugaki also believed that the *Yamato* was hitting her targets: "The First Battleship Division commenced firing with the fore turrets at a range of 33,976 yards, destroying a

---

[40] *White Plains* Action Report. Research has not uncovered any film or photograph of this salvo, but it would correspond to the *Nagato*'s first salvo fired at 0701, and she believed it was a straddle. Both the *Yamato* and the *Nagato* fired at the same target.

[41] United States Strategic Bombing Survey (USSBS): Interrogations of Japanese Officials, Vol. 1, pp 32-52.

ship with two or three salvos the target was changed to another one. The enemy turned back spreading a smoke screen and began retreating to the east, taking advantage of a rain squall."[42]

ON BOARD THE *NAGATO*

At 0704, Kobe recorded in *Nagato*'s logs, "Combined with continuing rain squalls the visibility is seriously limited. An enemy destroyer is making smoke, a carrier received a hit, and the enemy formation was retiring in the southeast direction." Soon after 0704, the *Nagato* fired her second salvo, and at 0705, a third. A fourth salvo was fired and may have fallen ahead of the *White Plains* at 0707 or 0708, and then she lost sight of her target and checked fire.[43]

Figure 14: Fifth view of the *Yamato's* second salvo, *White Plains* as observed from *Kitkun Bay* at 0700. Neither carrier nor *Samuel B. Roberts* on the horizon to the right had begun to make smoke. *Kitkun Bay's* deck was full of planes scrambling to take off. Note the three tall splashes with three shorter splashes which may indicate a mix of Type 3 and Type 1 shells. There are seventeen planes on the *Kitkun Bay* at 0700 and seventeen planes can be seen on her flight deck. Their positions help determine the order in which photos were taken.

---

[42] Ugaki, *Fading Victory*, p 492.

[43] *Nagato* Detailed Action Report.

Figure 15: *White Plains* launched her first plane (visible just above the horizon) at 0702. *White Plains* was not making smoke, and *Kalinin Bay's* flight deck was full of aircraft.

ON BOARD THE *WHITE PLAINS*

Captain Sullivan documented at 0704: "Straddled again. This salvo measured the carrier as calipers, diagonally from port quarter to starboard bow, four shells dropping microscopically close forward and aft. One of the latter two exploded below the surface under the port side of the stern. Splash water from forward whipped across the bridge. The vessel was shaken and twisted violently throwing personnel in some parts of the ship from their feet and much gear to the deck from normal horizontal stowage. Steering control was lost, gyro and radar failed, damage received in starboard engine room and all lights were extinguished throughout the ship. All electrical power was lost for several minutes until it was discovered the generator circuit breakers had been opened by the shock. The engineer officer was ordered to make smoke and the stacks were promptly set so as to emit smoke from one stack to port and one to starboard. No color was observed in the major caliber salvo that landed close aboard this ship."[44]

---

[44] *White Plains* Action Report.

29

Figure 16: The *White Plains* can be seen in the background from the *Kitkun Bay* at 0703. Faint smoke can now be seen. The *Fanshaw Bay* was the carrier to the right, and she has no smoke. The *Samuel B. Roberts* was the destroyer escort between the two carriers. The *Kitkun Bay* has launched two planes since the earlier photo at 0700, and fifteen planes remained.

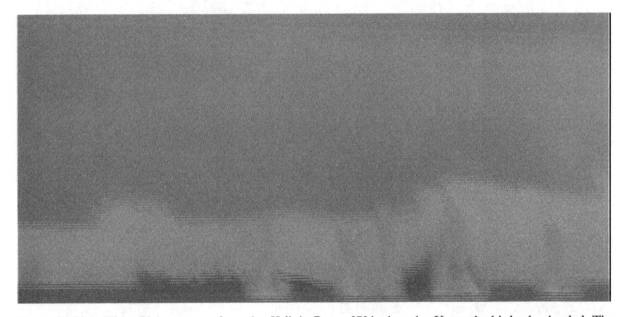

Figure 17: The *White Plains* as seen from the *Kalinin Bay* at 0704 when the *Yamato*'s third salvo landed. The tail end of the *Johnston*'s smoke indicated she had just started to emit smoke prior to this salvo landing. The *Nagato's* logs mentioned this at 0704.

Figure 18: A second view of the *Yamato's* third salvo. Note that the closest splash on the port side wasn't vertical but up and to the right side of the photo. It crosses in front of the number two splash closest to the *White Plains* on the port side.

The *White Plains* action report continued, "The second salvo[45] fired at this vessel was a six gun salvo and a perfect and close straddle, believed to be major caliber (AP) shells. The ship was severely shocked and twisted. One shell apparently exploded under the ship at the turn in the bilge, about frame 142 port, with the resulting mining effect. Shock threw out both generators resulting in complete loss of power. The ship twisted and lifted, crushing and tearing expansion joints at frame 101 and 146 port and starboard. Bottom shell plating in C-902V between frames 136-152 and port shaft alley and turn in bilge dished up 6 inches. Frames and web framing torn loose and buckled, numerous welds torn loose from overhead and bottom plating and buckling from bottom plating slightly forward of after engine room and boiler room. Fragment 8" diameter causing deep dent at frame 141. Turn in bilge prevented fragment from penetrating shell plating. Oil leaks in storage rooms C-401A and bottom shell plating buckled in C903 between frames 148-149 and starboard shaft alley also buckled in. Salt water leak in gasoline void A-406 flooding to 36" deep. Both gasoline educators were frozen and warped and the after elevator was out of alignment. The hangar deck shell plating cracked from deck level to one foot forward of expansion joint 146. Forty eight hours after the battle more cracks developed indicating hull stresses. All bed plate bolts to the starboard

---

[45] Though the second salvo (0700) was a close straddle, it was the *Yamato's* third salvo (0704) that placed the shell below the keel and the overall fourth salvo the *White Plains* had suffered. This is an error in the *White Plain's* report.

main engine were stretched and one sheared off, the engine out of alignment, sprung crank shaft, air ducts to boilers No. 3 and No. 4 completely blown out, main circulator governor damaged."[46]

Captain Sullivan noted in his report, "The salvo which so severely shook the ship fell as the fighters were being launched or were about to be launched. During the resultant undulation of the deck one of the fighters parted its single wing lines, jumped its chocks and its propeller chewed about three feet off the port wing of the fighter ahead. The remaining fighters were then six including one on the hangar deck. Though the ship was twisting and turning her course was essentially into the wind and we launched the five fighters, top-side with a relative wind of approximately thirty knots. The launching record shows the time of launching to be between 0702 and 0706:30."[47]

Figure 19: A third view of the *Yamato's* third salvo. The closest splash on the port side has already disappeared which may be an indication that the force of this explosion was blocked by the ship itself.

[46] *White Plains* Action Report.
[47] Ibid.

Figure 20: A fourth view of the *Yamato's* third salvo. The *White Plains* was seen from *the Kitkun Bay* at 0704 when the *Yamato's* third salvo landed. The *Fanshaw Bay* is to the right. On the horizon between the carriers the faint outline of the *Samuel B. Roberts* can be seen. This photo was over-exposed slightly, but the *White Plains* has emitted some smoke that appears as a faint shadow behind her. The *Fanshaw Bay* had not begun to make smoke nor had the *Kitkun Bay*. The *Kitkun Bay* has launched one more plane from the previous photo at 0703 and now has fourteen planes.

Captain Sullivan received a report from his Chief Engineer, "At approximately 0700 flank speed was registered on the engine order telegraphs and speed was increased on both engines to 150 or 155 RPM. Quickly following the order for flank speed the ship was badly shaken by two violent concussions spaced at about thirty second intervals. The circuit breakers on both forward and after distribution boards tripped out and lights and power leads were lost throughout the ship. The emergency battle lights functioned promptly and at no time throughout the engagement was either engine room in total darkness. The over speed trips on #1 Fire Pump and both main circulators tripped out.

"The air pressure of Nos. 3 and 4 boilers dropped from nine inches to four inches and steam pressure on these boilers began to fall rapidly necessitating a reduction in speed on the starboard engine 130-133 RPM. Less air pressure was due to the rupture of the canvas expansion joints in the forced draft air ducts. Steam leakage developed in the governor of #2 main circulating pumps when foreign matter became lodged beneath the pilot valve. Saltwater leakage developed in a gauge connection on the sanitary line in the starboard engine room. No other steam or saltwater leakage developed throughout the engineering spaces during the engagement. All asbestos insulation on engine cylinder heads was torn loose and the engine rooms were darkened considerably by dust, soot, and asbestos jarred loose by the concussions. The deck at the starboard engine throttles together with several loose floor plates and gratings around the main engine were airborne but no injuries to personnel were sustained.

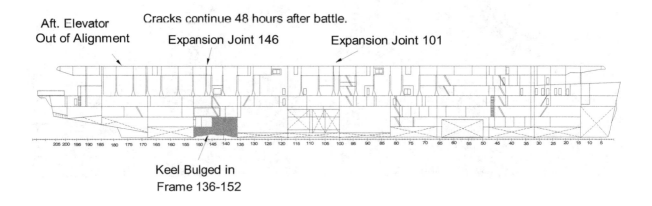

Figure 21: The *White Plains* hull damage

"All communications between engine room control, bridge, central control and other spaces were disrupted excepting the IJV circuit to the bridge. A steel nipple in the suction side of #2 evaporator feed pump ruptured and the after evaporator set had to be secured. Immediately following the concussions repairs to damaged equipment was in progress. Circuit breakers on both distribution boards were quickly reset and light and power was restored within three minutes. Communication between Bridge and Central Control was re-established within the same length of time. The over-speed trips on main circulating pumps were re-set and pumps placed in service before any vacuum loss was observed.

Figure 22: Damaged Keel. This damage can be argued as a near miss or a hit from the *Yamato*. The AP projectile probably never made physical contact with the hull; however, the shell detonated beneath the hull, and the resulting gas bubble and shock wave were directed up toward the ship. The eighteen-foot-long depression of bent keel plates and cracks in her sides show that the hull girder was severely compromised. A non-contact below-the-keel explosion is probably the most damaging form of attack against a surface ship. The *White Plains* survived due to the modest explosive charge in the 18.1-inch projectile compared to a torpedo or mine, but her physical response to the explosion was the same. Had the shell detonated a few yards forward or further aft she probably would have lost her aft engine room or both propeller shafts would be more severely twisted. This would have crippled her, and she would have suffered the same fate as the *Gambier Bay*. For those who consider this a hit it means the *Yamato* scored the longest-range hit by a battleship (34,587 yards) in the history of battleship warfare. The shell's success here was due entirely to its design. The Type 1 projectile was engineered to dive, maintain a stable trajectory underwater, and take advantage of the 0.4-second fuze delay to give it time to reach this point. The Japanese officers who designed this type of projectile believed it dramatically increased the danger space to a given target if a shell should land short. During this battle many U.S. ships suffered hits below the waterline, and it would be these hits that resulted in the most significant damage.

"Blankets were obtained through Repair Five and emergency repairs to air ducts were effective by wrapping and tying blankets around ruptured joints. Following this repair, the air pressure on No. 3 and No. 4 boilers was raised to about six inches and speed on the starboard engine was increased to 140 RPM. Repair parties from Repair Five affected a more substantial repair to air ducts with canvas and sheet metal strips within thirty five minutes when full air pressure was restored and the starboard engine speed increased to 153.4 RPM.

"Excessive vibration was noted throughout starboard engine room subsequent to concussions, being more pronounced as speed of engine was increased. An examination of this engine disclosed a broken holding down bolt on the after inboard side of the engine. All holding down bolts were loose and after end of the engine raised approximately one-eighth inch off the foundation. An up-down movement approximating one-sixteenth inch between engine and foundation was observed at the after inboard side. The holding down bolts on the starboard main condenser was sheared off and movement in conjunction with the engine was observed. Vibration of the main engine cylinders was severe at 153 RPM.

"The holding down bolts on main thrust and spring bearing pedestals were examined. No movement or overheating was apparent. A slight increase in the temperature of oil from main engine was noted and small metal deposits were found in the oil strainers. The suspension rod in the spring lead hanger on the main steam line at the inlet to starboard engine throttle carried away in the thread connection, permitting the main steam line to nag considerably at this point. All other hangers on this line were holding and in good order. The pre-coat on the screens in condensate filters held firmly and no difficulties with this equipment were experienced throughout the engagement.

"Speeds of approximately 160-163 RPM on the port engine and 153-155 on the starboard engine were maintained throughout the engagement. While all personnel were momentarily dazed and shocked at the force of the concussion there was no indication of panic or confusion. Their reaction was quick and all hands went about their duties in a highly commendable manner throughout the engagement."[48]

Captain Sullivan ordered his ship to commence making smoke at 0705. Then by 0706, he had completed launching five fighters, so he gave orders to commence violent changes in course. This was an attempt to throw off the Japanese gunnery. Her damage-control teams were working as hard as they could, and by 0708 electrical power was completely restored, and by 0710 radar was in full operation. Captain Sullivan noted in his report, "The perfect straddle immediately followed by the erratic steering, manner of making smoke and immediate launching of aircraft are believed to have been assurance to the enemy firing ship of a kill and resulted in either ceasing fire or passing on to the next target by this heavy battery, as there were no more straddles or near heavy caliber misses."[49]

---

[48] Ibid.

[49] *White Plains* Action Report.

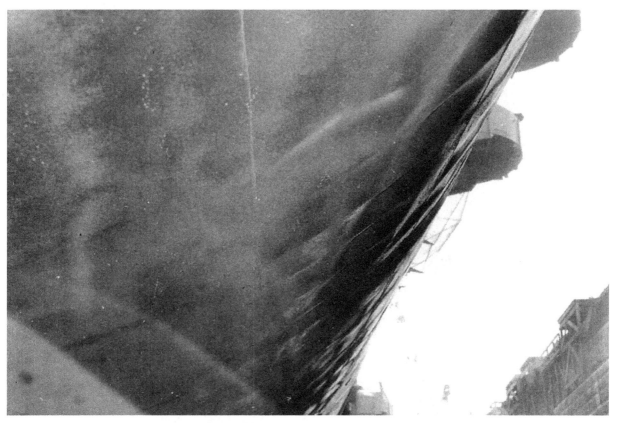

Figure 23: Cracks developed in *White Plains's* outer shell as underwater shock weakened the hull girder. These cracks continued to grow even forty-eight hours after the battle. These cracks represent hinges from the sheering force caused by the keel being forced up. Had the explosion been powerful enough to break her keel, the ship would have broken in half along these cracks. (See Keil, A. H. "The Response of Ships to Underwater Explosions." Department of the Navy, David Taylor Model Basin, 1961.) Upon her arrival at Manus Island, it was determined she needed to leave the combat zone immediately for repairs. This was fortunate, as she would avoid the November typhoon that the U.S. fleet would endure in just a few weeks. With her hull girder compromised, such severe stresses due to the high waves of the typhoon on her hull may have caused the ship to break up. The *White Plains* would never see combat operations again only being used as a ferry to the rear areas.

Figure 24: The *White Plains,* seen at 0704.5 just after the *Yamato's* third salvo landed, with the *Fanshaw Bay* to the right.

Figure 25: *Nagato's* second salvo (four shells) landed at 0705 between *Kitkun Bay* and *White Plains* (just out of the picture to the right). The destroyer to the left of the shell splashes is the *Johnston.* Center aircraft along back edge of flight deck has moved up from previous photo taken from *Kitkun Bay.* She now has thirteen planes on her flight deck. The *White Plains* recorded only pink-dyed shell and no-color shell splashes, indicating the *Yamato* and the *Nagato.* Japanese records also state that *Yamato* and *Nagato* fired on the same target.

Figure 26: The *Nagato's* third salvo landed astern of the *White Plains* at approximately 0706 when the *White Plains* turned radically and had begun to emit a dark cloud of black smoke. Heavy cruisers gunfire landed off her port side. This radical turn and the heavy black cloud convinced the Japanese that she had been severely damaged. The *Haguro* records reported that the first documented 8-inch gun fire was at 0705. The 8-inch shell splashes reached slightly above the carrier's flight deck while battleship-caliber shell fire reached three to four times the level from the waterline to the carrier's flight deck.

ON BOARD THE *YAMATO*

At 0706, the *Yamato* fired her fourth main-battery salvo at a carrier 33,428 yards away. At 0709, the *Yamato's* logs noted: "Enemy is making smoke, target is lost, last salvo from main battery fired at carrier 36,387 yards away, checked fire."[50] Kurita sent a message to *Noshiro* and *Yahagi* ordering their destroyer squadrons to follow in the rear of the battleships.[51] Kurita thought that the battleship and cruiser gunfire alone could destroy the enemy fleet and wanted the destroyers available to mop up

---

[50] *Yamato* Detailed Action Report.

[51] Ibid.

the Americans as their ships became disabled. His other concern was that the destroyers running at high speed would use up their fuel reserves so by following in the rear this reduced their speed from thirty-one knots to twenty-two knots. Kurita appeared not to have explained his reasons with Ugaki. His confidence in the *Yamato*'s guns may have come from the initial salvos at such a great range and the belief that they had already inflicted a fatal blow to one carrier within minutes of her opening fire.

Ugaki wrote in his diary after the battle, "Though its reasoning was unknown, the fleet order called for battleship divisions and heavy cruiser divisions to attack and the destroyer squadron to follow. The fleets attacking directions were conflicting and I feared the spirit of an all-out attack at short range was lacking."[52]

Figure 27: The *Yamato's* fourth salvo fell to port with one splash astern of the *White Plains* at approximately 0706-0707.

---

[52] Ugaki, *Fading Victory*, p 493.

Figure 28: A closer view of the *Yamato's* fourth salvo with possibly her secondary battery of 6.1-inch shells landing shortly after her main-battery salvo.

Figure 29: *Nagato's* fourth salvo straddled *White Plains*. *Nagato* then checked fire due to losing sight of the *White Plains* in the smoke. The *Samuel B. Roberts* is on the horizon.

CHAPTER 2. THE RUN TO THE EAST: 0645-0715

ON BOARD THE *FANSHAW BAY*

Clifton Sprague didn't hesitate and at 0650 ordered his task force to alter course to 090° true. The run to the east had begun. His task force turned to port and his ships took the following disposition: the carriers *Gambier Bay* and *Kalinin Bay* in the lead, followed by the *St. Lo* and the *Kitkun Bay*, with the *White Plains* and the *Fanshaw Bay* in the rear. The *Dennis, Raymond, Hoel,* and the *Samuel B. Roberts* made up the port side screen. The *Heermann, John C. Butler,* and the *Johnston* made up the starboard side screen.[53]

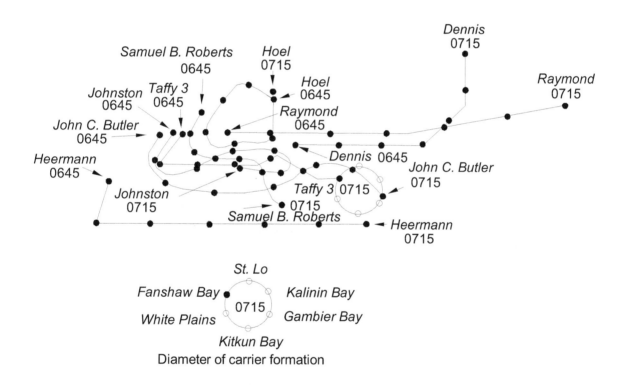

Figure 30: U.S. track chart 0645-0715.

At 0652, Clifton Sprague ordered all units to launch planes for an attack on the enemy fleet with the objective to distract and turn the enemy away. He ordered his own ships to retire at best speed, seventeen knots. Still in a state of disbelief at 0655, he ordered all planes to make positive

---

[53] *Fanshaw Bay* Action Report.

identification before they attacked. By 0656, Clifton Sprague ordered all screen units to make smoke behind the carriers to disrupt enemy gunfire.[54]

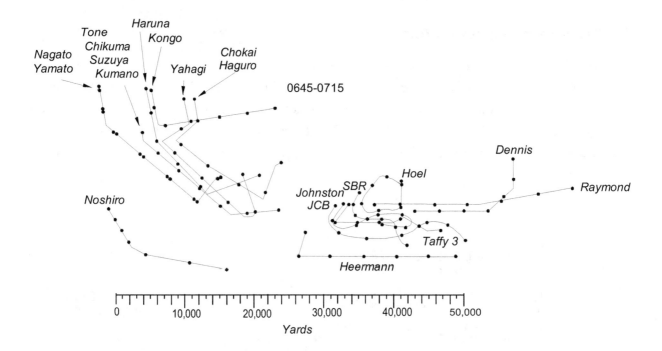

Figure 31: Track charts for 0645-0715, plotted from Japanese and U.S. action reports.

At 0658, the *Fanshaw Bay* reported that the enemy had opened fire with the first salvo falling short. Immediately Clifton Sprague ordered every plane that remained on board, eleven torpedo bombers and one fighter, to be launched with whatever fuel or armament they currently had. He also instructed all units to begin salvo-chasing, towards or away from the last salvo to throw off enemy gunnery. When the first salvo crashed around the *White Plains* just to starboard of the *Fanshaw Bay*, Clifton Sprague thought his force would not last another fifteen minutes. Desperate, he got on the radio and in plain language plead for help, "To any or all, we have an enemy fleet consisting of battleships and cruisers fifteen miles astern and closing us. We are being fired upon."[55]

Time was what he needed, and it was quickly running out. By 0700 the enemy was bearing 288°, distance 29,000 yards. Clifton Sprague recorded his thoughts:

> *"Out of the fog loomed his big battle-wagons—pagoda masts and all—and opened with their 14- and 16-inch guns at 25,000 yards. He had committed his whole task force to an attack on us!*

---

[54] Ibid.

[55] *Fanshaw Bay* Action Report.

Wicked salvos straddled the White Plains, and then colored geysers began to sprout among all the other carriers from projectiles loaded with dye to facilitate the spotting of gunfire. In various shades of pink, green, red, yellow, and purple, the splashes had a kind of horrid beauty. No, I wouldn't say it was like a bad dream, for my mind had never experienced anything from which such a nightmare could have been spun. Neither could such dream stuff have been recalled from my reading in some history book, because nothing like this had ever happened in history. "Bearing down on us at thirty knots were four new Jap super-battleships, in action for the first time: the Yamato, Nagato, Kongo, and the Haruna (32,720 to 45,000 tons[56]), averaging eight 14- and 16-inch guns; sixteen to twenty 5.5-inch and eight 5-inch guns, seven cruisers of the Nachi, Mogami, and Tone classes (8,850 to 12,000 tons, speed thirty-five knots), averaging eight 8-inch and eight 5-inch guns and eight to twelve 24-inch torpedo tubes; eleven destroyers, averaging 1,700 tons, five 4-inch guns, and four torpedo tubes. Well, anyhow, I thought, we might as well give them all we've got before we go down, so the minute the Japs were sighted I took several defensive actions in quick succession. I instructed my carriers to throw up all possible smoke from their stacks and break out tanks of screening chemical ordinarily used by the planes. Open to the air, these tanks were soon billowing clouds of vapor over the stern. At the same time, I ordered all the escorts to get on the stern of the formation and whip up all smoke they could muster."[57]

PILOTS OF VC-68, THE *FANSHAW BAY*

At 0645 four FM-2 fighter pilots of VC-68 then flying CAP over Taffy 3 turned toward the enemy fleet. The pilots were Lt. C.C. Sanders, Lt. (jg) Hoppe, Lt. (jg) Dickey, and Lt. (jg) S. Legatos. At approximately 0715 they picked out a *Yamato*-class battleship, began a strafing run at 6,000 feet and pulled out at 1,500 feet. Next they attacked a light cruiser (class unknown) and continued to strafe until their ammunition was exhausted. Finally they headed to Tacloban airfield to refuel and re-arm.[58]

---

[56] The *Yamato*'s true size and armament were not known to any of the officers involved in the battle at the time. Clifton Sprague believed the *Yamato* was a standard 45,000-ton battleship armed with 16-inch guns and similar in size to an American *Iowa*-class battleship.

[57] Sprague, "They Had Us on the Ropes."

[58] Composite Squadron VC-68, *Fanshaw Bay*, Lt. C. C. Sanders, Lt. (jg) Hoppe, Lt. (jg) Dickey, and Lt. (jg) S. Legatos.

Figure 32: The *Yamato's* fifth salvo straddled the *Kitkun Bay* at 0709. Three shells landed to port, and the other three landed to starboard. The *Yamato* remained the only battleship firing six-gun salvos. All other Japanese battleships were firing four-gun salvos. These photos were taken from the *Kalinin Bay*. The *John C. Butler* can be seen between the two most forward shell splashes, and she has not begun to produce smoke.

Four other VC-68 pilots also flying CAP received orders to make strafing attacks on the Japanese. Lt. Cdr. R. S. Rodgers, Lt. R. Anderson, Lt. W. H. Botzer, and Ens. Robinson were flying FM-2 fighters when they noticed a four-shell salvo land close to one of their carriers below. They proceeded at full power toward the enemy whose bearing was 200°, distance ten miles. Lt. Cdr. Rodgers led the four planes against the lead battleship, focusing their gunfire on the bridge area. Diving at 60° from 6,000 feet they opened fire at 4,000 feet and pulled out at 1,000 feet. They made a second run on a heavy cruiser and several more on a destroyer, causing an explosion on an anti-aircraft gun mount and expending all their ammunition.[59]

ON BOARD THE *KITKUN BAY*

Captain J. P. Whitney ordered a change course to 090° at 0650. Three minutes later the leading ships of the enemy force were sighted. Whitney sounded "General Quarters." At 0658 he observed

[59] Composite Squadron VC-68, *Fanshaw Bay*, Lt. Commander R. S. Rodgers, Lt. R. Anderson, Lt. W. H. Botzer, Ens. Robinson.

the enemy had opened fire with salvos landing within the disposition. He increased the ship's speed to maximum, about 18.5 knots. By 0700, course was changed to 070° to commence flight operations. She had eleven FM-2 fighters and six TBM torpedo planes aboard and began to launch them immediately. Evasive action consisting of turns of 5° to 60° were employed as enemy salvos landed between 2,000 yards and fifty yards from the ship with at least two straddles.[60]

PILOTS OF VC-5, THE *KITKUN BAY*

Lt. Cdr. R. L. Fowler, commanding *Kitkun Bay*'s air-wing, got his first indication of the Japanese fleet at 0653. He took off at 0700, leading six TBM bombers with four 500-lb bombs each and eleven fighters with full service ammunition. Upon reaching altitude, he was able to get a fairly good picture of the enemy units that were rapidly closing. With no other friendly units in sight, he kept his group together. They charged towards the approaching Japanese ships which were in very heavy weather at the time and not easily visible.[61]

ON BOARD THE *KALININ BAY*

Capt. Williamson received word at 0654 of an aircraft reporting an enemy task force of four battleships, six heavy cruisers, and numerous destroyers bearing 270°, distance twenty miles. He ordered, "All engines ahead at flank speed. Sound General Quarters! C/C to 090° true and all prisoners released from the brig." This information was conveyed to the rest of the ship over the Inter-fighter Director net (37.6mcs). Japanese voices were then heard over the IFD net on same frequency. In accordance with Clifton Sprague's orders, all available aircraft were launched with instructions to attack, then proceed to Tacloban airfield to re-arm and re-gas.[62] At 0705 three Japanese cruisers were sighted bearing 270°, distance 34,500 yards.[63]

---

[60] *Kitkun Bay* Action Report.

[61] Composite Squadron VC-5, *Kitkun Bay*, Commander R. L. Fowler.

[62] *Kalinin Bay* Action Report.

[63] Ibid.

Figure 33: Shell splashes near the *St. Lo.* Two splashes that have almost disappeared off *the St. Lo's* bow at 0708 are caught on film taken from *Kalinin Bay*. *Raymond* is making smoke on the left-hand side of the photo.

PILOTS OF VC-3, THE *KALININ BAY*

At 0700 two TBM-1c torpedo bomber loaded with two 500-lb GP bombs and eight 5-inch rockets, six TBM torpedo bombers loaded with six 100-lb bombs and eight 5-inch rockets, and thirteen FM-2 fighters with full service ammunition were on board. All were ordered to launch immediately. Due to the rain squalls and smoke screens the pilots joined up in small groups rather than one large formation. Lt. Cdr. Keighley, in command of VC-3, had a radio failure, so the lead was turned over to Lt. Patsy Capano. Four more TBM pilots joined: Lt. (jg) J. E. Merchant, Lt. (jg) J. J. Perrell Jr., Lt. (jg) E. J. Green, and Ens. R. G. Altman.[64]

Another group of TBM-1C torpedo bombers, led by Lt. W. D. Crockett, included Lt. (jg) E. L. Archer, Jr. and Ens. J. R. Zeitvogel and Ens. G. N. Smith. They rendezvoused, climbed to 7,000 feet in the direction of the enemy force, proceeded to a point about a mile astern of the enemy disposition, and spotted a hole in the clouds. When the planes appeared through this hole in the clouds, they encountered heavy and accurate AA gunfire.[65]

---

[64] Composite Squadron VC-3, *Kalinin Bay*, Lt. Cdr. Keighley, Lt. Patsy Capano, Lt. (jg) J. E. Merchant, Lt. (jg) J. J. Perrell Jr. Lt. (jg) E. J. Green, and Ens. R. G. Altman.

[65] Composite Squadron VC-3, *Kalinin Bay*, Lt. W. D. Crockett, Lt. (jg) E. L. Archer Jr., Ens. J. R. Zeitvogel and Ens. G. N. Smith.

ON BOARD THE *ST. LO*

The enemy was spotted from the Signal Bridge, and General Quarters was sounded. Despite poor visibility the distinctive pagoda-style superstructures of the battleships could be seen astern. The CIC reported the enemy formation at 30,000 yards and closing. Captain F. J. McKenna received word at 0653 of Japanese radio transmissions being received on SCR 808. Subsequently, anti-aircraft fire from Japanese ships was seen on the horizon. At 0658 the first shell splashes were observed on the *White Plains*. Three salvos fell short of the *Fanshaw Bay*. Captain McKenna observed dye colors of red, yellow, and blue around the *Fanshaw Bay*.[66]

At 0707 a salvo was observed to splash ahead of the *St. Lo* slightly off the starboard bow. A series of four splashes in a line fell close, the first about 200 yards from the ship. A second salvo similar to the one prior was observed the same distance ahead and slightly off the port bow at 0708. By 0713 the *St. Lo* had entered the rain squall, and all carriers had laid smoke. During the rain storm, the visibility closed to zero, and the *St. Lo* had begun to launch four torpedo bombers and fifteen fighters. The range to the enemy at this time was approximately 22,000-25,000 yards. Captain McKenna continued to observe main-battery salvos from the enemy battleships and enemy cruisers to land within the formation and noted that during this period many straddles were observed that missed only slightly in deflection on the *St. Lo* as well as other ships within the formation.[67]

---

[66] The shell colors of red, yellow, and blue indicate the *Fanshaw Bay* was being targeted by the *Kongo* and the *Haruna*.

[67] *St. Lo* Action Report.

Figure 34: The bow of the *St. Lo* now seen coming into view on the left as the camera pans aft.

PILOTS OF VC-65, THE *ST. LO*

Lt. Van Brunt flying sector 1 (000° to 090°) heard Ens. Brooks's contact report and immediately flew to the area where the enemy had been reported. Lt. Brunt picked out what he thought was a heavy cruiser and launched an immediate attack. He pushed over from 8,000 feet in a steep glide and released his three depth charges at about 1,800 feet. His gunner reported seeing three splashes alongside the target which threw water over her deck, but no damage was noted. He then pulled up into the clouds and circled the formation for an hour taking photos with a K-20 camera. He landed on the *Marcus Island* and left the negatives on board.[68]

---

[68] Composite Squadron VC-65, *St. Lo*, Lt. Van Brunt.

Figure 35: The *St. Lo* didn't begin to launch aircraft until the task force entered the rain squall. Note her flight deck was full of planes. The tail end of the *Raymond*'s smoke screen is seen, alerting us she had just begun making smoke when this photo was taken.

Lt. (jg) MacBride on sector 2 (090°-180°) made a quick search of his assigned area and then went to the scene of the action. He joined with five FM-2 fighters making a strafing attack. He saw splashes alongside a heavy cruiser but was unable to determine if they were from his depth charges or from another plane. After this attack he continued to make strafing runs until his ammunition had been completely expended. He then flew to Tacloban airfield for re-fueling and re-arming.[69]

Lt. (jg) Fields flew sector 3 (180° to 270°). Likewise, he made a quick search within his sector and then peeled his plane in the direction of the enemy. He located the Japanese force and made an attack on what he believed to be a heavy cruiser. He didn't see any other planes in the area and reported the AA as being of all sizes, very intense, and hits were made on both wings. His depth charges landed ahead of the enemy ship which ran over them. Shortly thereafter the ship made a radical turn to port but there was no evidence of damage. Fields still couldn't find any other aircraft; nevertheless, he continued to make strafing runs on the enemy until his ammo had been expended, and then he returned to Taffy 2 and landed on the *Ommaney Bay*.[70]

---

[69] Composite Squadron VC-65, *St. Lo*, Lt. (jg) Mac Bride.
[70] Composite Squadron VC-65, *St. Lo*, Lt. (jg) Fields.

Lt. Cdr. R. M. Jones was the first to take off from the *St. Lo*. It was known that he made at least one attack on a Japanese battleship and was heard to say that he got three hits, but no further information from him was received, and his plane was reported as shot down. During his first attack he was joined by Lt. (jg) J.H. Gore and Lt. (jg) Kash. The three pilots proceeded immediately to the Japanese force and launched an attack. The pilots picked out a heavy cruiser and dove from 10,000 feet.[71]

When Lt. Gore came out of the clouds, he was met with an intense AA barrage of all sizes. Colored bursts of red, blue, orange, and yellow exploded close to his plane. He expected his wings to be blown off at any second, but his plane was never hit. He dropped all eight bombs. Three landed short, but the other five strung out on the decks. He pulled up sharply and headed back up to the clouds. He lost sight of the other planes but heard Lt. Cdr. Jones make a second attack. He tried to find the other planes but couldn't locate them, so he strafed other Japanese ships until his ammunition was exhausted and then flew to Tacloban airfield.[72]

Lt. (jg) Kash took off without any bombs or rockets but had a full load of service ammunition. He attacked a *Nagato*-class battleship and made several strafing runs. On the second run his port side guns jammed. He continued strafing runs until his starboard ammunition was exhausted. Alone, with his port wing holed, he landed at Dulag where he and his crew were given a foxhole and rifles and told they expected a Japanese counterattack at any time.[73]

Lt. (jg) L. E. Waldrop had eight 100-lb bombs and two rockets. Unable to locate other planes in the heavy squalls, he launched a single-handed attack on four heavy cruisers. On two runs he didn't release his bombs because he was unsure of making hits. On two other runs he released four bombs each. After this he made two more attacks: he fired a single rocket and then strafed his target. Finally, he made two more runs strafing the target. Anti-aircraft fire was intense. His port wing was hit by fragments making a three-foot hole in the wing. After these attacks he returned and circled Taffy 3.[74]

ON BOARD THE *GAMBIER BAY*

Captain W. V. R. Vieweg received a report from his lookouts at 0640 that anti-aircraft fire was observed to the northwest. Then at 0643 he intercepted an almost unintelligible and excited VHF transmission from one of Taffy 2's anti-submarine aircraft reporting that it had sighted a large Japanese surface force thirty miles from Taffy 2, which was then operating ten miles south of his

---

[71] Composite Squadron VC-65, *St. Lo*, Lt. (jg) J. H. Gore and Lt. (jg) Kash.

[72] Composite Squadron VC-65, *St. Lo*, Lt. (jg) J. H. Gore.

[73] Composite Squadron VC-65, *St. Lo*, Lt. (jg) Kash.

[74] Composite Squadron VC-65, *St. Lo*, Lt. (jg) L. E. Waldrop.

position at the time. Simultaneously, a local ASP pilot reported an enemy force consisting of four battleships, eight heavy cruisers or light cruisers, and four destroyers.[75]

Captain Vieweg later wrote, "To make certain of the situation required no great amount of thought since about that time major caliber salvos commenced falling in the center of our formation. Just prior to this contact we had been on a northerly course, which as I recall it, was 040°. Only a few minutes before contact we reversed course and were headed in a generally southerly direction. Immediately this contact was made and identified as enemy. The officer in tactical command ordered a course change which brought us generally to the east, and was near enough to the wind to permit launching. Without waiting for instructions I commenced launching all planes on deck since I was under immediate threat of losing everything due to a shell hit on deck and setting the planes on fire."[76]

Orders were given at 0652 to jettison three napalm bombs located on No. 5 sponson. At 0654, gun flashes were observed to the northwest, and large-caliber salvo splashes were soon seen falling near the ships on the northern side of the formation. Captain Vieweg observed that the enemy's initial firing range was approximately 35,000 yards. Ranges closed rapidly. By 0655 all planes on the flight deck—ten FM-2 fighters and seven TBM-1C torpedo bombers—were ready for launch. These all took off within ten minutes, leaving four TBM-1C aircraft in the hangar deck. By 0708 the first of these was brought up on the forward elevator.[77]

PILOTS OF VC-10, THE *GAMBIER BAY*

Lt. Cdr. E. J. Huxtable had gone below to get some breakfast at 0655 when General Quarters was sounded; he immediately returned to the pilot ready room. He was the squadron leader for VC-10. When he reached the ready room, he was informed that the Japanese fleet was twenty miles astern and that all pilots were to man their planes for immediate launch. He took the lead torpedo plane, but this plane had no bomb load; he asked the air officer for a bomb load but was instructed to launch immediately. As he taxied onto the catapult the first enemy salvo landed near the *White Plains*. Take-off was at approximately 0700, and within five minutes he gave instructions for immediate rendezvous. Four torpedo planes made rendezvous in right echelon. With him were Lt. H. B. Bassett, Ensign R. L. Crocker, and Ensign W. C. Shroyer. Orders from the *Gambier Bay* instructed the pilots to attack immediately, and the enemy at the time seemed to be only twelve miles away. Lt.

---

[75] *Gambier Bay* Action Report.

[76] Captain W. V. R. Vieweg's transcript of the Battle off Samar, taken 18 December 1944, Office of Naval Records and Library.

[77] *Gambier Bay* Action Report.

Bassett and Ensign Shroyer had a bomb load of two 500-lb. bombs. Ensign Crocker was launched without any bombs or torpedoes and only had two rockets plus his machine gun ammunition.[78]

Lt. C. R. Ellwood was the third plane launched, and as he turned away from the formation, eight planes joined up with him. Lt. E. W. Seitz was catapulted almost as soon as he had started the engine, and when he looked back, he saw one of the carriers within the formation being straddled by large shell splashes. Ensign J. D. McGraw joined in his FM-2 fighter and provided escort for the torpedo bombers. Ensign C. J. Dugan also joined and despite the poor visibility he noted that the gun flashes of the enemy ships made them clearly visible. Lt. R. W. Roby, Ensign J. F. Lischer, and Ensign P. A. Bennett also joined the group.[79]

Several pilots got separated and were unable to join the other aircraft until later in the battle. Lt. (jg) Hunting took off between 0700 and 0710 but didn't meet with other aircraft until 0745. Ensign Dillard became separated as he climbed up into the overcast clouds. Ensign Osterkorn didn't find anyone, so he immediately flew toward the enemy alone. Lt. (jg) Phillips also flew toward the enemy alone. As he came over the Japanese fleet, he picked out a Japanese destroyer, made a strafing attack until suddenly all but one gun stopped firing. Undaunted, he made two more strafing attacks with his single gun and then attempted to return to base. He couldn't land on the *Gambier Bay*, so he eventually headed to Tacloban airfield where he landed at 1000.[80]

Ensign Wallace picked out what he believed was a *Fuso*-class battleship and began his strafing attack from 10,000 feet.[81] He made a total of eight strafing attacks on the battleship and a *Mogami*-class cruiser and, after his ammunition was exhausted, flew to Tacloban where he landed at 1000. Ensign Osterkorn came out of the clouds and proceeded into an attack glide. His bombs were armed with nose and tail fuses. In the first run, he attempted to release his bombs, but nothing happened. He climbed back into the clouds and join up with a group of fighters that were making an attack on a cruiser. He followed them in, and this time one of the bombs fell, but there was no explosion. He climbed back up and began a third run, and his second bomb dropped, but again no explosion was seen or felt. He then headed for Tacloban airfield to re-arm and re-fuel. Upon arrival he circled and lowered his landing gear but wasn't given permission to land, and then a few minutes later, the bases AA fire opened up on him. He proceeded to Point King and circled eventually receiving a signal from Lt. Comdr. Huxtable to land at Dulag.[82]

---

[78] Composite Squadron VC-10, *Gambier Bay*, Lt. Cdr. E. J. Huxtable.

[79] Composite Squadron VC-10, *Gambier Bay*, Lt. C. R. Ellwood, Lt. E. W. Seitz, Ensign J. D. McGraw, Ensign C. J. Dugan, Lt. R. W. Roby, Ensign J. F. Lischer and Ensign P. A. Bennett.

[80] Composite Squadron VC-10, *Gambier Bay*, Lt. (jg) Hunting, Ensign Dillard, Ensign Osterkorn.

[81] The *Nagato* class and *Fuso* class had a pagoda superstructure, single stack, and aft superstructure in common making the *Nagato* a possible candidate for Ens. Wallace's "*Fuso*"-class battleship.

[82] Composite Squadron VC-10, *Gambier Bay*, Ensign Wallace.

Lt. R. W. Roby at approximately 0710 broke into the clear and saw below him a portion of the Japanese force that consisted of four or more destroyers. He immediately made a strafing attack and made three more runs after his first. He then climbed to 9,500 feet and was able to join up with a fighter and a torpedo plane and made a vertical runs with this group but became separated. He was able to find a third group and attacked with them for four more strafing attacks. Ensign J. F. Lischer was with Lt. R. W. Roby for the first attack on the destroyers, but he became separated after the first run.[83]

Ensign B. F. Dillard climbed to 9,500 feet and, finding a hole in the clouds, dived to strafe the lead Japanese cruiser. As he dived, pink and orange AA fragments surrounded his plane. As he began to recover from his dive, he lost consciousness at approximately 800 feet. He awoke to find a 4-inch hole in the port side of the cockpit, while his cockpit hood, goggles, and helmet were missing. A pilot of another plane from the *Fanshaw Bay* which witnessed the incident believed his plane was out of control for two to four minutes. The two pilots headed for Tacloban airfield when a Japanese Tony fighter attacked but missed and then fled when they returned fire. He landed safely at Tacloban with only minor cuts to his face.[84]

Ensign P. A. Bennett was the last plane launched in the first group of planes that were on the *Gambier Bay*'s flight deck. The ship had closed on a rain squall, and almost immediately after launch he had to go on instruments. By the time he came into the clear the other planes were already on their way, and by the time he reached the Japanese the attack was underway. At this time he was joined by a FM-2 fighter who flew around him and in a lead position headed for the enemy, so Ensign P. A. Bennett followed him in. He had no bombs, only machine gun ammo, and together they made a strafing attack on the lead Japanese cruiser with no AA response from the ship. After he recovered from this attack, he became separated from the FM-2 fighter. A Japanese battleship emerged from the rain squall behind the cruisers, so he immediately made a strafing attack on this ship. This time the AA was very heavy, and shells detonated below and to starboard of his plane. Luckily, only a small hole in the right aileron was seen after the attack. His rear gunner strafed the target as they passed. He didn't feel they had done much damage but did draw AA fire from other attacking aircraft.[85]

ON BOARD THE *YAMATO*

At 0710, Kurita ordered the fleet to make a simultaneous turn 90° to port. U.S. aircraft approached the *Yamato*, and she opened fire with her AA batteries. This engagement lasted from

[83] Composite Squadron VC-10, *Gambier Bay*, Lt. R. W. Roby.

[84] Composite Squadron VC-10, *Gambier Bay*, Ensign B. F. Dillard.

[85] Composite Squadron VC-10, *Gambier Bay*, Ensign P. A. Bennett.

0710-0715. By 0714, Kurita ordered the fleet to make a simultaneous turn 20° to starboard. An enemy cruiser was sighted one minute later, and orders were given to immediately engage the cruiser with secondary guns. The *Yamato* fired eleven salvos from her 6.1-inch guns at the cruiser on her starboard bow, distance 25,646 yards, results were not observed, since the target disappeared into a rain squall.[86]

ON BOARD THE *NAGATO*

At 0711, the *Nagato*'s sighted three approaching SB2C's and three TBF aircraft to starboard, bearing 013°, distance 14,248 yards. At 0712, Rear Admiral Kobe ordered his anti-aircraft gunners to prepare to engage the aircraft. Five more aircraft were spotted to starboard, bearing 030°, distance 38,360 yards. By 0713 her lookouts reported that the enemy carriers were entering a rain squall. Then at 0714, Kobe gave orders to commence independent firing on the aircraft on the starboard side bearing 030°.[87] Then suddenly at 0715, Kobe saw a lone U.S. destroyer approaching and ordered the *Nagato* to open fire from her main battery at the enemy destroyer laying a smoke screen (one salvo fired) and noted that the *Yamato* was firing at the same target.[88]

ON BOARD THE *JOHNSTON*

Cdr. Ernest E. Evans, a Native American with Cherokee family heritage, was the first and only commander of the *Johnston*. When the Japanese fleet was discovered, he immediately gave orders to the engine room to light off all the boilers and make maximum speed. He also gave orders to the engine room to begin to make funnel smoke and ordered the smoke screen generators to make smoke. He then commenced zigzagging back and forth between the enemy and the carriers, laying a heavy smoke screen.[89]

By 0710, the range to the closest enemy cruiser had closed to 18,000 yards, and fire was opened with the 5-inch battery on this cruiser.[90] Evans turned his ship around in a starboard turn and began his charge toward the enemy warships on his own initiative. The U.S. planes were, at this time, striking the Japanese force, completing their strike at 0715. As soon as the *Johnston* commenced firing on the enemy, she was in turn taken under fire by more than one Japanese unit. Many projectiles straddled the ship during this period.[91]

---

[86] *Yamato* Detailed Action Report. The "cruiser" is the destroyer *Johnston*.

[87] This would be with her main battery at the ranges reported.

[88] *Nagato* Detailed Action Report. Her target was the *Johnston*.

[89] *Johnston* Action Report.

[90] The *Suzuya* logs also report the *Johnston* opened fire at 0710.

[91] *Johnston* Action Report.

Cdr. Evans ordered the torpedoes to be set on low speed, that they may have the maximum range. The bombardment was intense, and he wanted to get the torpedoes off before his ship was seriously damaged. The *Johnston* closed to within 9,000-10,000 yards of the leading cruiser which was the *Kumano*. The target angle was 040°, target speed twenty-five knots, depth of torpedoes was six feet, spread of 1°; torpedo mount one was trained at 110° relative, and torpedo mount two was trained at 125° relative. Now the crew waited for Evans to give the word to fire the torpedoes.[92]

ON BOARD THE *KONGO*

Kongo initially engaged the U.S. Carriers, and Rear Admiral Shimazaki noted the *Haruna* and the ships of Cruiser Division Seven were firing at the same target.[93] Results couldn't be observed. Since the enemy was entering a squall area, tracking was getting exceedingly difficult. The *Kongo* was quickly heading for the rain squall herself. Because of her turn to the east, she was the most northerly Japanese ship, the farthest from the U.S. formation. Then at 0713, U.S. planes attacked from astern.[94]

ON BOARD THE *HARUNA*

At 0706, the *Haruna*'s lookouts reported, "Enemy is making smoke." By 0708 lookouts reported, "Two enemy torpedo bombers bearing 040° port." Four minutes later the *Haruna*'s AA guns opened fire, and the enemy planes withdrew. At 0711, Shigenaga issued an order for the *Haruna* to turn to port. Then at 0713, she fired her fifth main-battery salvo at the U.S. carriers and then checked fire. Due to the poor visibility she had lost her target. A minute later the *Haruna* spotted a U.S. destroyer closing on an opposite course, distance 25,646 yards. New orders were given to shift fire to this target, and the *Haruna* opened fire at 0714 with her main battery at the charging U.S. destroyer.[95]

ON BOARD THE *HAGURO*

Capt. Sugiura on board the *Haguro* at 0706 reported, "Five aircraft coming to attack approaching from the bow." He then described the effectiveness of his anti-aircraft fire as "shooting blanks." Then at 0708, another signal from the *Yamato*, this time addressed to 2nd and 10th squadron, "Follow my squadron to the rear." At 0709, Capt. Sugiura ordered the main battery to open fire

---

[92] Ibid.

[93] This was the *Fanshaw Bay*.

[94] *Kongo* Detailed Action Report.

[95] *Haruna* Detailed Action Report. Her target at 0714 was the *Johnston*.

against the aircraft.[96] He then changed course to 20° true. At 0710, another signal from the *Yamato* was received, "Six enemy aircraft carriers confirmed."[97]

By 0711, two U.S. aircraft attacked off the bow of the ship. The *Haguro*'s AA guns opened fire; as one plane passed her port side, it was hit and observed to fall into the sea. At 0713, an enemy destroyer was spotted. Capt. Sugiura noted, "We fired upon it violently, visibility was narrow." At 0714, he commanded, "Gun battle to starboard side." The *Yamato* ordered the *Haguro* to turn towards the enemy. So he changed course to 65° true. By 0715, she had come to a 90° orientation on the enemy destroyer. Capt. Sugiura gave the order to open fire with the main battery at a distance of 13,261 yards. He noted, "Guns fired, three salvos together, all hit." Then the U.S. destroyer turned around and disappeared into a smoke screen.[98]

ON BOARD THE *SUZUYA*

The *Suzuya* was the second ship in a line of four heavy cruisers as part of the Seventh Cruiser Division. The *Kumano* was in the lead as flagship. The *Suzuya* was followed by the cruisers *Chikuma* and the *Tone*. Captain Masao Teraoka had commanded the heavy cruiser *Suzuya* since September 1944. He noted that the enemy smoke screen was expanding. He then gave orders to prepare to attack an enemy destroyer but was currently out of range. He observed the battleships as they opened fire, and he waited for the range to close. By 0710, a U.S. destroyer had turned around and was now charging the Japanese fleet, and the range closed rapidly. When the range decreased to 10,960 yards Captain Teraoka gave permission to open fire. He also observed that the enemy destroyer opened fire at the same time.[99]

The *Suzuya* main battery fired five salvos at the charging enemy destroyer with at least two salvos coming close to the enemy warship. He could see as the gun battle continued that the U.S. carrier formation was now retiring to the east. Then his attention was diverted to the sky as his lookouts warned of twenty enemy aircraft coming through the clouds, diving on his and the other ships of the Seventh Cruiser Division. Captain Teraoka immediately ordered his AA guns to open fire, and the air battle was joined.[100]

---

[96] Ensign Crocker's plane of VC-10 *Gambier Bay* had his radio and instruments knocked out when a heavy cruiser opened fire with her main battery on his plane.

[97] *Haguro* Detailed Action Report.

[98] Ibid.

[99] *Suzuya* Detailed Action Report. The *Johnston* opened fire at 0710 with her 5-inch guns.

[100] *Ibid.* The enemy destroyer was the *Johnston*.

ON BOARD THE *NOSHIRO*

Captain Kajiwara had been in command of the *Noshiro* since 29 December 1943. He reported at 0705, "Enemy opened fire with guns, a carrier was hit and begins to turn, vessel course 100°." Then at 0710, his lookouts reported, "Seven aircraft coming to attack." At the same time he received orders from the *Yamato* to follow in the rear of the battleship divisions. Captain Kajiwara ordered the speed of the *Noshiro* reduced to twenty-four knots at 0713 and by 0714 noted that an enemy cruiser was closing and that she was opening fire on the Japanese formation.[101]

ON BOARD THE *KISHINAMI*

Captain Tokujiro Fukuoka commanded Destroyer Division 31 in his flagship *Kishinami* which was part of the Second Squadron with the light cruiser *Noshiro* as overall flagship. Captain Fukuoka watched the battleships and cruisers engage at 0704, and by 0706 the enemy carriers were bearing 095°, and the *Kishinami*'s speed was thirty-two knots. By 0708, he observed an enemy destroyer closing the Japanese formation and gave orders to prepare to attack as the range decreased rapidly. Then at 0710, he received orders from the *Yamato* to follow in the rear of the battleship divisions. Speed was reduced, and then her lookouts reported four planes were coming to attack, and she opened fire with her AA guns.[102]

ON BOARD THE *YAHAGI*

Captain Masatake Yoshimura had been in command of the *Yahagi* since 29 December 1943. He received new orders from the *Yamato* at 0706, "Destroyers to stay in the rear of formation." By 0710, the first U.S. aircraft that were launched from the U.S. carriers had reached the Japanese fleet and were beginning their attack runs. The *Yahagi* opened fire on the aircraft. At 0711, another message came from the *Yamato*, "Take up position in rear of Third Battleship Division." The *Kongo* was the flagship of this division and she was on the port side of the Japanese formation. Captain Yoshimura gave orders to turn his squadron around just has he was gaining the starboard flank of the enemy. Now, he had to head north and chase the *Kongo* which was heading east.[103]

ON BOARD THE *HOEL*

Cdr. Kintberger received word at approximately 0650 by voice radio that an ASP plane was being fired upon by an enemy surface force. Simultaneously a lookout reported anti-aircraft bursts to the northwest, and gunfire splashes were seen falling near the carriers. Word was received by voice

---

[101] *Noshiro* Detailed Action Report. The enemy "cruiser" was the *Johnston*.

[102] *Kishinami* Destroyer Division 31 Detailed Action Report. The enemy destroyer was the *Johnston*.

[103] *Yahagi* Detailed Action Report.

radio, "We are being pursued by a large portion of the Japanese Fleet." Cdr. Kintberger ordered, "General Quarters" and orders were given to light off all boilers and prepare to make maximum speed. The enemy force was to the northwest at a range of 33,000 yards on a course of 110° true, the northern column was making twenty-seven knots and the central and southern columns were making thirty knots.[104]

Cdr. Kintberger then received orders from Clifton Sprague to lay a smoke screen. The *Hoel* left its screening station turning to port and laying a smoke screen between the enemy and the carrier formation following the *Johnston* and the *Samuel B. Roberts*. At approximately 0710 Cdr. Kintberger on his own initiative turned the *Hoel* and began her torpedo approach on the leading battleship setting a course of 000° true. The range at this time was 18,000 yards, and Cdr. Kintberger gave orders for the torpedo speed to be set on intermediate, and orders were given to fire a half-salvo as at least two columns were required to be slowed or stopped.[105]

ON BOARD THE *HEERMANN*

At 0645 Cdr. Hathaway's crew observed that SG radar was being jammed. At 0651, an enemy fleet was reported fifteen miles astern. Cdr. Hathaway was called to the bridge. By 0655, shell splashes falling to port from unknown source, initially believed to have been bombs. At this time true bearing of the enemy wasn't known as the *Heermann* was maneuvering and radar contact had not been made. Cdr. Hathaway gave orders for the ship to go to General Quarters. Then at 0656, he received a message from Clifton Sprague which stated Taffy 3 was under fire from an enemy fleet. By 0700, the formation headed into wind to launch all aircraft. Hathaway gave orders at 0702 to commence laying smoke.[106]

---

[104] *Hoel* Action Report.
[105] Ibid.
[106] *Heermann* Action Report.

Figure 36: *White Plains* under fire. Three shell splashes, most likely from a heavy cruiser, fall ahead of the *White Plains* and well aft of the *Kitkun Bay*. The *Johnston* was laying down both black and white smoke to the *White Plains's* starboard side on the horizon. Smoke to her port side belongs to the *Fanshaw Bay*. The *Kitkun Bay* has seven aircraft remaining to launch.

ON BOARD THE *SAMUEL B. ROBERTS*

Lt. Cdr. Copeland got at 0650 over TBS that one of the American aircraft had contacted the enemy task force. Immediately thereafter the *Samuel B. Robert's* lookouts sighted anti-aircraft fire to the northwest and the fighting tops of the larger units, which the Gunnery Officer immediately identified as Japanese. Copeland gave orders to go to General Quarters at 0655. He noted at this time the carrier force was on a course of 090° true and the carriers immediately started launching all available aircraft. He then ordered full speed. At 0658, Lt. Cdr. Copeland noted splashes from heavy-caliber shells with both green and purple dye markings, falling close to the *Johnston*, the rear carriers, and this ship. This was communicated to the Unit Commander on TBS. At this time CIC plotted Japanese force at thirty-three knots.[107]

---

[107] *Samuel B. Roberts* Action Report.

Figure 37: Another cruiser salvo landed to the *White Plains's* port side as she makes an erratic turn to starboard. Seven planes still remain to be launched. The *White Plains* noted in her logs that after the initial salvos she was targeted largely by heavy cruisers.

At 0700, orders were received from Clifton Sprague to lay a smoke screen astern. Copeland observed *Johnston* immediately commence laying funnel smoke, and this was followed by smoke from *Samuel B. Roberts,* followed by funnel smoke from *Hoel.* A few minutes later he noted that *Samuel B. Roberts* commenced making heavy black funnel smoke, which laid down on top of the white chemical smoke which adhered to the water's surface, providing one of the most effective smoke screens that anyone on *Samuel B. Roberts* had ever observed. It was noticed that the smoke screen caused a slackening of enemy fire and a seeming uncertainty in their fire control. About this time, the task unit entered a rain squall in which it remained for some ten or fifteen minutes, during which time enemy fire slackened to almost nothing.[108]

---

[108] Ibid.

Figure 38: A salvo from either the *Kongo* or the *Haruna* falls around the *Fanshaw Bay*. In her action report she says that the first four salvos directed at the ship were battleship-caliber projectiles from a range of 29,000 yards. She noted three colors, red, green, and yellow. The *Kongo's* color was red/purple, and the *Haruna's* color was a yellowish/green.

ON BOARD THE *DENNIS*

At 0650, Lt. Cdr. Hansen changed base course to 220° true, observed some gunfire in distant port quarter, probably AA gunfire. At 0650 a carrier plane reported large enemy force as follows: "Four battleships, twelve cruisers, and numerous destroyers, fifteen miles astern of you!" Hansen quickly received word from Clifton Sprague, "re-check of the sighting," which was immediately and definitely confirmed by the pilot making the original report. By 0652, Hansen changed course to 090°, and this would allow the carriers to launch all planes in ready condition. At 0655, he sounded General Quarters and observed AA fire forward of the port beam. There were no targets on radar screen in direction of the enemy.[109]

---

[109] *Dennis* Action Report.

Figure 39: The *Fanshaw Bay* as another 14-inch salvo lands close by.

He noted that the weather was very squally. At 0702, he changed course to 050° true. At 0705, he saw what was to him the first salvo by the enemy landing in the center of the American formation. He received orders from Clifton Sprague and commenced laying a smoke screen. The carriers continued to launch aircraft. By 0710, he received word, "Target bearing 325° true, distance fourteen miles, picked up on radar (SL) screen; the van of the enemy force." At 0711, he changed base course to 000° true to take cover in rain squall.[110]

[110] Ibid.

Figure 40: The *Kitkun Bay* launching planes, one of which has just taken off and looks like a small black streak. As she enters the rain squall, she pours out black smoke.

ON BOARD THE *JOHN C. BUTLER*

At 0649, the *John C. Butler*'s lookouts sighted anti-aircraft fire on horizon bearing 300° true and reported this to Clifton Sprague. Lt. Cdr. Pace issued orders so that *John C. Butler* maneuvered on various courses to interpose effective smoke screen between own force and enemy. At 0708, formation course changed to 080° true. The enemy ships were closing at an estimated speed of thirty knots. Many shell bursts were observed, but no hits were observed. Several salvos landed within three to four hundred yards of the *John C. Butler*, and several fell close astern of the *Kitkun Bay*.[111]

---

[111] John C. Butler Action Report.

Figure 41: Left to right, Rear Admiral Thomas L. Sprague, Rear Admiral Clifton A. F. Sprague, Rear Admiral Felix B. Stump

ON BOARD THE *SANGAMON*

When Rear Admiral Thomas Sprague heard Rear Admiral Clifton Sprague's pleas for help at 0702, he radioed Vice Admiral Kinkaid requesting permission to launch special torpedo attacks on the enemy fleet to relieve the ships of Taffy 3. He also redirected the planes he had already launched and re-directed them toward Taffy 3. As the senior commander of TU 77.4 which included all three carrier groups, he ordered Rear Admiral Felix Stump of Taffy 2 to go to the assistance of Taffy 3 and send additional planes.[112]

ON BOARD THE NATOMA BAY

At 0708, Rear Admiral Felix Stump received Clifton Sprague's pleas for help. Clifton Sprague's nickname was "Ziggy", and this was how Felix Stump referred to him as he radioed back to re-assure his friend. "Don't be alarmed, Ziggy; remember we're back of you, DON'T GET EXCITED! DON'T DO ANYTHING RASH!"[113]

Clifton Sprague replied with more information, "We estimate four battleships, at least eight cruisers, and some other unidentified units, Course and speed of enemy 090° at thirty knots!" Stump immediately sent a message to Kinkaid, and requested permission to launch all available aircraft and attack the enemy. He was fully aware that his force would be required to turn back the enemy and immediately began preparations to launch an air strike. At 0705, Felix Stump received Rear Admiral Thomas Sprague's order, "Launch as many VT and VF as possible, Go after them!"[114]

---

[112] CTU 77.4.1 Action Report.

[113] Morison, Samuel Eliot. *Leyte: June 1944-January 1945*. University of Illinois Press, 1958, p 252.

[114] CTU 77.4.2 Action Report.

ON BOARD THE *HAGGARD*

On board the *Haggard* in the Taffy 2 screen, Cdr. Harris noted, "The first indication that the enemy was in the vicinity was when some fragmentary TBS transmissions were intercepted from Taffy 3 at 0700." Soon thereafter Harris asked Rear Admiral Stump, "Have you intercepted recent transmissions from Clifton Sprague on this TBS circuit?" Almost immediately thereafter Stump reported over TBS, "Enemy course 090° speed twenty-five knots, bearing 330°, distance fifteen miles." This was the first positive indication that the enemy was dangerously close. Cdr. Harris ordered battle stations which were immediately manned.[115]

ON BOARD THE *WASATCH*

By 0710, still unaware that Taffy 3 was under attack, Kinkaid kept his focus on what remained of the Japanese southern forces. At 0712, Kinkaid received his answer from Halsey concerning Task Force 34. It read, "Your 241912 negative, Task Force 34 is with carrier group now engaging enemy carrier force." With this information Kinkaid immediately sent orders for a search to the northeast to Rear Admiral Thomas Sprague to locate the Japanese Central Force, but it would never be carried out. Within minutes Kinkaid would learn exactly where the Japanese Center Force was as time had already run out.[116]

---

[115] *Haggard* Action Report.
[116] CTU 77 Action Report.

CHAPTER 3. *JOHNSTON* AND *HOEL* COUNTERATTACK: 0715-0745

ON BOARD THE *YAMATO*

From the *Yamato*'s bridge, the enemy fleet was now obscured from view with white smoke that clung to the water surface and black funnel smoke that hid the horizon which was covered with a dark gray rain squall. Their targets appeared and disappeared within this backdrop, so a continuous rate of fire became impossible. Therefore, the Japanese gunners were forced to seek targets of opportunity as they presented themselves and could rarely observe the effectiveness of their gunfire. Kurita pursued the Americans east and into the rain squall in hopes to gain the windward side of the U.S. formation so the smoke screens being laid down by the Americans would be less effective.[117]

Figure 42: Smoke screens left by the U.S. escorts obscured the horizon making it difficult for the Japanese ships to target the American carriers.

---

[117] *Yamato* Detailed Action Report.

At 0721, the *Yamato*'s lookouts spotted the same cruiser they had seen at 0714 and opened fire with her secondary battery. The *Yamato* then ordered the fleet to make a simultaneous turn to 90° true at 0722. The *Yamato*'s logs read at 0725, "Open main battery gunfire on enemy cruiser." The next entry was at 0727, and it read, "Enemy cruiser warship, one count, hit and sinks." Within the *Yamato*'s communication logs Kurita at 0725 lists message 250725, "Have sunk an enemy cruiser within minutes."[118] What exactly did Kurita witness?

Samuel Eliot Morison in his book, *Leyte: June 1944-January 1945*, wrote on pages 254-255, "There was something the matter, too, with Kurita, for at 0725 he informed his force from flagship *Yamato*, "I have sunk one heavy cruiser!" He then writes on page 258, "*Hoel* may have been Kurita's imaginary 'cruiser observed blowing up and sinking at 0725,' but she wasn't sunk yet."[119] Morison implies that Kurita was imagining events, which was simply not true.

What Kurita witnessed was the *Johnston* being hit at 0727, and the *Yamato*'s main and secondary battery were responsible for her damage. (The *Hoel* would be fired upon by the *Haguro*, not the *Yamato*.) The range between the two ships was estimated to be 20,313 yards. BuShips estimated that the trajectory of the shells through the *Johnston* had an 18° angle of fall, which they estimated for a 14-inch projectile would be at a range of 21,000 yards. The *Yamato*'s range of 20,313 yards with an angle of fall of 17.5° for *Yamato*'s 18-inch shells. BuShips also calculated the bearing of the shell hits one through six as all coming from 190° relative which points directly back to where the *Yamato* was located and also means all six shells came from the same ship.[120]

From Kurita's perception standing on the *Yamato*'s flag bridge, he saw a charging U.S. warship making smoke and under fire from several Japanese ships from a distance of ten miles. To Kurita she was nothing more than a black dot on the horizon. She turned into her own smoke screen after she fired torpedoes. For a moment the enemy warship disappeared but as she came out from behind her own smoke she re-appeared and was once again was taken under fire by the *Yamato*'s secondary guns at 0721. At 0725, Ugaki gave permission to engage the enemy cruiser with the main battery at a distance of 20,313 yards. At 0727, the *Yamato* fired one salvo at the enemy cruiser and hit her, so the perception was she exploded and sank. Elated with the results Kurita sent a message to Tokyo, "The *Yamato* sank an enemy cruiser."[121]

---

[118] *Yamato* Detailed Action Report.

[119] Morison, Samuel Eliot. *Leyte: June 1944-January 1945*. University of Illinois Press, 1958, pp 254-255, 258.

[120] Bureau of Ships, Navy Department, "War Damage Report No. 51, Section IV, Loss of the *Johnston*," 25 January 1947.

[121] *Yamato* Detailed Action Report.

ON BOARD THE *JOHNSTON*

Lt. Hagen reported, "At 0720, Cdr. Evans ordered the torpedoes fired in three second intervals. All were observed to run hot straight and normal." The 5-inch guns were firing at a Japanese cruiser, and during the run in and over 200 rounds were fired. An excellent solution was continued throughout and numerous hits were visually observed. It was believed this heavy cruiser was severely damaged by at least forty 5-inch AA common projectiles. The *Johnston* swung to port and behind her own smoke screen after she launched her torpedoes. She didn't see the effect of her torpedoes still being within her smoke screen when men deep within her hull heard two possibly three underwater explosions when the torpedoes were scheduled to hit at 0727. Emerging from the smoke screen they could see the leading enemy cruiser was on fire.[122]

Just as the crew celebrated their success three massive explosions rocked the ship throwing her onto her side, quickly followed by three more explosions around her forward stack and bridge. The crew was thrown to the deck or onto bulkheads by the force of the impacts and the shock waves that were transmitted throughout the ship. With her crew dazed and stunned the *Johnston* disappeared into a torrential downpour of rain shielding her from a follow-up attack and giving her crew precious time to recover and ascertain what condition their ship was in.[123]

Hagen wrote in *The Saturday Evening Post*, 26 May 1945, "The *Johnston* was a mess. There were dead men on the deck and gaping holes from the 14" shells through which a fat man could have plummeted. In some sections below deck, as I learned later, almost every man had been killed. The bridge looked like a kid's B-B target. Lt. (jg) Jack Bechdel, my assistant gunnery officer whom we called 'Junior,' was lying on the bridge fatally wounded; so was the machine-gun officer, Ens. Gordon Fox. Lt. (jg) Joe Pliska, standing near to the skipper, had been killed outright. The skipper was standing bareheaded and bare-chested. His helmet and all but the shoulders of his shirt had been blown away; the hair on his chest was singed and blood was gushing from his left hand where two fingers had been shot away. Shell fragments had ripped his neck and face. The doctor rushed to his aid, but the skipper waved'him back saying, 'Don't bother me now. Help some of those guys who are hurt.' The skipper then wrapped a handkerchief around the stumps of his fingers and carried on."[124]

Lt. Hagen, who wrote the *Johnston*'s action report, originally estimated the shell caliber that caused the damage to the *Johnston* at this time was 14-inch.[125] In fact, the *Yamato* had struck the *Johnston* with

---

[122] *Johnston* Action Report.

[123] Ibid.

[124] Hagen, Robert C. "We Asked for the Jap Fleet—and Got It." *The Saturday Evening Post*, 26 May 1945, p 8.

[125] *Johnston* Action Report. This estimate taken on face value without determining who was actually shooting at the correct time has led to the dogma that the *Kongo* was responsible.

three 18.1-inch (AP) rounds.[126] Hit one struck the main deck at frame 156 under the No. 6 depth charge projector, hitting between bulkhead C-202 and C-203 breaking open one depth charge and tearing a hole in the main deck three feet wide by six feet long. The shell hit the bench along the forward bulkhead of the machine shop, tearing a hole about four feet in diameter in the bulkhead and then hitting the main reduction gear for the port engine and detonating. On passing through the main deck the shell cut plumbing and main drain from ships head. Compartment C-202 commenced flooding through a ruptured sea chest at end of the main drain from head. Flooding was controlled by stuffing rags and wooden plugs into ruptured sea chest. Compartment C-203 was flooded due to ships zigzag motion, water passing through hole in main deck into C-202 and C-203 through large hole in bulkhead C-203 and C-202. Water washed up into hole in main deck when ship would turn to starboard. This motion put 3-4 inches of water in C203. Several salt water lines and fire main loading to deck plug frame 137 were shattered by fragments, also electrical wiring from No. 2 engine room through C-202 aft. This hit reduced the ships speed to seventeen knots, and the starboard engine was increased to 350 rpm which was sustained.[127]

The second hit struck at frame 144 port side between No. 2 and No. 4 depth charge projector passing through main deck about one foot inboard down into No. 2 engine room detonating on hitting the main steam turbine. On passing through the deck this shell cut main steam strainer, the main steam line to cruising turbine, one of the two main steam lines leading to the H.P. turbine, and all electrical cables running aft that came through bulkhead near main cruising turbine. All lights were extinguished and the after engine room filled with escaping steam. Seams ruptured in the shell of the ship near frame 146 below the reduction gear and the compartment started to flood slowly.[128]

Hit 3 penetrated the main deck and uptake space at junction of uptake space vertical bulkhead and main deck frame 127-128 port side. On passing through deck shell sheared auxiliary steam line in uptake space, passing down into No. 4 boiler and detonating. Boiler was demolished and the compartment filled with steam. On detonating shell ruptured bulkhead leading to No. 2 engine room port side about five feet up from bottom of shell plating. Fires in both boilers except one burner in No. 3 boiler were extinguished by concussion. Master fuel oil valve was closed from

---

[126] Lt. Hagen wrote the *Johnston*'s action report as the senior surviving officer. His estimate that 14-inch shells struck the *Johnston* is based simply on his knowledge at the time. He wasn't aware the *Yamato* was armed with 18-inch guns. After the battle he describes *Yamato*, "The *Yamato*, a 40,000-tonner, had nine 16" guns which throw a one-ton shell; the other battleships had both 16" and 14" guns"; See Hagen, "We Asked for the Jap Fleet—and Got It," p 6. There would never be an 18-inch projectile estimate as none of the U.S. officers present at the battle writing these action reports knew the *Yamato*'s true armament. This and Samuel Eliot Morison's account resulted in the *Yamato* never receiving credit for these direct hits.

[127] *Johnston* Action Report.

[128] Ibid.

topside by hand, and all topside steam valves were closed. The ship had been on split-plant operation, and all valves leading aft from No.1 engine room were closed.[129]

Hits 4-6 came from the *Yamato*'s 6.1-inch secondary battery. Hit 4 struck No. 2 stack under the director platform. The binnacle was demolished and platform bent upward on both sides of stack. Shell detonated after hitting the stack, but location was never ascertained.[130]

Hits 5 and 6 hit the port side of the bridge, one passing through the bridge aft of the port torpedo director and one detonating on the bridge, injuring Cdr. Evans and the other crewmen. The ship had whipped so violently that the SG radar antenna was snapped and fell on the yardarm. The master gyro frame, capable of withstanding 2,000 ft. lbs. of shock was cracked in half, and all power was lost. Repair parties soon attended to the wounded and attempted to rescue men from the lower compartments using asbestos suits. Electrical fires soon began in the after engine compartments and these men attempted to control these fires by using CO_2. No. 3 handling room directly above No. 2 engine room had to be abandoned for a time due to escaping steam.[131]

Cdr. Evans immediately ordered steering to be executed using manual control. Teams of men would operate the ship's rudder ten minutes at a time. This would exhaust the men's physical strength very quickly. As one team's strength diminished, another team would replace them and let them rest and regain their strength. Power from No. 1 engine room was repeatedly attempted to complete a circuit aft but it was later determined that all electrical lines aft of No. 2 engine room were cut and the attempts to rout power aft were contributing to the electrical fires in No. 2 engine room.[132]

---

[129] Ibid.
[130] Ibid.
[131] Ibid.
[132] Ibid.

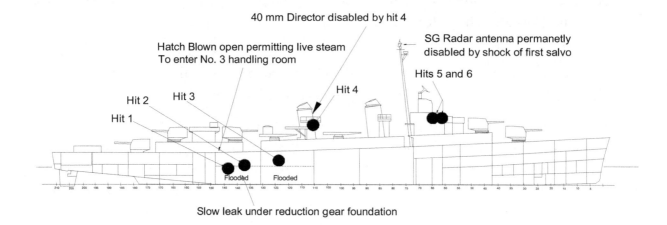

Figure 43: The *Johnston* battle damage hits 1-6.

All electrical power to all the guns was gone. Hoists were jammed due to shock and had to be operated under manual control. No. 3 shell magazine began to flood so that within an hour 6 feet of water was being carried in this compartment. 5-inch guns No. 3 and No. 5 were still receiving indicating signals. 5-inch gun No. 4 fired under local control for the remainder of the action. FD radar was non-operational for about five minutes after the hits.[133]

The FD radar was back in operation, and at about 0735, the lead Japanese destroyer was taken under fire at a range of 10,000 yards by modified radar control.[134] Then on her radar scope she observed another ship closing the formation. The *Johnston*'s crew believed this ship was a cruiser but neither the destroyer before or this cruiser was actually ever seen. When this cruiser had closed to approximately 11,000 yards fire was switched to this target.[135]

---

[133] Ibid.

[134] The *Johnston* couldn't see the "Japanese Destroyer" due to the rain and smoke; the ship on her radar was the *Haruna.*

[135] *Johnston* Action Report.

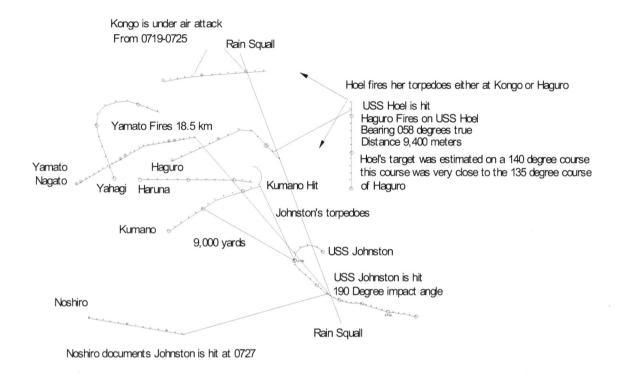

Kongo is under air attack
From 0719-0725

Rain Squall

Hoel fires her torpedoes either at Kongo or Haguro

USS Hoel is hit
Haguro Fires on USS Hoel
Bearing 058 degrees true
Distance 9,400 meters

Yamato Fires 18.5 km

Hoel's target was estimated on a 140 degree course
this course was very close to the 135 degree course
of Haguro

Yamato
Nagato   Haguro
        Yahagi Haruna   Kumano Hit

Johnston's torpedoes

Kumano

9,000 yards   USS Johnston

                               USS Johnston is hit
                               190 Degree impact angle

Noshiro

Rain Squall

Noshiro documents Johnston is hit at 0727

Figure 44: Position of the *Johnston* and the *Hoel* in relation to Japanese units 0715-0727.

ON BOARD THE *NAGATO*

Rear Admiral Kobe received a signal from *Yamato* at 0715 that she had counted six enemy aircraft carriers. Kobe ordered *Nagato* to check fire on the U.S. destroyer at 0717 and to prepare secondary battery for action. Then a few minutes later at 0723 lookouts reported, "Four SB2C aircraft were sighted preparing to dive from between the clouds on the port side, bearing 100°, distance 10,960 yards." Kobe gave the order, "Commence firing AA guns."[136]

ON BOARD THE *HARUNA*

Rear Admiral Shigenaga on board the *Haruna* received reports at 0716 informing him that *Haruna* was quickly approaching a rain squall zone dead ahead. At 0717, she fired a second main-battery salvo at the charging U.S. destroyer and then checked fire as the destroyer disappeared from view.[137]

---

[136] *Nagato* Detailed Action Report.

[137] *Haruna* Detailed Action Report. Her target was the *Johnston*, and she checked fire after *Johnston* fired her torpedoes and disappeared behind her own smoke screen.

PILOTS OF VC-10, THE *GAMBIER BAY*

Lt. Cdr. E. J. Huxtable climbed to 2,000 feet and noted that the carrier formation below was on a course of 090° heading east. Huxtable's orders were to attack immediately, and his fighters had already begun heading for the enemy. The first thing he saw was one of the U.S. escorts on a course of about 120°, she was firing and under fire at the same time. Further west, the Japanese cruisers with a *Mogami*-class cruiser in the lead on a course of 060° moved at flank speed. Astern of these cruisers on a course of 090° was a column of four Japanese battleships with a "*Fuso*" class battleship in the lead.[138] Huxtable headed on a course of 290° climbing to 2,500 feet through a rift in the clouds. He noted at the time that the cruisers were maintaining fire but the battleships were not firing at all, so he decided to attack the cruisers. He climbed to 3,000 feet which was solid overcast, turned back to attack from the west and dropped to 2,000 feet where the overcast was thinner. No fighters had joined, but he didn't feel he could delay. At 4,000 yards the Japanese cruisers opened fire with a terrific barrage of both heavy and medium AA.[139]

He approached the cruisers starboard bow, instructed those planes with bombs to focus on the lead cruiser which was the closest, and then he made a feint to the rear cruiser in order to draw the AA gunfire away from those planes that had bombs. The cruisers maintained gunfire on him until he was 6,000-7,000 yards distant. When the enemy changed course to 030°, he radioed back to the *Gambier Bay*. He had become separated from the other planes and the *Gambier Bay* recommended flying to Tacloban airfield, but he decided to stay over the Japanese fleet and organize strafing attacks.[140]

Lt. H. B. Bassett followed Huxtable. As they headed for the Japanese cruisers he was instructed to attack the lead ship which was a *Mogami*-class cruiser while Lt. Comdr. Huxtable swung to the left. Lt. Bassett climbed to 2,800 feet just below the cloud bank, nosed over into a dive, and soon realized the AA gunfire was very intense. His dive was approximately 35°; he released a bomb at 2,000 feet and suddenly the plane shuddered from a hit. He immediately released his second bomb at 1,500 feet and climbed back into the cloud bank. The weather prevented his crew from observing the results of the bombing run, but none of the crew had felt any explosions. In the rush to take off Lt. Bassett believed the bombs had hydrostatic fuses for anti-submarine operations.[141]

He climbed to 8,000 feet on instruments but once in the clear the crew looked for damage to the plane. Other than a binding when he pulled the stick back, all seemed okay. Orders were received to head for Tacloban airfield. He proceeded alone and informed the airfield he could only make an

---

[138] *Haruna* would have been in the lead at this time.

[139] Composite Squadron VC-10, *Gambier Bay*, Lt. Cdr. E. J. Huxtable.

[140] Ibid.

[141] Composite Squadron VC-10, *Gambier Bay*, Lt. H. B. Bassett.

emergency landing. He circled until 1100 and then headed for Dulag where other members of VC-10 had landed. He arrived shortly after 1100. After they landed they discovered an explosive shell had blown a 10-inch hole below and an 18-inch hole above in the starboard horizontal stabilizer. It completely severed two of the fore and aft bracers and produced a bulge in both the leading edge and the after braces. The latter bulge forced against the elevator and caused the binding previously mentioned. Another fragment had come through the glass window next to the radioman's seat but caused no other damage and his plane was repaired by Army personnel.

Ensign Crocker was told not to attack because he had no bomb load, so he flew alongside the Japanese formation to draw their AA gunfire away from the other planes. Indeed he did, for a Japanese heavy cruiser opened fire on him with her main battery. The blast wave concussion blew out his instruments and radio, but otherwise his plane escaped damage. Ensign Shroyer came in and strafed the cruiser but didn't drop his bombs due to the poor weather that reduced visibility. The AA fire was tremendous, but he dove along the water at very low altitude to escape.[142]

Lt. J. R. Jackson, Jr. was in a TBM-1c and had a full load of ammunition plus two 500-lb. bombs. He joined up with the Lt. Cdr. E. J. Huxtable and two other TBM's flown by Lt. Bassett and Ensign Shroyer. He leveled off at 7,000 feet and circled to the west side of the Japanese formation and noted there were very few AA rounds coming up at him. He picked out a *Mogami*-class cruiser and nosed over and into a dive. While his dive was in progress he saw a bomb from another plane hit the cruiser's stern. The Japanese must not have seen him for the only AA fire he received was described as scattered. At 2,500 feet he released a bomb and, as he looked back, saw it hit just forward of amidships near the bridge. There was a sheet of red flame, and black smoke rolled up. A few seconds later he heard another plane report that a cruiser was putting out smoke both on her stern and forward, so he was positive he had scored a hit.[143]

ON BOARD THE *HAGURO*

Captain Sugiura's lookouts warned of four aircraft bearing 60° to starboard attacking through the clouds at 0717. Captain Sugiura ordered his AA guns to open fire immediately, but the aircraft managed to drop four bombs around his ship, but no damage was sustained. Then at 0718 came a new warning when one of the lookouts sighted an enemy destroyer or cruiser bearing 43° to starboard and closing. He ordered his main battery to engage the charging enemy warship. No sooner had his attention been fixed on this warship when his lookouts reported at 0719 a large number of torpedo strike aircraft bearing 45° starboard at a distance of 21,920 yards and closing.

---

[142] Composite Squadron VC-10, *Gambier Bay,* Ensign Crocker.
[143] Composite Squadron VC-10, *Gambier Bay,* Lt. J. R. Jackson, Jr.

The enemy destroyer was returning fire and was bearing 30° relative to starboard. Captain Sugiura believed he saw two shells hit the enemy ship.[144]

ON BOARD THE *SUZUYA*

At 0727, the *Kumano* just ahead of the *Suzuya* was hit in the bow by a torpedo and rapidly lost speed. Her forward watertight compartments were flooded, and her maximum speed was reduced to twelve knots. Captain Teraoka maneuvered the *Suzuya* around the stricken flagship. Then a few minutes later at 0735 about ten enemy aircraft attacked the *Suzuya*. A near-miss bomb landed on her port side aft which damaged the port outside propeller shaft. Captain Teraoka pulled his ship out of formation to port allowing the *Chikuma* and the *Tone* to continue. He received a signal from the *Kumano* to transfer Vice Admiral Kazutaka Shiraishi, commander of the Seventh Cruiser Division, to the *Suzuya*. With one port shaft disabled her maximum speed had been reduced to twenty knots. Captain Teraoka maneuvered his ship back toward the damaged *Kumano* to take the admiral on board. This delay effectively took the *Suzuya* out of the battle. The Seventh Cruiser Division was down to the *Chikuma* and the *Tone*, and the Fifth Cruiser Division remained the *Haguro* and the *Chokai*.[145]

ON BOARD THE *NOSHIRO*

Captain Kajiwara at 0717 ordered his destroyers to line up according to ship number. His new orders forced him to slow down and take up position behind Battleship Division 1. Currently Battleship Division 1 was behind him slightly to the north. At 0718, he saw an enemy cruiser bearing 70° distance 20,276 yards. Then at 0720.5 his lookouts report, "Two enemy aircraft proceeding bearing 140° to port." This was followed by at 0723, "Count ten enemy aircraft approaching." At 0724, his lookouts reported, "Enemy aircraft trailing, passing by"; then at 0727, "Large enemy cruiser was hit and sunk."[146]

ON BOARD THE *KISHINAMI*

The destroyer *Kishinami* fired on the enemy aircraft that attacked her at 0710. Captain Fukuoka observed the *Johnston* ahead and ordered his ship to fire briefly at 0725 but checked fire at 0726. Then at 0728, he recorded, "The *Yamato* sank one enemy cruiser, and two enemy aircraft carriers were on fire, advance bearing 110°."[147]

---

[144] *Haguro* Detailed Action Report. No hits were scored on the *Johnston* at this time.

[145] *Suzuya* Detailed Action Report.

[146] *Noshiro* Detailed Action Report. She witnessed the *Johnston* being hit.

[147] *Kishinami* Destroyer Division 31 Detailed Action Report.

ON BOARD THE *HOEL*

Cdr. Kintberger gave orders to open fire when the range had decreased to 14,000 yards with her 5-inch battery at the approaching battleship. At 0725, the *Hoel* received her first two hits near the bridge and main-battery director. The Mark 37 director, FD radar, PPI scope, machine-gun control, and all voice radio communications were taken out of commission. The director was frozen in train making it necessary for the main battery to shift from modified radar control to a plot solution using SG radar ranges, gun No. 2 relative bearings, and gunnery officer's target angles. Immediately after these hits, the forward fire room was hit two feet above the waterline on the starboard side by an 8- or 16-inch shell leaving a hole two feet in diameter between No. 1 and No. 3 blower rooms with no loss in the fighting efficiency of the ship.[148]

At 0726, the after fire room, after engine room, and number 3 handling room all took 8-inch shell hits from port causing the loss of steam to the port engine and after generator, loss of the port turbine from a direct hit, and fire in the No. 3 handling room. Escaping steam from the after engine room along with the magazine fire made No. 3 gun untenable. The fire was extinguished by the aft repair party in three minutes, using the after main deck hoses. The after fire room immediately commenced flooding. The after engine room began to flood as well. The diesel generator immediately started taking over all emergency power and lights aft.[149]

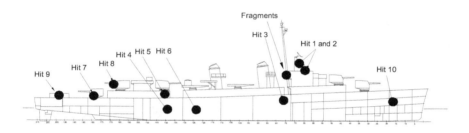

Figure 45: *Hoel*'s battle damage after 0740.

With his ship taking hits Cdr. Kintberger gave orders to launch a half salvo of torpedoes at 0727. *Hoel* launched five torpedoes at the leading Japanese battleship at 9,000 yards. Results were unobserved because as soon as she finished launching the torpedoes she took more hits. Three 8-inch shells struck aft striking No. 5 gun at the base freezing it in train, hitting No. 4 gun barrel cutting half the barrel off, and completely demolishing number five and seven 20 mm gun mounts

---

[148] *Hoel* Action Report. The *Hoel*'s report is written from memory as all logs went down with the ship. At 0725 there were no Japanese ships to the *Hoel*'s starboard side, so if this hit occurred at 0725 it must have come from port, or the hit took place later around 0755 when she presented her starboard side to the *Yamato* and the *Nagato*. Most probably this hit occurred at 0755 when the *Nagato* fired at her at point-blank range.

[149] *Hoel* Action Report.

and the smoke screen generators on the fantail. Power was lost to the steering engine room at this time making it necessary to shift to hand steering. At 0740, she received an estimated 5-inch shell hit in compartment A-304 on the port side cutting the forward fire main and causing the compartment to flood.[150]

Cdr. Kintberger ordered his ship to retire to the southwest using one engine and hand steering. However, the ship was boxed in with enemy ships on both sides. Japanese battleships were on her port side, and enemy cruisers were to her starboard quarter. Within the rain squall, most of the enemy gunfire stopped.[151] By turning southeast he cut in front of the oncoming Japanese cruisers. After he was past this line he could turn back to the southwest and, with five more torpedoes at the ready, look for another target for a second torpedo attack. The two forward guns continued to fire expending about 250 rounds during this time period.[152]

ON BOARD THE *HAGURO*

Captain Sugiura's lookouts warned at 0722 of three enemy aircraft to port bearing 090°. He ordered his AA guns to immediately open fire, and one aircraft was hit. He also changed course to 095° and then at 0723 changed course to 135° and checked fire at 0724. By 0725, he received a message from the *Yamato*, "Six enemy carriers bearing east." His lookouts observed an enemy warship was on fire to starboard. Then at 0726, a new enemy cruiser was sighted bearing 058° true to port, distance 10,300 yards, and she was launching torpedoes. Captain Sugiura ordered his main battery to engage the new target and four salvos were fired with hits being scored on each salvo.[153] He commented, "All hit very well!" and changed course to 045° true to head for the new enemy cruiser. The *Haguro* was fast approaching a rain squall, and visibility was reduced. By 0730, he was handed another message from the *Yamato*, "Change course to 110° and attack with all force, six enemy aircraft carriers are escaping in smoke, we are pursuing." Then his lookouts observed the *Chokai* to the rear was under attack by U.S. aircraft. At 0731, he ordered a course change to 070° and prepared for a starboard gun battle. By 0735, the *Haguro* changed course to 080°. Then at 0740, nine enemy aircraft attacked through the clouds bearing 050° to port and her AA guns immediately opened fire. Two more aircraft attacked from starboard, distance 1,096 yards at 0742. The American ships now appeared and disappeared within the rain squalls and smoke. At 0744, Captain Sugiura

---

[150] *Ibid.* It is not known if *Hoel* launched her torpedoes at *Kongo* or *Haguro* but her records give a target course of 140° which was close to *Haguro*'s course of 135°.

[151] A very important observation that the Japanese gunfire stopped, which is consistent with Japanese logs. Visibility was extremely reduced for both sides.

[152] Ibid.

[153] *Haguro*'s target is the *Hoel*. The *Haguro* is responsible for the initial hits on *Hoel*.

received another message from the *Yamato* that she detected six enemy aircraft carriers to starboard bearing 100° at 18,768 yards.[154]

ON BOARD THE *KONGO*

The *Kongo* was under intense air attack beginning from 0713 and was firing her AA guns in defense. The *Kongo* was hit by a bomb on the port side of her stern. According to her damage report this was a very close near miss which sent fragments into the officer's quarters along her stern. At 0722, she was attacked by more fighters who strafed her and disabled her main-gun rangefinder. Then at 0724, she received a lamp signal from the *Yamato*, "Enemy carriers heading east." Shimazaki ordered her gunners to hold fire at this time. At 0725, the *Kongo* entered the rain squall area and visibility was reduced.[155] At 0728, all guns had checked fire, and the air attack was over.[156]

By 0729, the *Kongo* received another radio signal from the *Yamato* that all units were ordered to advance east. Then at 0733, four torpedo wakes were sighted ahead. The *Kongo* steadied on a course of 090° true with a speed of twenty-eight knots.[157] By 0743, Shimazaki observed that the *Nagato* had opened fire on aircraft. Once the *Kongo* entered the rain squall, she ceased all fire and would not re-open gun fire again until after she left the rain squall. The *Kongo* remained the farthest Japanese ship to the north and furthest away from the U.S. carriers.[158]

---

[154] *Haguro* Detailed Action Report.

[155] The *Kongo*'s records do not reflect that she engaged the *Johnston* at the time *Johnston* was hit. It focuses on the fact she is under intense air attack. The BuShips estimate of a 190° bearing from the *Johnston* to the firing ship does not line up with the *Kongo* who is at a greater distance and ahead of the *Yamato* at the time the *Johnston* is hit. The *Johnston* would be pointed south and would not have entered the rain squall and the angle of fall would have been greater if the *Kongo* was the firing ship. The *Yamato* is at the correct bearing and range; she documents that she is shooting and that she scores a hit at the right time. All evidence points to the *Yamato* scoring the hits on the *Johnston*. It is virtually impossible for *Kongo* to even see the *Johnston* as she has entered the rain squall prior to *Johnston* being hit and can't even see *Hoel* who is only 9,000 yards away. *Kongo* has lost her main-gun rangefinder, making her least likely candidate out of all the Japanese battleships based on her location, weather conditions, battle damage suffered, range, bearing, and what was documented in both *Kongo*'s logs and *Johnston*'s logs.

[156] *Kongo* Detailed Action Report.

[157] The *Kongo* never reports seeing the *Hoel* in her action report, just sighting the torpedoes. Most accounts have a slight maneuver for Kongo at this time to evade torpedoes. It is not reflected in her action report but the author maintained this since all previous sources had it. As she passed the *Hoel*, there was no record she ever fired on *Hoel*, and she didn't suffer any damage during this phase even though they passed each other at close range. *Hoel* reported that enemy gunfire on her stopped at this time. In addition as *Hoel* withdrew to the southeast, her own smoke screen would block her from view since *Kongo* was to her northwest with the wind coming out of the east-northeast. This makes the claim that *Kongo* did not see or fire on *Hoel* very consistent with this account.

[158] *Kongo* Detailed Action Report.

ON BOARD THE *YAMATO*

At 0728, the *Yamato*'s lookouts warned, "Enemy torpedo bomber attacking from port beam." At 0730, Kurita sent out another message to his fleet, "Simultaneous turn 20° to starboard, signal all units, attack with full speed, and pursue on course 110°. Six carriers escaping in smoke screen, we are pursuing." At 0735, the *Yamato*'s lookouts reported, "One enemy aircraft carrier sinks."[159] By 0738, Kurita sent a message to Admiral Toyoda, "First Mobile Squadrons (1YB) observed at 0653 three enemy aircraft carriers in the northeast of the Samar Island and opened fire at 0700. All of the fleet to follow us and attack the enemy." At 0750, Kurita sent out additional orders, "All vessels turn 20° to starboard."[160]

ON BOARD THE *NAGATO*

At 0732, the *Chokai* sent a signal about a bomb explosion followed by the *Tone* sending another signal about an aerial torpedo explosion at 0735. These signals may have been these ships reporting on the *Kumano*'s being hit by a torpedo and the *Suzuya* being hit by a bomb, but the records are not very legible. At 0735, a signal from Battleship Division 1, "Advance on bearing 110°." Then at 0740, her lookouts reported, "Enemy aircraft sighted above clouds." Kobe gave orders to open fire with her AA guns. During this phase in the battle the *Nagato* didn't engage any U.S. warships and was pre-occupied with repelling air attacks.[161]

ON BOARD THE *HARUNA*

At 0730, lookouts reported four enemy planes bearing 040° port, elevation 120°. It doesn't appear from her records she engaged them. At 0731, Shigenaga reported, "Main guns ready to fire." At 0734, he gave the order to fire on a cruiser on an opposite course to starboard, bearing 040°. Five salvos were fired at this cruiser, without observed results. Lookouts reported at 0740, "Five aircraft bearing 060° port, elevation 3°, launched from carrier."[162]

---

[159] It is not known what was observed to give the perception that an enemy carrier had been sunk at this time, but this is repeated within several Japanese action reports, so something they witnessed gave them this impression. The carrier force is turning to the southwest, and it may be this maneuver that caused a billow of smoke to rise, making it appear like an explosion. Visibility was extremely poor at this time in the engagement.

[160] *Yamato* Detailed Action Report.

[161] *Nagato* Detailed Action Report.

[162] *Haruna* Detailed Action Report. The cruiser may be the carrier formation which is in the process of turning to the southwest, and later at 0750 she will score a hit on *Kalinin Bay* but mis-identify her as a destroyer on the opposite course. This simply points to the fact that due to the rain squall and smoke screens ship identification was extremely difficult and they are simply seeing shapes within a fog of smoke and rain.

ON BOARD THE *NOSHIRO*

At 0730, Captain Kajiwara ordered, "Main battery to open fire on enemy cruiser, distance 18,632 yards." Next at 0732, "Enemy warship was heading to the right." By 0733, his lookouts reported, "One enemy aircraft shot down." He ordered a course change to 040° true at 0734. This would close the distance between his force and Battleship Division 1. He then received a message from the *Chokai* which warned she had spotted enemy aircraft. At 0739, lookouts reported that they have discovered the enemy fleet bearing 80°, distance 24,112 yards through the smoke. By 0741, more enemy aircraft bearing 20° passed by. Kajiwara changed his course to 90° true by 0743. He noted in his logs that the *Yamato*'s main battery fired, and that he could count two aircraft carriers, and one was hit and sunk.[163]

ON BOARD THE *YAHAGI*

Captain Yoshimura was traveling south at flank speed but his new orders to follow in the rear of the Third Battleship Division forced him to turn around and head back north. Much of the time during this phase in the action, the *Yahagi* and her destroyer squadron were made getting to the *Kongo*'s starboard quarter. At 0724, she received a message from the *Yamato*, "Enemy carriers pursue to East." Then at 0729 another message came from the *Yamato*, "All forces directed to the East." At 0730, Captain Yoshimura ordered, "No. 3 battle speed or twenty-six knots pursue in east direction."[164]

ON BOARD THE *HEERMANN*

Cdr. Hathaway received orders from Clifton Sprague directing the formation into the wind and ordering carriers to launch all aircraft, at the same time ordering the screen commander to lay smoke screen. Hathaway noted, "With the enemy thus blocked from view by our own smoke screen, contact wasn't gained until 0725 when CIC reported that contact with the enemy, bearing 320° true, 35,000 yards, was made with Sugar George radar. Enemy attempts at jamming were by this time successfully countered. Before radio contact report could be made we maneuvered at flank speed to form a column on the *Hoel* as directed by TBS transmission from commander screen, Cdr. William D. Thomas. During this time smoke from screening vessels and intermittent rain squalls made visibility extremely poor and uncertain, varying from 100 to 25,000 yards. While approaching the

---

[163] *Noshiro* Detailed Action Report. As the carrier force turned, their smoke screens billow up making it appear like an explosion has occurred.

[164] *Yahagi* Detailed Action Report.

enemy a true column was never formed on the *Hoel*. The *Heermann* had to maneuver around the *Samuel B. Roberts* and then proceed at full power to join the *Hoel*."[165]

ON BOARD THE *SAMUEL B. ROBERTS*

Lt. Cdr. Copeland received orders at 0735 from Clifton Sprague for Cdr. W. D. Thomas the screen commander, to deliver a torpedo attack. The *Samuel B. Roberts* called Cdr. Thomas and asked if DE's were to accompany DD's as the difference in speed, torpedo armament, and fire control made such action open to question. The Cdr. Thomas replied negative, directed destroyers to form in order, the *Heermann, Hoel,* and the *Johnston* for first attack, and for DE's to form up for second attack. This message was heard to be acknowledged over TBS by only the *Samuel B. Roberts* and the *Johnston*. After waiting about five minutes for some indication that the other DE's were forming for an attack, and finding none, Lt. Cdr. Copeland, finding his ship in an advantageous position from which to make a torpedo attack, called upon CIC for a torpedo attack course and followed in about 3,000 yards astern of *Hoel* and the *Johnston*.[166]

ON BOARD THE *RAYMOND*

Lt. Cdr. Beyer received the message at 0716 from Clifton Sprague which ordered the destroyers to make a torpedo attack and the destroyer escorts to make a second attack. The task unit having launched all available planes then changed course to 200° true, and the range closed on the enemy force astern. Beyer turned his ship about and raced to the southwest now that the carriers had changed course.

By 0730, he gave orders to commence systematic firing on an enemy cruiser bearing 310° true, range 14,000 yards and closing. At this time there was a moderate and intermittent heavy rain with clouds settling low overhead. This and the fact that all ships were making smoke reduced visibility considerably.[167]

---

[165] *Heermann* Action Report.

[166] *Samuel B. Roberts* Action Report. The *Samuel B. Roberts* was actually following the *Heermann* and the *Raymond* not the *Hoel* or the *Johnston* which had already delivered their first torpedo attacks and are nowhere close to the *Samuel B. Roberts*.

[167] *Raymond* Action Report.

Figure 46: The *Heermann* is the closer ship and the *Samuel B. Roberts* the farther ship in this photo. They maneuver through the U.S. formation and head towards the Japanese fleet to make their initial torpedo attacks. The photo was taken from the *White Plains*.

At 0743, he received orders from Clifton Sprague for the destroyer escorts to make a torpedo attack on the enemy cruisers. He gave orders to immediately check fire on the 5-inch battery and came to a course of 000° true to close range on the enemy cruiser. His target was then dead ahead and the *Raymond* commenced firing with her forward 5-inch guns while the range decreased rapidly to 10,000 yards or less. At this time the enemy launched a major torpedo attack at a range of approximately 14,000 yards. The enemy employed eight or nine destroyers in this attack. Torpedo wakes were observed coming toward the *Raymond*, one wake was observed to have passed close to port and another passed under this vessel heading for the carriers. None of these torpedoes were observed to have hit any U.S. ships.[168]

ON BOARD THE *DENNIS*

Lt. Cdr. Hansen gave orders at 0723 to change course to 110° true. Realizing he was now too far to the north, at 0730 he gave new orders to change course to 200° true. By 0735, he ordered flank speed and was maneuvering to take position 270° true on the carrier formation, to lay smoke between the carriers and the enemy on orders of Clifton Sprague. As the *Dennis* sailed southwest back toward the carrier formation Hansen noted at 0738 enemy salvos fell 1,000 yards astern of carrier group, and the enemy continued sustained fire. By 0740, he gave orders to open fire with his 5-inch guns on an enemy cruiser and destroyers as visibility permitted; opening range 15,200 yards.

---

[168] *Raymond* Action Report. It is not currently known who fired these torpedoes. It may have come from one of the Japanese ships such as *Noshiro*'s destroyers, *Chikuma*, or *Chokai*. None of the surviving Japanese records document a torpedo attack at this time, but one was made. These torpedo tracks were observed by several U.S. ships and U.S. pilots at this time.

He then received the order for destroyers to make a torpedo run on the enemy force. He noted that the entire area was heavily covered by smoke and rain squalls; enemy ships appear intermittently through the smoke. The effects of the destroyer torpedo attacks were unknown.[169]

ON BOARD THE *JOHN C. BUTLER*

Around 0718, *John C. Butler* entered a rain squall, and at approximately 0720 the formation course changed to 170° true. Lt. Cdr. Pace ordered *John C. Butler* to work away from the formation and toward its starboard beam. Enemy ships were closing at about thirty knots. Many shell bursts were observed around his ship, but no hits. Salvos landed within three to four hundred yards of *John C. Butler*, and several salvos fell close astern of *Kitkun Bay*.[170]

At approximately 0738, the *John C. Butler* came out of the rain squall. Pace noted that during this period there was no enemy fire observed. At 0740, he received orders from Clifton Sprague that, "All ships were ordered to open fire." Pace could see no enemy ships at this time since *Butler* had run out on the beam of the formation to lay smoke, and realizing she was out too far, he ordered her to come about and head back in to renew the smoke screen. By 0741, he received new orders from Clifton Sprague directing the screen to deliver a torpedo attack. Pace gave the order to prepare for torpedo attack, and course was changed, on advice of CIC, toward the enemy. The intention was to join the destroyers in the attack. Then by 0743, Cdr. Thomas ordered the destroyer escorts to form up for second attack. The *John C. Butler* had closed to about 13,500 yards from the enemy, and it had appeared the enemy had turned away. The *John C. Butler* then came about in an attempt to form up on the *Dennis*, the senior destroyer escort. Visibility was very poor, due to many smoke screens and rain. CIC had no information as to location of any of the other destroyer escorts.[171]

ON BOARD THE *FANSHAW BAY*

At 0721, the *Fanshaw Bay* entered the rain squall. By 0723, Clifton Sprague changed course to 110°. The main enemy battle force appeared to him to be split into three groups. Their battleships were bearing 306°, distance 30,000 yards, one cruiser unit was bearing 287°, distance 23,000 yards, and another cruiser unit was bearing 255°, distance 16,000 yards.[172] Clifton Sprague recorded what he was thinking at this time: "In the squall, I did some thinking. I didn't like my easterly course, because I felt the Japs were not being drawn as far from San Bernardino Strait as I'd like. I wanted to pull the enemy out where somebody could smack him, for if we were going to expend ourselves I wanted to make it count. Furthermore, I felt I should run southwest to meet whatever help might be

---

[169] *Dennis* Action Report.

[170] *John C. Butler* Action Report.

[171] *John C. Butler* Action Report.

[172] *Fanshaw Bay* Action Report.

coming to me out of Leyte Gulf. And still I wanted to keep myself between the enemy fleet and our landing operations to the southwest.

"It was a hard decision to make, but at 0730 I changed course to the southeast and then to the south. It was hard, because in so turning we moved in an arc—roughly semicircular—and I feared the Jap commander would cut across the diameter and blast us out of the water as we emerged from our little squall. Racking my brains for some trick to delay the kill, I resolved to throw my destroyers and destroyer escorts at him in a torpedo attack as we emerged from the rainstorm.

"As we came out of the squall, I was surprised to find that the Jap commander had not moved to cut us off but had stupidly followed us around the circle. However, going now at almost twice our top speed, he closed with depressing rapidity, slipping up to 25,000, then to 20,000, and soon to 15,000 yards. The volume and accuracy of his fire increased until, at one point, it did not seem that any of our ships could survive for another five minutes.

Figure 47: Formation turning. This photo taken from *White Plains* shows the carrier formation turning with *White Plains* shifting from the rear most aircraft carrier to the lead carrier in the formation. The two carriers are probably *St. Lo* and *Kalinin Bay*.

"Some urgent counteraction was demanded at once, and this was the time for my little group of seven escorts to charge our big tormentors. In they went, pressing their attack to close range in the most heroic fashion. And not a single one of these little ships was lost! Results were obscured in the heavy smoke screen, but we know that one destroyer got a direct torpedo hit on a battleship. More important, the escorts turned the battleship fleet away momentarily and created a diversion of immense value."[173]

Clifton Sprague gave orders at 0729 and changed course to 200° true, the ceiling was reduced to 500 feet, visibility reduced to half mile or less.[174] By 0732, Clifton Sprague noted that they had commenced running out of squall, and he changed course to 170°. At 0735, he sent another plain language message to Admiral Halsey informing him he was under attack by battleships and cruisers and requested help be sent immediately. He then ordered at 0740 the screen commander to deploy his destroyer screen and to make a torpedo attack on enemy battle line. By 0743, his destroyers turned towards enemy battleships and closed enemy for launching torpedo attack.[175]

Figure 48: As the carriers turn the *Kalinin Bay* becomes the rear carrier which will take up position directly astern of the *White Plains*. She becomes the main target of the Japanese fleet. As she turned she throws up a cloud of black smoke which may have been perceived by the Japanese that she had been hit and possibly sunk as she disappears behind the smoke temporarily. The shell splashes may come from the *Haruna*.

PILOTS OF VC-68, THE *FANSHAW BAY*

Ens. G. D. Thompson took off with two depth charges on what was supposed to be an anti-submarine patrol. He joined up with seven other TBM bombers, and they all began circling the enemy force. Picking out a group of four Japanese ships that appeared to be heavy cruisers, the first four planes attacked the lead cruiser, and the last four planes attacked the second cruiser. Ens. Thompson was the third man of the second group to dive. He released his two depth charges at 2,000 feet which detonated off the cruisers port bow. He didn't see any hits from his group's attack.

---

[173] Sprague, "They Had Us on the Ropes."

[174] This description of entering the rain squall shows just how much visibility was reduced.

[175] *Fanshaw Bay* Action Report.

After this attack he made several strafing runs on a battleship until all ammunition was expended. He then returned to the *Fanshaw Bay* to re-arm.[176]

Lt. W. J. Slone was launched at 0715 with a cold engine and equipped with four 500-lb. bombs.[177] The enemy force was twenty miles off our port quarter and shelling the ships before he launched. He headed for the enemy immediately and climbed to 8,000 feet behind cloud cover. Coming into the clear, he saw two destroyers entering a rain squall below. They were followed by a destroyer leader and four more destroyers. He started his attack on the destroyers and before he was in range they began firing heavy AA. At 4,000 feet a 20 mm shell hit his port wing and cut the main spar in half. He set the bombs in train at sixty feet and 200 knots and released at 3,000 feet. His gunner observed three hits, and one bomb didn't release. He remained in the area until 0900 and then flew to Tacloban airfield.[178]

Lt. (jg) Evans took off at 0730 and climbed to 7,000 feet. Alone he made a strafing run on a destroyer observing hits and then joined up with Lt. (jg) Allen and together made additional strafing runs on a Japanese battleship, heavy cruiser, and another destroyer which they both observed hits from their machine guns.[179]

ON BOARD THE *KALININ BAY*

As the *Kalinin Bay* ran to the east, Captain Williamson readied her planes and launched them as fast as he could. The *Kalinin Bay* was leading the formation while the carriers were headed east, and most of the enemy gun fire had been directed at the carriers to the rear of the formation. By 0723, this situation changed when Clifton Sprague changed course to the southwest. The *White Plains* in the rear of the formation would now take the lead with the *Fanshaw Bay* and then the *St. Lo* on her starboard side. The *Kalinin Bay* was directly astern of the *White Plains* and the *Kitkun Bay* and the *Gambier Bay* were on the port side of the formation. This placed the *Kalinin Bay* and the *Gambier Bay* on the most exposed position, and as the battle progressed, they would now receive the greatest attention from the Japanese gunnery officers.[180]

PILOTS OF VC-3, THE *KALININ BAY*

Lt. Cdr. Keighley's group from VC-3 sighted four Japanese cruisers, two *Nachi* class and two *Tone* class, two battleships, one *Nagato* class and one *Kongo* class, and numerous destroyers at 0740. His

[176] Composite Squadron VC-68, *Fanshaw Bay*, Ens. G. D. Thompson.

[177] A plane with a cold engine and fully loaded had a high chance of stalling on take-off. This highlights the emergency nature of the situation and the increased risk that pilots were taking.

[178] Composite Squadron VC-68, *Fanshaw Bay*, Lt. W. J. Slone.

[179] Composite Squadron VC-68, *Fanshaw Bay*, Lt. (jg) Evans.

[180] *Kalinin Bay* Action Report.

planes were at 8,000 feet, and the signal to attack was given. Lt. Cdr. Keighley picked out a *Tone*-class cruiser for his dive bombing attack. His six rockets straddled the stern going from starboard quarter to just aft of amidships on the port side. Three bombs were direct hits with the others falling short or over.[181]

USS Kalinin Bay

USS St. Lo

Time
0730

USS Fanshaw Bay   Moving Southwest   USS Gambier Bay

USS Kitkun Bay

USS White Plains

Figure 49: Carrier Formation at 0730

Ens. Altman glided down to about 5,000 feet, and when he was directly over a *Nagato*-class battleship, he pushed over, firing his 5-inch rockets and releasing two 500-lb. bombs. The rockets hit amidships causing an explosion and black smoke. The 500-lb. bombs hit on the port side of the ship, one hitting the bow and one falling within twenty-five feet of the port bow.[182]

Lt. (jg) Merchant picked out a *Nachi*-class cruiser and straddled it with six rockets and three direct hits. Lt. Patsy Capano leading the flight was observed going down on the leading cruiser with six rockets. After this attack he joined back up with Lt. Cdr. Keighley and made a strafing attack on a *Tone*-class cruiser. Lt. Capano pulled out to the left, and Lt. Cdr. Keighley to the right. Lt. Capano wasn't seen again. Lt. J.J. Perrell who had been launched without any ammunition headed south to look for Taffy 2 to see if he could be loaded there.[183]

Lt. Crockett signaled for the attack and he started his run on a *Kongo*-class battleship, the only battleship he could see through the clouds. At 1,000 feet other units of the Japanese fleet were seen,

---

[181] Composite Squadron VC-3, *Kalinin Bay*, Lt. Comdr. Keighley

[182] Composite Squadron VC-3, *Kalinin Bay*, Ens. Altman. The *Nagato* does not report being hit, but the *Kongo* does have two bomb hits on the bow but did not list the time or day these hits occurred. They were simply part of a sketch of her damaged locations.

[183] Composite Squadron VC-3, *Kalinin Bay*, Lt. (jg) Merchant, Lt. Patsy Capano, Lt. Comdr. Keighley, Lt. J.J. Perrell.

including three heavy cruisers just to port of the battleship, and ahead of this battleship was another *Kongo*-class battleship. Lt. Crockett made his run from stern to stem on the same course that the battleship was moving. His bombs were set at fifty feet, 300 knots in train and were released at 2,500 feet. Lt. Crockett after his release pulled up sharply into the clouds. Intense AA was encountered, and the TBM-1C that was following him was hit and crashed into the sea, and the third TBM was observed by his gunner to also get hit and went down smoking.[184]

Lt. (jg) E. L. Archer, Jr. joined with Lt. Crockett and upon reaching the same open space in the clouds observed eight destroyers in column. Lt. (jg) Archer attacked the last two destroyers in the column, strafing with 0.50-cal. from 6,000 feet to 500 feet, where he made a sharp climbing recovery into a rain squall. He climbed to 8,500 feet and joined seven torpedo planes and ten fighters headed to attack the cruisers and battleships. As the flight proceeded around a cloud, two cruisers and a battleship were sighted. The cruisers started a turn to the left. Archer was the third man down. He attacked two cruisers in column that were turning to port, dropping his bombs from 4,500 to 3,000 on the second cruiser. Archer continued his dive at about 30° into the leading cruiser, which he hit with eight 5-inch rockets, walking them up the deck. Two of the rockets hit right on the bridge, knocking part of it off and causing an explosion.[185]

Ens. G.N. Smith also joined up with Lt. Crockett and selected as his target a *Tone*-class cruiser which was closest to our own forces. The enemy apparently was unaware of his approach, for they didn't fire in his direction until he started firing his rockets. He released his two 500-lb. bombs at 4,000 feet, continuing his dive for a rocket run. Five of the eight rockets hit the superstructure. Two near misses were registered with 500-lb. bombs, one exploding fifteen feet from the stern and the other about thirty feet off the bow. He recovered from his attack at 1,500 feet and climbed to 2,000 feet out of range of the enemy AA.[186]

ON BOARD THE *ST. LO*

Captain McKenna received a signal at 0730 from Clifton Sprague which ordered a change in course to 180° true and a little later to 240° true as not to remain on the same course too long. The enemy had continued to close and was now northward, the range to the closest cruiser falling from to 23,000 yards. He gave the order for *St. Lo* to open fire with her single 5-inch/38-caliber gun on her stern. By 0733, the range to the closest cruiser had decreased to 19,500 yards bearing 275° true.

---

[184] Composite Squadron VC-3, *Kalinin Bay,* Lt. Crockett.

[185] Composite Squadron VC-3, *Kalinin Bay,* Lt. (jg) E. L. Archer Jr., Lt. Crockett.

[186] Composite Squadron VC-3, *Kalinin Bay,* Ens. G.N. Smith.

By 0738, the range was down to 14,000 yards bearing 302° true with all CVE's making maximum smoke and returning fire with their stern guns.[187]

Captain McKenna observed that his gunners singled out a Japanese heavy cruiser that didn't appear to be under fire from any other ship. Three hits were claimed by his men. The first forward of turret one on the bow which started a fire and two impacted between the bridge and the forward stack. In the meantime a Japanese cruiser and a large destroyer had gained a position abeam on the port side of the formation and were firing very deliberately full broadsides. Between the times of 0738 to 0750, many salvos were observed on all sides of the *St. Lo*, several not more than fifty yards away. It was also reported that another cruiser and several destroyers were moving up on the port side, but no salvos were observed coming from this direction at this time.[188]

ON BOARD THE *KITKUN BAY*

Captain Whitney reported, "At 0740 the ship opened fire with her stern 5"/38 caliber gun. The screen left the formation to launch a torpedo attack against the enemy. Evasive action, consisting of turns of 5° to 60° was employed, as enemy salvos landed between 2,000 yards and fifty yards from the ship with at least two straddles close aboard."[189]

PILOTS OF VC-5, THE *KITKUN BAY*

At approximately 0730, Lt. Cdr. R. L. Fowler with the rest of VC-5 had reached an altitude of 8,000 feet and was flying on instruments due to the very bad weather. It was necessary to keep all the Japanese units under radar surveillance at this time. Two large units appeared on his screen dead ahead at a distance of eight miles. He climbed the group up to 9,500 feet still on instruments. Then his group was met with heavy AA of all kinds. No holes were in the clouds, so an effective attack at this point was impossible. Fowler orbited the Japanese units for twenty minutes trying to find a hole in the clouds to dive through, but none was available.[190]

ON BOARD THE *GAMBIER BAY*

Captain Vieweg reported, "From 0715 to 0730 foul weather between own task force and closing enemy force momentarily checked fire and only a few salvo splashes were observed in the formation

---

[187] *St. Lo* Action Report.

[188] Ibid.

[189] *Kitkun Bay* Action Report.

[190] Composite Squadron VC-5, *Kitkun Bay,* Commander R. L. Fowler.

during this period." At 0723, He changed course on TBS signal to the south. By 0730, he picked up on SG radar two or three vessels bearing 170° true, distance nineteen miles.[191]

The enemy force had at least six separate tracks approaching from 270° around to about 060°. By 0731, he noted the advanced cruiser unit moving around the northeast flank. The estimated speed of this enemy unit was thirty knots. Weather had partially cleared. Salvo splashes began to fall intermittently near the *Gambier Bay*. The *White Plains* and the *Fanshaw Bay* came under concentrated fire.[192]

Captain Vieweg's log reported that at 0733 one TBM-1C took on a torpedo brought up from the hangar deck on the forward elevator. By 0734 commenced pumping aviation gasoline to the plane, now on the flight deck. At 0738 completed gassing and purged the gasoline system. By 0740, Rear Admiral Clifton Sprague gave TBS order to open fire with the "pea shooters" when range was closer. Captain Vieweg gave the order at 0741 to commence firing 5-inch gun at enemy cruiser, 17,000 yards away on port quarter." By 0745 *Gambier Bay* launched one TBM-1C aircraft and noted, "Enemy straddling the ship."[193]

PILOTS OF VC-10, THE *GAMBIER BAY*

Lt. (jg) R. E. Weatherholt didn't take off with the first group of planes. Four planes were brought up from the hangar deck. Ens. Gallagher took off with the first plane loaded with a torpedo but only had thirty-five gallons of fuel. He knew he had only enough fuel to make a one way trip to the enemy and not enough fuel to make it back. Around 0720, Ens. Gallagher took off with the first plane. Lt. (jg) R. E. Weatherholt took off with the second plane at about 0730 but he had a full fuel tank plus a torpedo. Two more planes were being readied on the flight deck, so he circled waiting for these two planes to be launched. Shell fire began to fall around the *Gambier Bay* some as close as seventy-five yards. Her circled for thirty minutes, but the other two planes were never launched, so he headed for the enemy alone.[194]

Ensign Crocker after his attack spotted Ensign Gallagher's plane smoking badly after he had made a torpedo run on the Japanese fleet. It was soon apparent to him that Ensign Gallagher's plane wasn't going to make it and saw him land in the water, flip over onto the plane's back, but saw all three crewmen get out of the plane. He dropped several dye markers, and his seat boat-pack to them.[195] He then climbed for altitude waiting for someone to join up with. Not finding anyone he

---

[191] *Gambier Bay* Action Report.

[192] Ibid.

[193] Ibid.

[194] Composite Squadron VC-10, *Gambier Bay*, Lt. (jg) R. E. Weatherholt.

[195] Ens. Gallagher and his crew were never rescued after the battle.

decided to attack alone and made a run on a Japanese destroyer firing his rockets and guns. His turret gunner also fired, and then the plane was hit in the port wing and engine, but with no loss of power. He and his crew witnessed another plane fire eight rockets into the water near a destroyer, so he turned back around, and he believed he sighted a submarine just below the surface, but he had nothing left to attack with.[196] He then headed for Dulag airfield and landed safely only for a fighter to crash into his plane damaging his propeller.[197]

Lt. Jackson watched the Japanese ship continue to shell the U.S. carrier formation. He then heard over his radio to take care and not to attack friendly units; the U.S. destroyers were to make a torpedo attack. He climbed to 10,000 feet, and there was an occasional AA burst in his vicinity from time to time. Then he heard by radio that Ensign Gallagher had been hit and was making a water landing. He soon received word to head for Tacloban airfield which he did landing at 0840.[198]

Ensign McGraw and Lt. (jg) Hunting teamed up to make several strafing runs on the battleships and cruisers. Ensign McGraw reported making eleven strafing attacks on what he identified as a *Fuso*-class battleship and three on a *Tone*-class cruiser.[199] He reported the AA gunfire as heavy but inaccurate. Lt. (jg) Hunting made five such strafing attacks on what he identified as a *Mogami*-class cruiser. Lt. (jg) Hunting then flew to Tacloban airfield where he landed safely at 0945.[200]

ON BOARD THE *WHITE PLAINS*

By 0720, the master gyro was back in operation with an estimated error of 15° easterly. It continued to fluctuate, so Captain Sullivan had to approximate all course changes from this time forward. By 0721, he turned his ship into the wind and launched two more torpedo bombers by 0726. After these two planes were launched he then issued orders to continue erratic steering until 0735 where he steadied her course and launched two more torpedo bombers. By 0736, he issued orders to change course to 180° south and by 0740 he received word from Clifton Sprague for the destroyers to make a torpedo attack.[201]

---

[196] The Japanese submarine *I-26* was operating close to Taffy 1, so it may be possible Ensign Crocker spotted her on his way to Dulag. There was no known Japanese submarine operating near Taffy 3 during the surface battle.

[197] Composite Squadron VC-10, *Gambier Bay*, Ensign Crocker.

[198] Composite Squadron VC-10, *Gambier Bay*, Lt. Jackson.

[199] The *Nagato*'s superstructure has the most in common with a *Fuso*-class battleship, making *Nagato* Ensign McGraw's most likely target.

[200] Composite Squadron VC-10, *Gambier Bay* Ensign McGraw, Lt. (jg) Hunting.

[201] White Plains Action Report.

94

ON BOARD THE *NATOMA BAY*

Rear Admiral Felix Stump expressed the situation: "At 0720, Clifton Sprague gave the position of the enemy as 11-44 N, 126-24 E. This was the first time we could determine the enemy bearing. At this time Taffy 2 was about thirty four miles from the main enemy disposition. It was apparent that this enemy force had passed through San Bernardino Strait during the night and was sweeping toward Leyte Gulf. It was likewise evident, with the enemy probably coming to a southerly course and with the wind being from 025° to 040° true that this task unit while launching planes would be on a converging course with the enemy force. While preparations for the first torpedo attack were being made this task unit at 0720 changed course to 120° true with a speed of seventeen knots in an attempt to conserve the ever decreasing distance between the enemy and this task unit. It seemed best to try to gain distance to the eastward away from Leyte Gulf the probable objective of the enemy. This was based on the hope that the enemy might not see us, or if he did do so he would send a small portion of his force which we could destroy and thus gain time to enable us to cripple him by air attacks. It was apparent immediately that the major burden of destruction of the enemy force must be the responsibility of Taffy 2."[202]

ON BOARD THE *HAGGARD*

At 0730 Cdr. D. A. Harris received orders from Rear Admiral Felix Stump to interpose with Destroyer Division 94 between enemy and main body. Immediately thereafter, Cdr. Harris ordered the *Hailey* and the *Franks* to form on the *Haggard*. At 0745, he noted that the vessels of Taffy 3 were sighted.[203]

[202] CTU 77.4.2 Action Report.
[203] *Haggard* Action Report.

Figure 50: The *Santee* is seen from the *Petrof Bay* a moment after she took a kamikaze plane hit at 0740, 25 October 1944.

ON BOARD THE *SANGAMON*

Rear Admiral Thomas Sprague of Taffy 1 was busy getting his carriers ready to launch a second attack. Suddenly at 0740, four Japanese planes attacked his task unit with complete surprise. Thomas Sprague believed the aircraft to be either Zekes or Judys. Each plane attempted a suicide dive into each of the four carriers. The *Santee* was hit on her flight deck, forward of the after elevator, causing a fire on the flight deck and hangar deck. At the same time the *Sangamon* and the *Petrof Bay* suffered a near miss each.[204]

ON BOARD THE *PETROF BAY*, TAFFY 1

Six TBM torpedo bombers and four FM-2 fighters were launched at 0728. They joined up with twenty more fighters and ten more torpedo bombers from the other three carriers. As these aircraft were making rendezvous, Taffy 1 came under air attack, and they were diverted to the southwest, and the fighters were recalled to defend the task unit. Only eleven fighters returned to cover the

---

[204] CTU 77.4 Action Report. This was the very first successful kamikaze attack of the war. Vice Admiral Kurita didn't know Vice Admiral Onishi had adopted these tactics. He received very little information from the First or Second Air Fleets and remained unaware of these air attacks during the battle.

sixteen torpedo bombers, and five of these were forced to abort due to low fuel. The delay in the strike prevented this strike from arriving over the target until 1050.[205]

Figure 51: On board the *Santee* as she was hit by the kamikaze aircraft. Crew members attempt to shield themselves from the fragments and from the explosion.

PILOTS OF VC-76, *PETROF BAY*, TAFFY 1

Four FM-2 fighters that had been launched by the *Petrof Bay* at 0552 on October 25 rendezvoused over Homonhon Island with six F6F fighters each carrying one 500-lb. bomb, and four additional FM-2 fighters joined them a bit later. When word was received that Taffy 3 was under attack by the Japanese fleet, this strike group was directed to proceed and attack the Japanese force.[206]

The strike flew a course of 042° true from Homonhon Island and sighted Taffy 2 which was known to be operating just south of Taffy 3. Course was changed to 300° true and thirteen miles further on, the flight spotted Taffy 3. Three of the carriers were being bombarded and were on fire and smoking. The planes let down under the clouds which were heavy over the target area and

---

[205] *Petrof Bay* Action Report.
[206] Ibid.

observed the Japanese forces about twelve miles beyond the CVE's. The strike pulled up into the clouds and prepared to attack. The time was approximately 0730.[207]

The F6F's went in first diving through the clouds. The pilots were unable to see their results due to cloud coverage. Lt. (jg) Crocker led his wing-man, Ens. Loverin, and the second section, Lt. Forsythe and Ens. Curtright, in on a battleship or a heavy cruiser on the first run. Dive angle was approximately 70° and pull-out made at 1,000 feet. Lt. (jg) Crocker pulled up into rain squall area, and as he leveled out, his wing man and the second section had disappeared. He joined up with the F6F's and made a second run on a battleship. Ens. Loverin made his second run independently on this same ship and joined back up after the second run. A third strafing run was delivered on a cruiser. The fourth attack was made on a group of destroyers who attempted to evade by forming a circle pattern. The fifth and final run was made on three destroyers which left the circle. Lt. (jg) Crocker and Ens. Loverin then withdrew and landed at Tacloban Field to refuel before returning to base.[208]

The second section of Lt. Marke and Ens. Brown made another run on a destroyer of a disposition coming in on the port side of the heavy formation. Cloud cover over the smaller Japanese element was about 3,500 feet and section burst out of the clouds at low altitude over the destroyer. A heavy cruiser beyond the destroyer was also strafed. A final run was made by Lt. Marke and Ens. Brown on the destroyer before they retired. All runs were made broadside to the ships attacked.[209]

TBM's of this squadron split with one section, Ens. E.B. Sawyer and W.L. Farmer, choosing lead ship as target. Section two with Lt. R. F. Tracy, Ens. R. P. Lodhole, and Ens. W. E. Niemann chose the leading battleship on the starboard side of the formation.[210] A third section with Lt. A. E. Schwarzwalder made a lone attack on the battleship on the port side of the formation. Enemy AA picked up the formations at 5,000 feet and a mile or more out as break-up commenced. AA bursts left purple and green smoke which remained visible for several minutes. The enemy also opened up with main batteries on the torpedo planes.

Lt. Schwarzwalder swung to his right and toward the lead ship of a smaller formation. The lead ship, a heavy cruiser, opened fire as he turned to his port and back in on the battleship. As he began his run he saw a TBM spin into the sea near a *Yamato*-class battleship. At his dropping point he was 30° to the bow of the *Kongo*-class battleship which had commenced a turn toward the attacking

---

[207] Ibid.

[208] Composite Squadron VC-76, *Petrof Bay, Lt.* (jg) Crocker, Ens. Loverin, Lt. Forsythe, and Ens. Curtright.

[209] Composite Squadron VC-76, *Petrof Bay,* Lt. Marke and Ens. Brown.

[210] Composite Squadron VC-76, *Petrof Bay,* Ens. E.B. Sawyer, W.L. Farmer, Lt. R. F. Tracy, Ens. R. P. Lodhole, and Ens. W. E. Niemann.

plane. Drop was made at 350 feet altitude with 240-250 knots indicated. The torpedo commenced a normal run, but Lt. Schwarzwalder couldn't keep track of the torpedo due to the intense AA gun fire that required him to maneuver. The range when he dropped the torpedo was approximately 1,100 yards.[211]

Lt. Schwarzwalder retired down the side of a *Kongo*-class battleship (*Haruna*, most likely his target) and in doing so flew past a second battleship (*Nagato*). As he passed the after island of this battleship, he observed a huge flag that particularly fascinated his attention. The ship was partially enveloped in a rain squall, and he was unable to identify it. Due to the intense AA, he didn't climb above 400 feet as he retired.[212]

Lt. Tracy, Ens. Lodhole, and Ens. Niemann made their attack on either the *Nagato* or the *Haruna* which they miss-identified as the *Yamashiro*. After the break-up a turn was made to the division's port, and then a turn to starboard so that the run was made at 50° angle to the starboard bow of the battleship. AA fire was intense. Drop was made from altitude of 700 feet with a speed of 285 knots and a range of 1,200 yards. During the turn into the target, Ens. Lodhole lost sight of Lt. Tracy and Ens. Niemann and never did see them again. Ens. Lodhole passed ahead of the battleship as the torpedo began a normal run. The target didn't take evasive action. To avoid flying over another battleship on the port side of the formation he turned and ran down the center of the formation through a hail of AA fire of all types. Breaking out into the clear he joined up with Lt. Schwarzwalder, and they both proceeded back to base.[213]

Ens. Sawyer and Ens. Farmer made a run on the leading *Yamato*-class battleship. At the break-up point this section pulled out toward their starboard and then turned in toward the target. The drop by Ens. Sawyer was made approximately 1,500 yards out, altitude 700 feet at an angle of 90°. Ens. Sawyer's torpedo made a normal run toward the target. Pilot was able to observe Ens. Farmer's torpedo also making a normal run toward the target. Both pilots were unable to observe results due to the intense AA that forced the planes to maneuver and getting out of there in a hurry. Pilots pulled out and ran across the bow of the *Nagato*.[214]

Ens. Farmer's plane ran out of gas, and he had to make a water landing eight miles from the *Petrof Bay*, and he and his crew were rescued by a destroyer. Ens. Sawyer landed on the *Petrof Bay* with ten gallons of fuel remaining. Lt. Schwartzwalder and Ens. Lodhole landed on the *Ommaney Bay* with only five and ten gallons of fuel remaining.[215]

---

[211] Composite Squadron VC-76, *Petrof Bay,* Lt. Schwarzwalder.

[212] Ibid.

[213] Composite Squadron VC-76, *Petrof Bay,* Lt. Tracy, Ens. Lodhole, and Ens. Niemann.

[214] Composite Squadron VC-76, *Petrof Bay,* Ens. Sawyer and Ens. Farmer.

[215] Composite Squadron VC-76, *Petrof Bay,* Ens. Farmer, Lt. Schwartzwalder, Ens. Lodhole.

ON BOARD THE *WASATCH*

Vice Admiral Kinkaid received a word at 0715 that the *Louisville* had launched a scout plane to search Surigao Strait, Bogod Bay, and Bohol Island areas. By 0719, the left flank had changed course to 155°, and at 0721 one of the Japanese destroyers seen burning earlier had sunk. Then at 0724, he learned that Taffy 3 was under attack. Kinkaid immediately contacted Rear Admiral Oldendorf to rendezvous his force to the eastern entrance of Leyte Gulf; he also called for all planes moving for strikes against the retreating enemy ships to the south to stop and attack the enemy task force attacking Taffy 3. He then radioed Halsey in plain language, requesting immediate help. Orders were given to Rear Admiral Thomas Sprague and Rear Admiral Felix Stump to come to the assistance of Taffy 3 with all available aircraft.[216]

By 0727, Oldendorf received Kinkaid's message to rendezvous to the eastern entrance of Leyte Gulf. At this same time Kinkaid sent a second plain-language message to Halsey, "Request Lee proceeds at top speed to cover Leyte, request immediate strike by fast carriers." By 0731, Oldendorf had changed course to 355° and was heading north back up through Surigao Strait.[217] Kinkaid then received a message that Taffy 1 was under air attack and that the *Santee* has been hit by a suicide aircraft and was burning. Kinkaid then sent a third plain-language message at 0739 to Halsey, "Help needed from heavy ships immediately."[218]

---

[216] CTU 77 Action Report.

[217] On 21 October 1944 at 0642 the *West Virginia* had run aground and damaged three of her four propellers reducing her maximum sustained speed to sixteen knots and in an emergency eighteen knots.

[218] CTU 77 Action Report.

CHAPTER 4. *YAMATO* FORCED NORTH: 0745-0815

ON BOARD THE *HARUNA*

Rear Admiral Shigenaga at 0747 shifted fire to what he believed was a destroyer on an opposite course, bearing 45° relative to starboard. At 0748, *Haruna* opened fire at a distance of 16,998 yards and fired two salvos, then checking fire at 0751. Smoke hid the results.[219]

Figure 52: This photo was taken by the *White Plains* when in the lead of the carrier formation with the *Kitkun Bay* closest and the *Gambier Bay* further aft.

ON BOARD THE *KALININ BAY*

Captain Williamson reported, "At about 0750, the *Kalinin Bay* received her first hit on the starboard side just aft of the forward elevator on the hangar deck with several near misses at the same time. No units were visible off the starboard side at this time; this hit may have come from a

---

[219] *Haruna* Detailed Action Report. The *Haruna* is actually firing on the *Kalinin Bay* which was hit by a battleship shell fragment at 0750.

Japanese battleship observed to be firing on us by a fighter pilot of the *Kalinin Bay*, who was attacking the enemy units. Fragments of a large-caliber shell were found on the hangar deck."[220]

The first damaging shell, battleship-caliber, was a near miss close to Sponson No. 1, part of the shell entering the ship about six feet above the hangar deck at frame 69 on the starboard side expending itself against the opposite bulkhead.[221]

Figure 53: The *Kalinin Bay* was hit, as viewed from the *White Plains* looking directly aft at approximately 0750. The *Kalinin Bay* was directly behind the *White Plains* in the rear of the formation with the *Fanshaw Bay* and the *St. Lo* on the *White Plains's* starboard side (left side of photo) and the *Kitkun Bay* and the *Gambier Bay* to port. This photograph was often labeled as a photograph of the *Gambier Bay* taking a hit to port; however, the *White Plains* was never in position to take such a photo. The *Kalinin Bay* was the only U.S. carrier to take a battleship-caliber hit to starboard. A U.S. plane can be seen overhead. The white and black smoke coming from the right side belongs to *Gambier Bay*. The *Haruna* fired two salvos from 0748-0751, and the heavy cruisers fired on the *Kalinin Bay* and the *Fanshaw Bay* from 0750-0755.

Williamson saw three heavy cruisers on the port quarter, and these were definitely identified by the recognition officer and other officers to be one heavy cruiser of the *Nachi* class and two heavy cruisers of the *Tone* class. When the enemy cruisers closed the range to 18,000 yards at about 0800,

---

[220] *Kalinin Bay* Action Report. The only Japanese battleship firing at this time was the *Haruna*, which fired two salvos at what she believed was a destroyer at 0748-0751. The range, 16,998 yards, corresponds to the distance of the Taffy 3 carrier formation. She was on the *Kalinin Bay*'s starboard side at 0750. All heavy cruisers were on the carrier formation's port side at the time and had taken both her and the *Fanshaw Bay* under fire. The remaining hits scored on the *Kalinin Bay* all come from port. This is the only hit that came from starboard.

[221] Ibid.

the *Kalinin Bay* was ordered to open fire. The cruisers closed to 17,300 yards. Fire was continued from the single 5-inch/38-caliber gun on her stern.[222]

Figure 54: A detail of the original photo shows that what appears to be a carrier viewed from astern when taking a hit on the port side was actually a carrier viewed from directly ahead. She was pouring out white and black smoke. The much wider shell splash may be two shells in line with each other making this a four-shell salvo instead of three-shell.

ON BOARD THE *HAGURO*

Captain Sugiura ordered the main battery to engage an aircraft carrier at 0750. From 0750 to 0755 she fired fifty-three projectiles with an estimate of six to nine hits. The distance was approximately 17,207 yards.[223]

---

[222] Ibid.

[223] *Haguro* Detailed Action Report.

Figure 55: *Kalinin Bay* turning to starboard as a heavy cruiser salvo falls to her port side, as seen from the *White Plains*.

Figure 56: The next five or six shells were probably *Haruna*'s second salvo landing ahead.

Figure 57: *Haruna* checked fire, and the heavy cruisers maintained their fire on *Kalinin Bay*.

ON BOARD THE FANSHAW BAY

At 0750, the *Fanshaw Bay* received a hit on the bow, apparently from an 8-inch shell; only one hit from a salvo of five. The shell struck the flight deck between frame 32 and 33 about twenty-eight feet inboard of the starboard gallery walkway. The trajectory was downward and forward passing through the top of bulkhead 32 at a point where it joined the overhead; this cut all power, lighting, and communication cables (34 circuits), causing an electrical fire that men from Repair Two put out with CO_2. The projectile penetrated door A-0201 and then the deck of A-0201 at frame 27 tearing a hole 24 inches by 36 inches. It then entered stateroom A-0103 and struck bulkhead 26, tearing a hole approximately 48 inches by 60 inches in stateroom 0101. It continued into the outboard bulkhead of compartment 0101, distorting and pushing this bulkhead outboard for four feet between frames 24-25. It penetrated this bulkhead, making a 24-inch by 40-inch hole, stuck a ventilator, and sheared it off at its base, killing and wounding several men in this area. The shell then penetrated the forecastle deck at frame 22 and into A-102-E, tearing a hole 24 inches by 24 inches. The projectile continued through bulkhead 20, tearing a hole 20 inches by 20 inches, and then penetrated the starboard side of the ship at frames 17-19, opening a hole 24 inches by 60 inches about two feet above deck level.[224]

Hit 2 passed under the barrels of 40 mm mount No. 4 and struck the crewman at the pointer position, killing him. The shell then struck the top corner edge of the gun shield which deflected the shell upward and broke it in half so that the nose entered the outboard bulkhead of compartment A-2011/2-2C (Radar Room 2) at frame 21. The nose of the shell created an 18-inch by 18-inch hole, penetrated bulkhead 20, causing a similar hole and then hitting the steel door of A-0201-2M which was against bulkhead 20. The impact tore the top part of the door off its hinges and dented it, but the fragment stopped here and fell to the floor. The remainder of the shell was believed to have ricocheted over the flight deck after hitting the gun shield.[225]

Clifton Sprague gave orders to change course to 195° at 0752 and then to 200° at 0755. By 0757 he changed course again to 180° and ordered the ship's 5-inch gun to fire at an enemy cruiser on the port quarter. At 0758 hit 3 soon struck the flight deck eight feet aft of frame 34 and entered thirteen and a half feet from the port side of the ship. It smashed the catapult track on the port side and the catapult machinery compartment A-202-E at frame 32. This one went through the brig and ricocheted through various compartments and outside through the skin of the ship, approximately twelve feet above the water line.[226]

---

[224] *Fanshaw Bay* Action Report.

[225] Ibid.

[226] Ibid.

All lighting and communication cables were cut (thirty-one circuits) causing an electrical fire which Repair Two put out with CO_2. The shell penetrated bulkhead 30 and entered A-201 3/4L which was the Flag office where a low-order detonation occurred wrecking all furniture within the compartment. One man was killed, and two others were wounded. Repair Two put out this fire with water fog and evacuated the wounded.[227]

Shell fragments or nose pieces then penetrated the forward bulkhead at frame 26, creating a large hole 48 inches by 48 inches entering A-0201 where it hit six boxes of .50-caliber ammunition and exploded, causing a fire in this area. Fragments then smashed through the flight deck web beam on the forecastle deck at frame 20, tearing a huge hole 48 inches by 48 inches, and a section of bulkhead 26 tore up through the deck of the above described area. Another fragment ripped a hole 24 inches by 36 inches in the overhead, demolishing a wardrobe locker, and fire spread there as well. One fragment continued and smashed into the top of the port side of the anchor windlass, gouging out a section of the port brake shoe drum, smashing the port wild-cat, completely cutting the anchor chain for the port anchor, dented the port wild-cat shaft collar, and sheared off the port forward hold down stud and bolts of the main shaft bearing. A section of the wild-cat was bent over, and into the intermediate drive gear.[228]

This fragment was still not finished, as it ricocheted upward and took out a 36-inch section of the bull gear, and a spoke of the bull gear tore away one support and distorted the bull gear shield, thence continuing upward through the starboard forward apron of the flight deck about twelve feet from the starboard edge and tearing a hole about 24 inches by 24 inches in the flight deck at frame 3. Other fragments which resulted from this hit penetrated the flight deck at frame 6 making a 12-inch by 12-inch hole. Another fragment penetrated #1 starboard longitudinal forward of the flight deck web support, tearing a 20-inch by 20-inch hole. Two officers and two enlisted men were severely injured, and five other enlisted men suffered minor injuries as a result of these fragments.[229]

---

[227] Ibid.

[228] Ibid.

[229] Ibid.

Figure 58: The entry hole in the flight deck for hit #3 and the torn-up catapult on the *Fanshaw Bay*. Unfortunately the entry hole was not shown in its entirety, so an estimate of the size of the hole remains in question.

The windscreen and cap head of hit 3 separated upon striking the flight deck and penetrated bulkhead 30, creating a 20-inch by 20-inch hole and then penetrated A-0201 3/4L (Flag Office) at frame 27 tearing another 20-inch by 20-inch hole and then entered Junior Officers Bunk Room A-0102 tearing an 18-inch by 24-inch section of the corrugated deck beam and breaking a 48-inch by 48-inch area of fiberglass insulation on the overhead; the projectile then weakly penetrated the light sheet metal bulkhead at frame 26 making a hole 8 inches by 12 inches, and the nose and windscreen came to rest on the upper bunk along this bulkhead in stateroom 0102.[230]

---

[230] *Ibid.* The damage inflicted by the shell of hit 3 raises doubts about the estimated shell caliber of 8-inch. An 8-mch cap head is 5.5 inches in diameter and 5 inches thick and weighs 7.9 lbs. A 14-inch cap head is 12 inches in diameter and 8 inches thick and weighs 63 lbs. An 8-inch windscreen is 16.6 inches in length while a 14-inch windscreen is 26 inches in length. Holes as large as four feet square and cap head penetrations of 20-inch diameter seem inconsistent with the smaller projectile. The last hole the cap head made was the exact measurement of a 14-inch cap head. However, the fact that the windscreen and cap head were reportedly recovered by the crew should have positively identified the caliber of shell; yet the documentation of this hit did not specify the shell's entry hole size in the flight deck, and the dimensions of the cap head and windscreen were not recorded. The damage photos lack sufficient detail to make a reliable estimate. So there is not enough information to determine if indeed this hit came from a battleship-caliber round.

Figure 59: *Fanshaw Bay* seen off *White Plains's* starboard quarter, under heavy cruiser fire. To north on the horizon, *Dennis* and *John C. Butler* withdraw after launching torpedo attacks.

Clifton Sprague changed course to 220° at 0759. At 0800, he sighted another group of ships bearing 165°, distance twelve miles heading north. At 0803, he changed course to 240°. Next he ordered all fire bombs jettisoned. Not wanting to stay on the same course for too long at 0814 he changed course to 205°. Clifton Sprague remarked, "After my task group had been under heavy surface fire for about an hour, I turned to William Morgan, my chief quartermaster, with the remark: 'By golly, I think we may have a chance.'"[231] So far none of his six carriers had been seriously damaged, and all could maintain their maximum speed. Though the Japanese salvos were landing very close, so far there had been relatively few hits made on the carriers themselves. Clifton Sprague fully expected help to be coming north from Leyte Gulf from Kinkaid and was also aware that Taffy 2 and Taffy 1 were launching everything they had.[232]

[231] Sprague, "They Had Us on the Ropes."
[232] *Fanshaw Bay* Action Report.

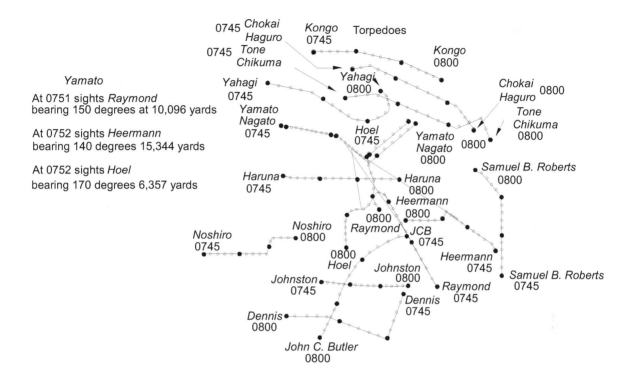

Figure 60: Position of Japanese and U.S. ships at 0745-0800

ON BOARD THE *YAMATO*

At 0750, the *Yamato* sent a flag signal for all vessels to turn 20° to starboard. By 0751, she opened secondary-battery fire against an enemy cruiser bearing 150°, distance 10,096 yards. This was the *Raymond* now charging in to make her torpedo attack. By 0752, the *Yamato* lost sight of the *Raymond* in the smoke screen, and the secondary battery changed to a destroyer bearing 140°, distance 15,344 yards. This was the *Heermann* also charging in to make her first torpedo attack. Before *Yamato* engaged the *Heermann*, she suddenly found another destroyer about to launch a torpedo attack, bearing 170°, distance 6,357 yards. This was the *Hoel* which launched her second torpedo attack at 0753.[233]

The *Yamato*'s secondary battery opened fire on the *Hoel*. Torpedo wakes were sighted bearing 100° to starboard. At 0754, the *Yamato* turned hard to port. At 0755, the *Yamato* opened with her 5-inch and light AA guns against the *Hoel*. The *Yamato* was then hit by an enemy 5-inch shell that

---

[233] *Yamato* Detailed Action Report. The *Hoel* in her action report documents her second torpedo attack occurred at 0735, a reversal of the 3 and 5. This time is incorrect and simply may be a typo. *Heermann* documents that *Hoel* fired her torpedoes at 0753. In addition the Japanese see more torpedoes at 0753 than the *Heermann* can fire alone, and the *Heermann* does not fire at the *Haruna* until 0800 which is seven minutes after the *Yamato* is forced north.

penetrated the ceiling for the crew kitchen making a two-foot hole in the uppermost deck. At 0756, the *Yamato* checked fire. Then at 0802, the torpedo wakes to port disappeared, and the *Yamato* turned to 000°. By 0804, the torpedo wakes to starboard disappeared, and the *Yamato* turned to starboard to reverse her heading, and settled on a course of 160°. By 0812, she turned 10° to starboard and launched the #2 air scout in an attempt to gain some intelligence on the enemy disposition.[234]

Ugaki recorded in his diary, "At 0754, when we were firing at an enemy destroyer at short distance, we found a torpedo trace to the starboard bow and we evaded it to the non-enemy side, turning to port with a direction of the commander in chief. This caused us a lot of trouble afterward because we were caught between four torpedoes on the starboard side and two on the port side. The enemy slow speed torpedoes running parallel to *Yamato* with twenty-six knots didn't permit her to turn for a pretty long time. It was about ten minutes but it felt like a month to me. After the traces disappeared we finally could turn to starboard and put all our power into the chase."[235] Ugaki may not have realized that *Haruna* blocked any turn to starboard. A turn toward the torpedo tracks would have caused a collision.. The turn to port was *Yamato*'s only option. In addition, *Yahagi* and her destroyers were to her port side, and this formation prevented her from simply turning 360° to port. Caught between *Haruna* to starboard and *Yahagi* to port, she could only parallel *Hoel*'s torpedoes until they ran out of fuel.

ON BOARD THE *HOEL*

Heading southwest after her initial torpedo attack, the *Hoel* cut in front of the onrushing battleships. At about 0750 she turned to make her second attack on a "heavy cruiser" which was actually the battleship *Haruna* or *Yamato*. Cdr. Kintberger at 0753 fired five torpedoes at a range of 6,000 yards, with a target angle of 050°. All torpedoes ran hot, straight, and normal, and Cdr. Kintberger witnessed a large column of water from the cruiser at about the time scheduled for the torpedo run.

The *Hoel* had two potential targets to fire her torpedoes at but she did not give a complete record for her second torpedo attack. If her target was the *Haruna* with a 050° target angle her course heading would have been 270° and the *Haruna* would be at 320° true at a range of 7,179 yards from the *Hoel*. The *Haruna*'s course was 090° at a speed of 28 knots and if the *Hoel* fired her torpedoes between 350°-000° at an intermediate speed of 33.5 knots they would travel 5,500 yards in 4.9 minutes and crossed the *Haruna*'s path which would travel 4,508 yards during this time frame. However, this does not match historical events and torpedoes fired at these bearings would travel

---

[234] Ibid.

[235] Ugaki, Matome. *Fading Victory: The Diary of Admiral Matome Ugaki 1941-1945*. University of Pittsburgh Press, 1991, p 493.

behind the *Yamato* as she was already ahead of the *Haruna* so the *Haruna* was not the *Hoel*'s intended target.

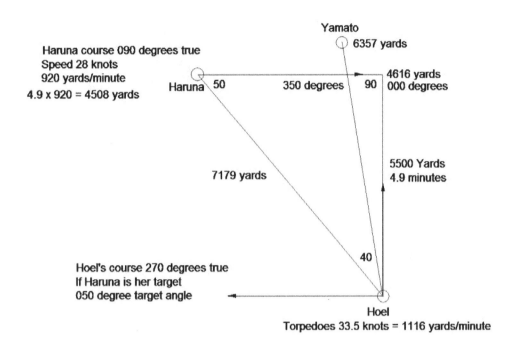

Figure 61: *Hoel's* **second torpedo attack at 0753**

From the *Hoel*'s position the *Yamato* was at a bearing at 350° true at the stated range of 6,357 yards but to gain a 050° target angle the *Hoel* would be on course 300°. This simply reflected her maneuvering to position herself to fire her torpedoes. The *Yamato* was on course 120° and was making 26 knots. If the *Hoel* fired her torpedoes bearing 020°-030° at 33.5 knots and the *Yamato* maintained her course of 120° the torpedoes would have crossed her path in 4,869 yards taking 4.3 minutes. If the *Yamato* makes a 090° turn to port to avoid these torpedoes she comes to a new course of 030° true and would have torpedoes running parallel with her on both sides. At 33.5 knots the torpedoes were travelling at 1,116 yards per minute. It would take the torpedoes nine minutes at this speed to run 10,000 yards which was the listed range of the torpedo at intermediate speed. If the first torpedoes were launched at 0753 they would complete their run at 0802 which was when the *Yamato* documented the torpedoes to port disappeared. It then would depend on how fast *Hoel* launched the remaining four torpedoes and based on the *Yamato*'s report it would appear it was over two minutes time so the last torpedo disappeared at 0804. This largely matched historical events so the *Hoel* must have fired her second torpedo attack at the *Yamato* as her intended target. This also shows that the torpedoes passed ahead of the *Haruna* and she did not have to make a violent maneuver to avoid them which was consistent with her logs.

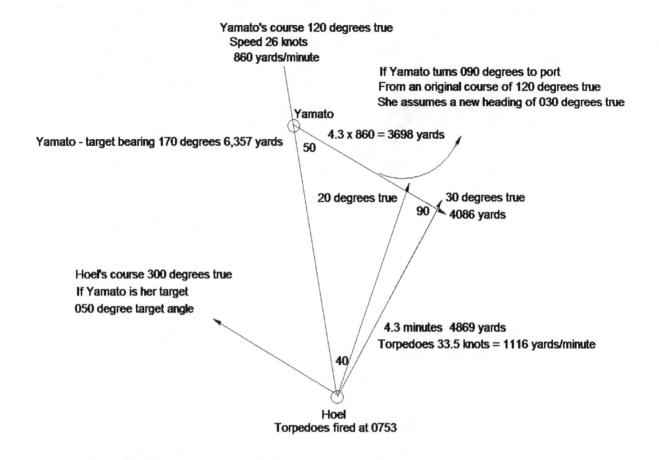

Figure 60: *Hoel's* **second torpedo attack at 0753**

Cdr. Kintberger reported, "Between 0740 and 0800 many estimated 5" and 8" shells were received above the water line as follows; torpedo shack, loading machine, base of after stack, three hits in forward stack sending much fragments into the signal bridge, galley, pay office, emergency radio, sick bay, number one and three 20 mm gun mounts, No. five 40 mm gun magazine, and starboard depth charge throwers that split several depth charges spilling them onto the deck. No fires were caused by these hits.

ON BOARD THE *NAGATO*

At 0746, Rear Admiral Kobe received *Yamato*'s order to set course 100° true. Then at 0749, *Yamato* gave orders for a 20° turn. As *Nagato* trailed her flagship, the surrounding sea was thick with smoke, and the rain squalls made visibility extremely difficult. Suddenly, the *Yamato* signaled a warning at 0753, "Torpedoes avoid," and the flagship turned to port. Kobe also turned the *Nagato* to port at 0754, and her lookouts spot three torpedo wakes bearing 045°. At 0800, the *Yamato* signals another warning to avoid torpedoes and turned to course 000°, and Kobe turned the *Nagato* to match course. By 0802, *Yamato* was beginning to reverse course, and Kobe ordered the *Nagato* to fall in behind her.[236]

At 0802, his lookouts reported an enemy cruiser bearing 096° relative partially hidden by smoke screens and rain squalls. Kobe gave the command to open fire on the enemy cruiser at 0803 using both main and secondary guns now bearing 090° relative. At 0804, the range to the enemy cruiser was 9,371 yards, and by 0805 hits were observed by the secondary guns, and the enemy cruiser was listing and on fire. By 0806, the enemy cruiser had disappeared behind a smoke screen, and Kobe ordered the main and secondary guns to check fire. As soon as this surface battle was over, the *Nagato*'s lookouts reported more aircraft attacking from astern. U.S. fighters made a strafing attack. The *Nagato* engaged with her AA guns. Kobe noted at 0811 that the *Yahagi*'s destroyers were attacking the same enemy ship covered in the smoke screen as they sailed south on the *Nagato*'s starboard side.[237]

ON BOARD THE *HARUNA*

At 0754, the *Haruna* received a signal from the *Kumano*, "Carriers are located on bearing 080, distance 17,536 yards from my location." Preliminary orders were given to fire using radar control, but Shigenaga canceled the order to spare ammunition. Then at 0756, she received an urgent signal from the *Yamato*, "Warning two incoming torpedo wakes!" Shigenaga made a minor adjustment in his ship's course so that the torpedoes passed ahead of his ship. At 0758, he directed the main guns at a new target, a cruiser bearing 030° starboard, distance 15,125 yards. At 0800, Shigenaga gave permission to fire from her main guns at this new cruiser.[238] At 0802, the main guns were fired, but the target disappeared behind a smoke screen. At 0804, Shigenaga observed that Cruiser Division 5

---

[236] *Nagato* Detailed Action Report.

[237] Ibid.

[238] This range and bearing points to the *Johnston* who would engage a *Kongo*-class battleship once she cleared the rain squall. It can't be stressed enough at how poor visibility was during this phase of the action for both sides.

and Cruiser Division 7 were engaging the enemy carriers. By 0806, Shigenaga gave the order to check main battery fire.[239]

ON BOARD THE *YAHAGI*

At 0755, as the *Nagato* and the *Yamato* turned to port, this forced the *Yahagi* and her destroyers to also turn to port, and they made a 270° turn. By turning the squadron this may have also avoided the *Heermann*'s last three torpedoes as they passed the port side of the *Yamato* and the *Nagato*. At 0805, Captain Yoshimura received a message from the *Yamato*, "All fleet attack." He ordered twenty-eight knots and "attack" to his destroyers; with this he stopped following the battleships to the rear of the formation, and he headed south at flank speed in an attempt to finally join the action.[240]

ON BOARD THE *HOEL*

The *Hoel* at 0815 had developed a 10° list to port, and the forward engine room was hit by an estimated 8-inch shell near the lube oil cooler causing a leak that was stopped by stuffing it with rags. This hit placed the forward engine and the forward generator out of commission, causing the ship to lose way. The diesel generator took over the entire emergency and lighting load. The *Hoel* maintained fire on the Japanese using her two forward 5-inch guns. Plot maintained communication with the bridge to the very end.[241]

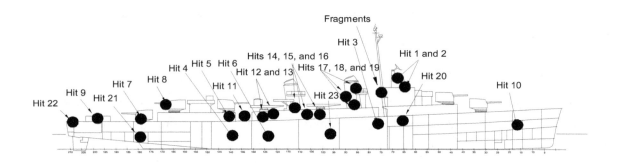

Figure 61: Hits 11-23 added to locations for 1-10 to the *Hoel* between 0740 and 0800.

---

[239] *Haruna* Detailed Action Report.

[240] *Yahagi* Detailed Action Report. Many secondary sources say that the *Yahagi* came under air attack at this time, but the *Yahagi* herself does not mention it in her action report.

[241] *Hoel* Action Report, the 8-inch estimate was more likely to be 6-inch projectiles, considering the ships actually firing at her. The 6.1-inch (AP) projectile fired by the *Yamato* is virtually identical to the larger 8-inch caliber.

ON BOARD THE *HEERMANN*

Cdr. Hathaway reported, "At 0750, the *Heermann* took the leading *Tone* class heavy cruiser under fire. This *Tone* class cruiser was leading a column of three other cruisers. At 0753, *Hoel* fired torpedoes.[242] At 0754, the *Heermann* fired seven torpedoes at this cruiser. The torpedo director set up was as follows. True bearing of target 355° true, depth setting six feet, distance 9,000 yards and closing, estimated target course 120° true, estimated target speed twenty-five knots, own ship course 300° true, track angle 93° relative or 033° true. Torpedo speed was set at intermediate. Commanding officer ordered half salvo fired at the enemy. Torpedo control ordered number one tube mount to be used. The tube trainer on number two mount hearing the commence fire one and the fire two didn't look at his firing lights and fired two torpedoes by percussion until he was stopped by the mount captain. These two torpedoes ran on parallel tracks to their corresponding numbers from mount one."[243]

ON BOARD THE *HAGURO*

At 0756, an enemy destroyer was sighted at 8,220 yards. Captain Sugiura shifted fire from the carriers to the charging destroyer firing fifteen rounds but the results were unclear. At 0757, the enemy destroyer was seen launching torpedoes and Captain Sugiura immediately ordered an evasive turn. At 0758, two torpedo tracks were observed to pass astern.[244]

ON BOARD THE *TONE*

Captain Haruo Mayuzumi at 0745 saw three torpedo planes and five bombers attack his ship as well as the *Chikuma*. The *Chikuma* turned hard to starboard, and Captain Mayuzumi ordered a hard turn to port to evade enemy torpedoes. The two ships separated for a short time but then turned to the southwest once the air attack was over. The *Tone* was approximately 6,576 yards behind the *Chikuma* after this maneuver. At 0800, the *Tone* was attacked again by U.S. aircraft, but no damage was inflicted.[245]

---

[242] This is the primary documentation which tells the time the *Hoel* fired her second torpedo attack. The *Heermann*'s torpedo attack at 0754 was directed at *Tone* and in no way would force the *Yamato* to turn north, and she will not fire her second torpedo attack at the *Haruna* until 0800.

[243] *Heermann* Action Report.

[244] *Haguro* Detailed Action Report.

[245] *Tone* Detailed Action Report.

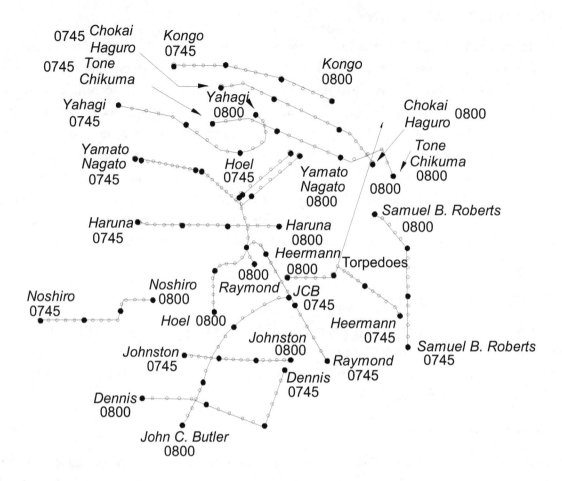

Figure 62: The *Heermann*'s first torpedo attack at 0754.

ON BOARD THE *RAYMOND*

Lt. Cdr. Beyer reported, "At 0756, we fired a spread of three torpedoes at an enemy cruiser at a range of 10,000 yards and closing fast." Raymond's course at this moment in time was 330°, speed 24 knots. The target was on course of 130° at a range of 10,100 yards with a speed of 25 knots. From these figures the target bearing was 50° relative with a torpedo track of 90°.[246]

---

[246] *Raymond* Action Report.

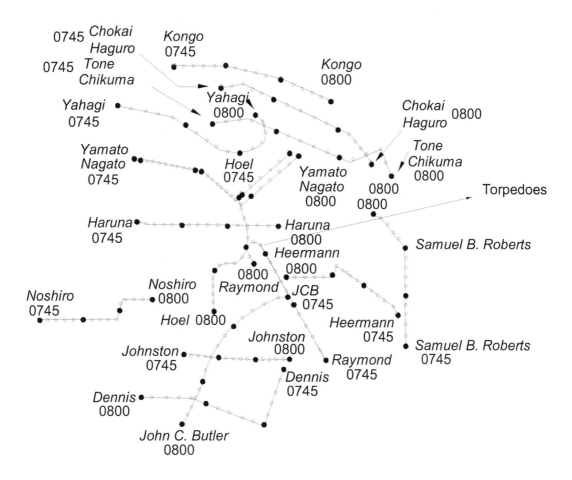

Figure 63: *Raymond's* **torpedo attack at 0756.**

The torpedo personnel misunderstood the bridge's "fire when ready" order and thought they were to fire entirely by local control. "As a result the tube captain set the problem on the sight, trained on the target, and fired on his own initiative without settings from CIC." Normally a torpedo speed of 46 knots, depth of 6 feet and a spread of 2° was maintained. With the torpedo control officer in the CIC at the time, torpedo speed was not confirmed before firing.[247] Beyer continued, "The target at this particular time was making an effort to close the formation and outflank the formation on the port side. DRT tracing of this action indicates that after we fired our torpedoes evasive action was taken by the enemy cruiser. This evasive action succeeded in closing the range at least 1,000 additional yards and made conditions more favorable for our torpedo attack. Several

---

[247] Ibid.

observers stated that we hit this cruiser, however, visibility was so reduced that there was uncertainty as to who may have hit the cruiser.[248]

"On the run in for this torpedo attack we were under fire from the enemy cruiser and numerous straddles were obtained by them on us. Just after we fired our torpedoes and before we changed course and returned to the formation, the commanding officer observed a destroyer escort, which appeared to be the *Samuel B. Roberts*, on our starboard beam under heavy fire from the enemy. The *Samuel B. Roberts* was firing rapid fire from her 5-inch guns and she appeared to be taking direct hits from the enemy. A curtain of flashes was observed surrounding this vessel and when we changed course to return to formation, we could no longer locate the *Samuel B. Roberts*."[249]

ON BOARD THE *DENNIS*

Lt. Cdr. Hansen reported, "At 0750, received orders to make torpedo attack with other destroyer escorts. Selected nearest ship, a cruiser, and commenced approach on course 310° true, range 18,000 yards. All enemy ships obscured by smoke and rain squalls; continued 5"/38 cal. Gunfire intermittently as targets appeared through the smoke and rain. Our speed was twenty-two knots. By 0755 maneuvered to avoid enemy torpedoes sighted on starboard bow. At 0759, at a range of 8,000 yards fired full salvo (three torpedoes); our firing course was 270° true. Second torpedo fired twenty seconds after first and third, five seconds after second. Base course of the torpedoes was 026° true. At 0802, changed course to 240° true; observed one of our destroyers hit by shell fire. By 0814 changed course to 205° true."[250]

ON BOARD THE *NOSHIRO*

Captain Kajiwara at 0754 changed course 10° true, and then at 0756.5 she changed course to 090° true. He spotted a charging U.S. destroyer at 0758 and saw her fire torpedoes in *Noshiro*'s direction.[251] At 0800.5 the enemy destroyer was bearing 150°, distance 8,000 yards. Captain Kajiwara immediately gave the order to open fire and observed his ship hitting the target.[252] He then turned his division to avoid the torpedoes, and by 0801 his course was 110°. By 0803, he ordered an increase in speed to twenty-eight knots. By 0804, the ship's course was 140° and still turning so that by 0809 the course was 220°. At this point three enemy destroyers were observed with the closest at

---

[248] *Raymond* Action Report.

[249] Ibid.

[250] *Dennis* Action Report.

[251] *Dennis* fired her torpedoes at 0759 toward the *Noshiro*.

[252] The *Noshiro* was describing the attack made by the *Dennis* which was the closest U.S. ship bearing 150° at this time. The *Dennis* was not hit. The *John C. Butler*, as she searched for the *Dennis*, was also firing at the *Noshiro* through the smoke.

6,576 yards.[253] Kajiwara gave orders to pursue, and by 0810 the ship's course was 240°, but he brought her slightly back to port at 0812 to 225°.[254]

ON BOARD THE *KISHINAMI*

Captain Fukuoka following the *Noshiro* sighted an enemy destroyer at 0805 and ordered his main battery to open fire. From 0805 to 0810 the main battery fired on the destroyer which was bearing 045° port, hits confirmed.[255] The target disappeared within a smoke screen at 0813.[256]

ON BOARD THE *JOHN C. BUTLER*

John C. Butler's skipper Lt. Cdr. Pace reported, "At 0753, we sighted an enemy destroyer on starboard quarter for short periods and opened fire at 18,000 yards. At 0759, we checked fire. By 0801 opened fire. Then at 0802 her guns checked fire. This was repeated at 0805 when her guns opened fire. By 0809 her guns checked fire. Range had closed to 16,000 yards. One hit was observed. The enemy cruiser was rapidly drawing toward our formation's port beam."[257]

ON BOARD THE *HEERMANN*

Cdr. A. T. Hathaway continues, "During the time the first half salvo was being fired CIC reported another heavy column to the southwest of the first unit which we had under fire. While our torpedoes were in the water, the gunnery officer observed an enemy battleship sharp on our port bow. Course was immediately changed to the left and the remaining torpedoes were readied for an attack on the enemy battleship. 5" fire was also shifted to this same target, which was already firing on us. The target which was the leading ship in a column of four was identified by the gunnery officer as a *Kongo* class battleship. The second ship in column was identified by the Officer of the Deck as a battleship but the class was never ascertained.[258]

---

[253] The three U.S. destroyers are the *Dennis*, *John C. Butler*, and *Hoel*.

[254] *Noshiro* Detailed Action Report.

[255] The Second Squadron is likely engaging the *Hoel*.

[256] *Kishinami* Destroyer Division 31 Detailed Action Report.

[257] *John C. Butler* Action Report.

[258] *Heermann* Action Report.

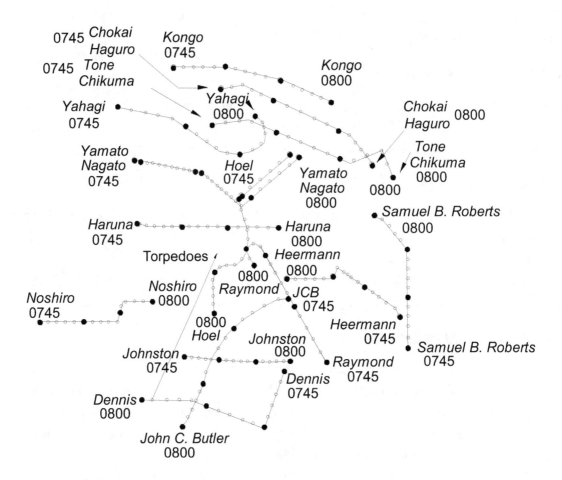

Figure 64: *Dennis's* **torpedo attack at 0759.**

"Torpedo director set up for this firing was as follows. Bearing to target 350° true, range 4,400 yards, estimated target course 100° true, speed twenty knots, own ship course 270° true, track angle 080° relative, depth setting six feet. Torpedoes were set on high speed. Identification as a battleship wasn't made in time to change the depth setting. All torpedoes ran hot, straight, and normal. About three minutes later the gunnery officer and rangefinder operator observed a torpedo hit on the starboard quarter under No. 4 gun turret of the target.[259] During this phase of the engagement the right hand and window of the rangefinder was hit and the starboard boat holed. Action with the enemy battleship was broken off at 0803 after which time we proceeded to the starboard quarter of the carrier formation."[260]

---

[259] *Haruna* didn't report any torpedo hit, and this may have been a near-miss bomb dropped by an aircraft.

[260] *Heermann* Action Report.

ON BOARD THE *SAMUEL B. ROBERTS*

Lt. Cdr. Copeland reported, "At 0753-54 the *Samuel B. Roberts* passed the *Heermann* as she turned away after launching her torpedoes. The approach was made on the starboard bow of the Japanese cruiser column, through the cover of smoke previously made by the *Heermann*, *Raymond*, and the *Samuel B. Roberts*, and was apparently wholly undetected by the enemy. For this reason the decision was made not to open fire with the No. 1, 5"/38 cal. gun, although excellent targets were presented. All fire control data however was set up and guns were loaded and ready for firing if we were detected. The *Samuel B. Roberts* was able to approach to 4,000 yards without being detected although it had been originally intended to launch from 5,000 yards. An unexpected delay in interior communications with the ships closing at a relative speed of about forty seven knots shortened the range below that intended. It was intended to fire torpedoes at high speed setting, but passing the *Heermann* which was under fire a stray shell hit the radio antennae which in falling fell across the tubes and dislodged the speed setting wrench. Consequently torpedoes had to be fired at intermediate speed. Flame smoke and a column of water were observed near the water line below the secondary control of the *Aoba* class heavy cruiser leading this column, between three and four minutes after firing. The other two torpedoes were believed to have hit nothing, although all torpedoes ran hot, straight, and normal. When this cruiser column was next seen, after the *Samuel B. Roberts* had completed retiring into smoke from the torpedo run, the '*Aoba*' class cruiser was no longer in column and the column now being led by a *Tone* class heavy cruiser. It was believed that some major damage was done to this particular cruiser '*Aoba*.'[261] At 0805, the *Samuel B. Roberts* opened fire for the first time with her 5" battery, opening at a range of 10,500 yards which was rapidly closed to 8,500 yards."[262]

ON BOARD THE *HAGURO*

At 0800, Captain Sugiura witnessed a huge explosion on an aircraft carrier, and at the same time the *Haguro* was hit by a salvo of shells that damaged the radio transmitter and communication cable.[263] In addition, U.S. aircraft suddenly attacked, and she took a direct hit from a bomb on her number two main gun turret. He immediately ordered the magazine to number two powder magazines to be flooded as the turret was completely gutted by fire. Thirty men had been killed within the gun house and barbette structure, but the quick closing of the anti-flash doors to the powder magazine prevented further damage.[264]

---

[261] *Haguro* had been in the lead but was overtaken by the *Chikuma* and *Tone* at this time. *Haguro* was the cruiser that *Samuel B. Roberts* identified as an *Aoba*-class cruiser.

[262] *Samuel B. Roberts* Action Report.

[263] This gunfire is likely from the *Samuel B. Roberts* who was the closest U.S. ship to the *Haguro* at this time.

[264] *Haguro* Detailed Action Report.

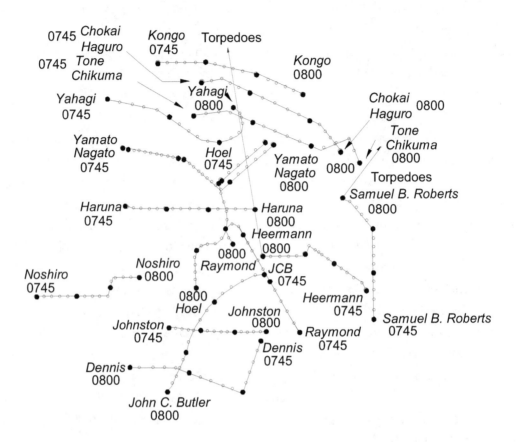

Figure 65: *Samuel B. Roberts*'s torpedo attack and *Heermann*'s second torpedo attack at 0800.

As Sugiura determined the damage to his ship, a message from the *Tone* reported at least two enemy carriers were on fire. At 0801, he ordered a course change to 120° true, and then at 0802 ten more U.S. aircraft attacked. They came from all directions. He maneuvered his ship violently to avoid the bombs, firing everything she had. At 0810, a light bomb hit her stern resulting in a small fire but little damage. After this attack the *Yamato* signaled for the cruiser divisions to attack. Despite the loss of one main gun turret, the *Haguro* continued to fight and her speed and maneuverability had not been diminished.[265]

PILOTS OF VC-68, THE *FANSHAW BAY*

Lt. (jg) J. B. L. Bunyon had taken off from *Fanshaw Bay* at 0645 but became lost in the rain squall. He flew his fighter over the Japanese force at 1,200 feet and found another plane on anti-submarine

---

[265] Ibid.

patrol flying 500 feet below him. He signaled to the other pilot to join up which he did. Unfortunately the other plane had already dropped his depth charges, so Bunyon left him to see if he could join up with other planes for an attack. At this time Japanese AA fire was exploding above him. Not able to locate anyone, he picked out two heavy cruisers that were closing the carriers on their port quarter. He pushed over and began to make his run on the second cruiser. He completed three runs and started a fourth when a shell exploded between his port wing and his tail flipping the plane 90°. He was able to recover control of his aircraft, but after this close call, he headed for Tacloban airfield.[266]

Lt. Johnston's TBM bomber was loaded with four 500-lb. bombs. He waited until after a coordinated attack of fighters and glide-bombing had been completed. Cloud cover was used as much as possible. When he broke out into the clear about five miles from the target, he used a slow weave coupled with a fast descent from 9,500 feet. No advantage could be taken of the sun as it was on opposite side of approach line. Due to the necessity of delivering an immediate attack, too much time would have been wasted in getting in sun position.[267]

He pushed his plane over at 7,500 feet and released at 3,000 feet. Just after release, heavy AA fire caused the aircraft to flip over in half a spin turn. The port side of the cockpit hood was blown off and shrapnel hit the extreme end of the fuselage.[268] The dive was made from the starboard quarter to the port bow. The first bomb landed close if not right against the starboard hull in line with the bridge. The next two stuck close to the No. 2 gun turret with heavy black smoke that blotted out the bridge area. The fourth bomb landed in the water to port.[269]

ON BOARD THE *HARUNA*

By 0807, the weather begins to improve and a new target was sighted bearing 060° relative to the starboard bow. Originally the target was thought to be a cruiser but was later identified as a carrier. At 0808, Rear Admiral Shigenaga gave permission to use the main battery, and at 0809 her first salvo was fired and appeared to hit the target with two shells.[270] The forward secondary guns also engaged

---

[266] Composite Squadron VC-68, *Fanshaw Bay*, Lt. (jg) J. B. L. Bunyon.

[267] Composite Squadron VC-68, *Fanshaw Bay*, Lt. N. D. Johnston.

[268] *Ibid.* Miraculously Lt. N. D. Johnston wasn't seriously injured, and he recovered control of his plane.

[269] Composite Squadron VC-68, *Fanshaw Bay*, Lt. N. D. Johnston. This was the attack on the *Haguro* which claimed her number two main gun turret. The explosion directly next to her hull by the first bomb appeared like a torpedo hit to the crew of the *Samuel B. Roberts*. A few minutes later the *Haguro* was hit on the stern by a bomb starting a fire, and this was exactly what the crew of the *Samuel B. Roberts* described.

[270] *Gambier Bay* was hit at 0810. The damage to her flight deck was consistent with a 14-inch projectile. The largest 8-inch shell penetration into the flight deck of the *Fanshaw Bay* or the *Kalinin Bay* was 2 feet by 4 feet. This shell created a hole 6 feet by 8 feet in the *Gambier Bay*. A 14-inch projectile was almost twice the size of an 8-inch projectile—5 feet tall by 14 inches in diameter compared to 3 feet by 8 inches. These holes were not caused by explosions, just entry holes in the wood and thin sheet metal flight decks.

and fire three salvos with a straddle on the third salvo. Just as she gained this success, aircraft attacked her from aft; she engaged them with her AA guns.[271]

Then at 0810, Shigenaga saw a new group of carriers and destroyers off the port bow at a distance of 36,168 yards. Shigenaga reported this new carrier group to Admiral Kurita immediately and gave orders to prepare for gunnery action to port. This new group of carriers was Felix Stump's Taffy 2, and as they were not making any smoke, *Haruna*'s lookouts had a clear view of them. Shigenaga then gave permission to open fire with the main battery at 0813 at a range of 35,400 yards. At the same time he was also engaging an enemy destroyer with his secondary guns to starboard. The destroyer to starboard was likely the *Johnston* who reported as she came out of the rain squall engaging a *Kongo*-class battleship at short range.[272]

ON BOARD THE *GAMBIER BAY*

Between 0745-0810, shortly after fire was opened with the 5-inch gun, Captain Vieweg observed salvos falling nearby. He maneuvered the ship to avoid them. At 0746, he changed course to 210° true, though this course provided insufficient wind to launch a loaded TBM.[273]

Captain Vieweg explained what occurred at this time, "By this time the officer in tactical command had changed course in small increments towards the south and when my planes were brought up on deck we had very little relative wind movement over the deck. According to the tables we didn't have enough wind to launch a fully loaded and fully fueled torpedo plane. The first torpedo plane to be launched with a torpedo was Ens. Gallagher's aircraft with only thirty-five gallons of fuel. Notwithstanding the fact that it didn't have enough wind over the deck, it went off all right. I permitted the full loading of the second plane and it was successfully launched as well. We changed course again further to the south and the wind came almost directly astern with only a five knot relative wind over the deck. I knew that meant certain death for the crew. I pulled the crew out of the plane and catapulted the plane without a crew just as a means of jettisoning it since we were by that time threatened with hits."[274]

---

[271] *Haruna* Detailed Action Report.

[272] *Haruna* Detailed Action Report.

[273] *Gambier Bay* Action Report.

[274] Captain W. V. R. Vieweg's transcript of the "Battle of Samar," taken 18 December 1944, Office of Naval Records and Library.

Figure 66: The *Santee* was hit by a torpedo from *I-26* at 0752 on 25 October 1944. The photo was taken from the *Petrof Bay*.

Figure 67: Flooding enters the *Santee* after the torpedo hit.

Captain Vieweg jettisoned the plane at 0750. This left one plane aboard on the hangar deck near the forward elevator. Three unidentified ships were sighted on the horizon dead ahead of formation.[275] He sent a signal challenge by way of 24-inch searchlight. All three ships responded immediately with the correct reply. The Captain then signaled "WE ARE UNDER ATTACK". The center vessel acknowledged. By 0800, course was changed on to 200° true and then at 0805 course was changed again to 240° true. Then at 0810, the first hit was scored on the after end of flight deck, starboard side, near Battle II. Fires were started on the flight deck and the hangar deck; luckily, personnel casualties were small.[276]

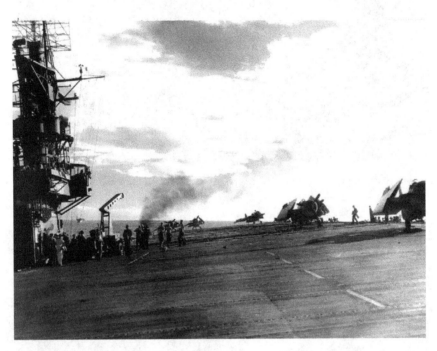

Figure 68: The *Santee* lists to port after the torpedo hit.

The shell hit about six feet aft of the after elevator near the center-line of the flight deck, tearing up the flight deck planking and creating a 6-foot by 8-foot jagged entry hole in the flight deck. The projectile continued on to the after athwart-ship passage, and then exploded in or near this passage, starting a fire on the flight deck as well as in this passage. Hangar deck personnel observed smoke and flame appearing through the after bulkhead of the elevator well at the level of the gallery deck. Repair One and Repair Three fought the fires which were under control within five minutes. At 0815, the *Gambier Bay* changed course to 205° true.[277]

---

[275] The three ships are the *Haggard*, *Hailey*, and *Franks* of Taffy 2.

[276] *Gambier Bay* Action Report.

[277] Ibid.

ON BOARD THE *SANGAMON*

As Rear Admiral Thomas Sprague received reports on the damage to the *Santee*, she was suddenly hit by a torpedo at 0752 from an undetected submarine.[278] She lost steering control and developed a 6° list due to the flooding. Then air alerts sounded as an enemy air attack approached. A suicide bomber hit *Suwannee* at 0759. The bomb exploded on the hangar deck, causing many casualties and extensive structural damage to the ship. A periscope was sighted by the destroyer *Trathen*, and an emergency 90° turn to starboard was made. The *Trathen* attacked at 0818 but with inconclusive results. The *Trathen* remained over the contact until 1121. At 0806, the *Santee* reported her No. 1 boiler room was out. Her maximum speed was sixteen knots. By 0815, the *Santee* reported her fires were under control.[279]

Figure 69: *Suwannee* of Taffy 1 under attack at 0759. The kamikaze (right side) is in its dive above the carrier. A U.S. fighter (left) arrives too late to intercept.

ON BOARD THE *NATOMA BAY*

Read Admiral Felix Stump heard from Taffy 3 at 0814 reporting their position and a course change to 205° true. The enemy force was between the two task units, at a position estimated to be abaft the port beam of Taffy 3 and on the starboard quarter of Taffy 2. Distance had closed between the enemy and Taffy 2. Felix Stump ordered Destroyer Division 94 under the command of Captain Reynolds (Division Commander) in the *Haggard* along with the *Franks* and the *Hailey* to take up a position about three miles astern of the carriers to intercept any light forces in the van of the enemy's main force that may attempt to attack Taffy 2. As these events were taking place preparations were being made to launch a second strike.[280]

---

[278] The Japanese submarine *I-26* scored the hit on the *Santee*.

[279] CTU 77.4 Action Report.

[280] CTU 77.4.2 Action Report.

ON BOARD THE *HAGGARD*

Cdr. Harris observed shell splashes landing around the ships of Taffy 3 at 0756. By 0810, an enemy vessel was sighted. Then at 0812, enemy planes were reported approaching Taffy 2 from 330°, low over the water. Cdr. Harris couldn't locate these reported enemy aircraft. At 0814, first radar contact was made on the enemy force bearing 356° distance 27,600 yards. Course and speed of the enemy units couldn't be accurately determined. Cdr. Harris made all preparations to attack the enemy with torpedoes and gunfire.[281]

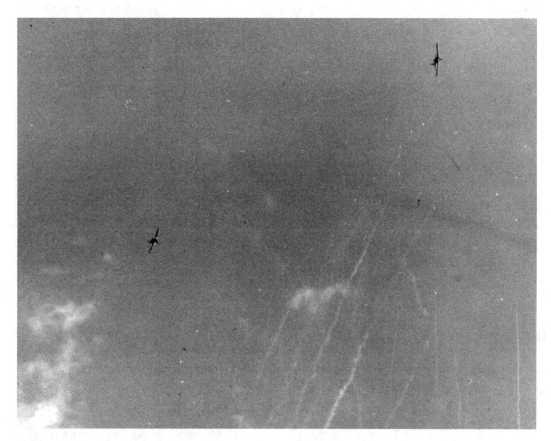

Figure 70: Anti-aircraft fire from the *Suwannee* attempts to shoot down the Japanese plane.

ON BOARD THE *WASATCH*

At 0754, Kinkaid sent all available destroyers plus the cruiser *Nashville* to TG 77.2 so they could join Oldendorf's battle-line and sortie with them. He then received further reports that Taffy 1 was under attack from Japanese submarines and planes and that the *Santee* and the *Suwannee* had been hit. To make matters worse, TG 77.2 radioed at 0815 that they were under air attack. Admiral Kinkaid at

---

[281] *Haggard* Action Report.

this moment in time didn't know the level of the Japanese counter-attack, but two of his three carrier groups were under assault, his main battle line was under air attack, and he still had not received any word from Third Fleet.[282]

Figure 71: Damage to the *Suwannee's* flight deck after the kamikaze hit.

---

[282] CTU 77 Action Report.

CHAPTER 5. *GAMBIER BAY'S* PLIGHT: 0815-0845

ON BOARD THE *YAMATO*

Kurita had finally gained the windward side of the U.S. formation, and the *Yamato* was now driving south in an effort to close on the enemy carrier formation. Free of the rain squalls at last, the weather began to improve, but smoke screens were still providing good cover for the U.S. carriers. At 0822, the *Yamato* opened fire using her radar, with her forward main battery against an enemy "battleship" bearing 210°, distance 21,920 yards. The target was not visually sighted until a minute later at 0823 when the target was properly identified as a burning carrier. The *Yamato* had the inside track to the U.S. formation and the most oblique target angle.[283]

A shell side-swiped *Gambier Bay*'s hull or detonated alongside, ripping out a 4-foot by 4-foot section outboard of her forward engine room. Her records give various times for the hit: 0816, 0820, and 0825. The 0820 time was the most common time reported, but for this analysis 0822 will be used because this was when *Yamato* gave her range to the enemy carriers. *Kongo* at 0826 gave a range of 26,304 yards. *Kongo*'s records were not specific in that she says she was shooting at a carrier at 0802 (no range given) and that at 0826 she was shifting fire from a destroyer to a carrier. At 0816 *Haruna* fired on the three destroyers from Taffy 2 and then documented at 0822 that she was shifting fire to the middle of the new target. At 0824, she re-opened fire from her main guns at a range of 33,743 yards. The *Heermann* documented yellow splashes falling around her at this time, so the *Haruna*'s target seemed to be the *Heermann*.[284]

Nagato, heavily engaged in protecting herself from air attack, was not shooting at any of the American ships. Heavy cruisers had *Kalinin Bay*, *St. Lo*, and *Fanshaw Bay* under fire. *Kongo* and *Yamato* both claimed the hit to *Gambier Bay*. *Kongo* fired from a greater range, with her main rangefinder still out of action.[285] Given *Yamato*'s oblique target angle, she seems the more likely source of a shell that stayed alongside the hull without entering, and her larger projectiles had the better chance of inflicting the damage recorded by the *Gambier Bay*.[286]

---

[283] *Yamato* Detailed Action Report.

[284] Data taken from *Gambier Bay, Yamato, Kongo, Haruna,* and *Heermann* Action Reports.

[285] In addition *Kongo* had lost her primary rangefinder, which had not yet been repaired at this time.

[286] Data from *Nagato, Kalinin Bay, St. Lo, Fanshaw Bay, Kongo, Yamato,* and *Gambier Bay* Action Reports.

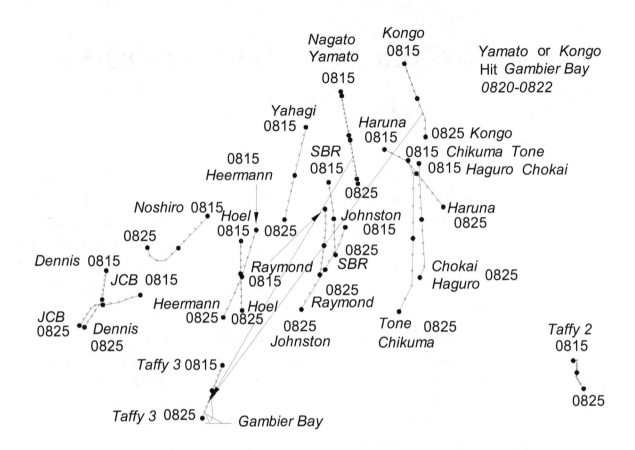

Figure 72: U.S. and Japanese tracks from 0815-0825.

ON BOARD THE *KONGO*

At 0815, the *Kongo* had been heading south, still on the far outside track. The *Haruna* passed in front of her at 0822 and took up a position ahead and to her port side. At 0826, *Kongo* shifted fire from a destroyer to a carrier at a range of 26,304 yards. Then at 0830 more U.S. aircraft attacked. Rear Admiral Shimazaki ordered his AA guns to open fire. The planes withdrew, and no damage was sustained. In the *Kongo*'s logs—not in her time line but in the section where she claimed her results in the fight—Shimazaki claimed that his ship had sunk an enemy aircraft carrier at 0825. While no U.S. carrier was actually sunk at this time, it does correspond to when the *Gambier Bay* received her critical hit and began to fall out of formation.[287]

---

[287] *Kongo* Detailed Action Report.

ON BOARD THE *GAMBIER BAY*

At 0817, the second hit glanced off a flight deck support on the forecastle deck at frame 30 on the port side. It continued to the overhead and then down, piercing the deck and exploding in the chain locker. No fires or underwater flooding were observed. There was some buckling of the forecastle deck. The fire main riser to the flight deck located at frame 30 port side was ruptured. The personnel of Repair Two closed the fire main riser valve to prevent a loss of pressure.[288]

Figure 73: The *Gambier Bay* as seen from the *Kalinin Bay*, straddled by a six-shell battleship salvo at approximately 0820-0825. Subsequent photos taken from the *Kalinin Bay* show that the *Gambier Bay* began to fall back out of formation after this photo was taken. Shell splashes are bright white and do not appear to be dyed. If this photo shows the salvo that crippled the *Gambier Bay*, it provides additional evidence that *Yamato* inflicted the crippling damage.

At 0820, a third shell affected the forward engine room on the port side. This wasn't a direct hit into the engine room itself as no fragments entered that space, but an impact explosion opened a gap in the skin of the ship approximately four feet square between frames 96 and 98. The center of this hole was about twelve feet below the waterline. Very rapid flooding occurred in the engine room and fire room, and in about five minutes the water was up to the fire box in the boilers, necessitating the securing of both boilers and No. 1 main engine at 0825.[289]

---

[288] *Gambier Bay* Action Report.
[289] Ibid.

Upon receiving word of the forward engine room flooding, the crew in the after engine room started No 2 bilge pump to drain water from the forward engine room drain wells. No. 1 bilge pump was also started. The capacity of these two pumps combined was about 1,200 gallons per minute. In the forward engine room, the main injection to No. 1 main condenser was closed, and attempts were made to open No. 1 main drain connection to the main circulator. However, due to the rush of flooding water, this wasn't accomplished. The concussion was sufficient to blow a foamite generator located at frame 97 against the main condenser and crack the 275-pound superheated steam line to the main circulator. This line was cracked at the first platform deck level and admitted steam into the forward engine room.[290]

The forward engine room was abandoned shortly after 0825. The safety valves on the boiler were lifted by hand, the booster pump was secured, and the fires were out in the boilers, this later being done by closing the fuel oil quick-closing valve. The main condensate and standby feed booster pumps were left running as flooding made securing them difficult. At the time of abandonment of the engine room the water was at a height of approximately five feet. No. 2 bilge pump continued to pull suction on the forward engine room. Two electrical submersible pumps were lowered down into the escape trunk to help control flooding. The discharge line from one pump was split, and the pump had to be secured and a new discharge line put on.[291]

At this time the assistant engineering officer and personnel took station on the second deck and assisted with the placement of submersible pumps. Repair Two and Repair Five were sent to check the forward and aft bulkheads to the forward engine room and check for leaks and possible shoring of the bulkheads. Repair Five reported leaks in the forward bulkhead of the machine shop and were directed to use mattresses for shoring and stopping the leaks. This work was begun but never completed.[292]

Since the hit was reported to damage control, the electrical officer shifted power from No. 1 to No. 3 generator. There was no noticeable failure in the lights at this time, though there had been several shorts in the circuit as the ammeter registered between 900 to 2,000 amperes. This was a probably the reason for the faulty operation of the portable submersible pumps which couldn't maintain suction continuously.[293]

At 0824, a fourth hit entered the skin of the ship on the port side of the machine shop at about frame 110, seven feet below the waterline, and exploded in the vicinity of the fresh water tank C-406-W. At this time the lights in this compartment went out, and emergency lights came on. Men

[290] Ibid.
[291] Ibid.
[292] Ibid.
[293] Ibid.

from Repair Five that were engaged in plugging and shoring in this compartment were killed or seriously wounded by this explosion. A party from Repair Five that was proceeding to the machine shop for shoring was dazed by the concussion but succeeded in removing the wounded. Damage control wasn't notified of this hit. It was at this time that the tie breakers and electrical panels went out and power was lost in the forward part of the ship. Later it would be restored.[294]

At the same time of 0824, a fifth shell hit compartment A-203-L on the port side nine feet above the deck at frame 33. This shell didn't explode but continued through the compartment going out the starboard side at frame 34, four feet above the deck. It was believed this hit was part of the same salvo that hit the machine shop.[295]

By 0825, the captain informed OTC by TBS that ship had been hit hard and had lost one engine. The engine room had flooded to the burner level. All boilers within the compartment were secured. At 0826 all loads shifted to after generators and engine room. The forward engine room was secured. The ship slowed to eleven knots and dropped astern of the formation.[296]

ON BOARD THE *TONE*

Captain Mayuzumi took a bullet from a strafing American fighter in the right thigh at 0828. The ship's surgeon was called to the bridge, and they attempted to stop the bleeding as the Captain refused to leave the bridge. The *Gambier Bay* began to fall out of formation, and fire was shifted to this carrier. As the range closed, the *Tone* was able to consistently hit her target. Captain Mayuzumi identified the carrier as a "*Ranger* class" and believed his ship had inflicted fatal damage by 0838; he so signaled the rest of the fleet.[297]

ON BOARD THE *GAMBIER BAY*

At 0828 another shell exploded on impact at frame 66 port side eleven feet above the hangar deck. This hit gave forth smoke and momentary flame but did no great damage. At the same time another shell hit the flight deck at frame 75. This shell impacted ten feet from the center-line and

---

[294] Ibid.

[295] *Ibid.* These hits likely came from the battleships. *Haguro* did not shift fire to the *Gambier Bay* until 0842. *Tone* did not shift until 0828. Photos show the *Gambier Bay* under fire from the battleships, and her documents say she was under fire from the Japanese main body. Due to her predicament, her crew did not have time to do a detailed damage analysis other than location of hits. Her crew did not estimate shell caliber or give measurements of shell damage. The heavy cruisers had initially the *Kalinin Bay*, *St. Lo*, and *Fanshaw Bay* under fire, as shown in photos as well as documented within their reports. The *Yamato* and *Kongo* are the two ships likely scoring the initial hits on the *Gambier Bay*. Both the *Yamato* and the *Kongo* claim they sank her, as did *Tone*; it is quite possible that they all inflicted damage as she fell back. As the *Gambier Bay* fell back at 0826, the *Kitkun Bay* which was ahead of the *Gambier Bay* documented the leading enemy cruiser (*Chikuma*) took her under fire.

[296] Ibid.

[297] *Tone* Detailed Action Report.

started a large fire. Repair One attempted to fight the fire but there was no water pressure from the fire hoses that were supplied by the forward half of the ship. This was probably due to the main fire risers being cut. They then attempted to install a jumper from the aft part of the ship, but by the time this was accomplished, the after engine room was hit, and all pressure was lost.[298]

At 0830, a shell exploded in the CPO galley. The interior bulkhead of the pantry was bellied out, and this blocked the passageway leading to the forward mess hall. At 0832, another shell hit the starboard bulkhead of the forward mess hall at about frame 114 which exploded on impact tearing a hole 3 feet by 4 feet out of this bulkhead. Damage control did not receive word of this hit at the time it happened.[299]

At 0837, a shell struck compartment C-202-2 which was the steward mate's compartment. The shell exploded on impact, the lights went out, and the compartment filled with smoke. The ship lost steering control forward at this time, perhaps due to concussion from this hit or due to the rupture of liquid lines by shell fragments from hits near the island structure. At the same time, another shell hit and exploded against the after messing compartment bulkhead at frames 159-165. The port ladder to the hangar deck was torn off. Five or six men were dazed. This was the main station for Repair Three and was used as an after battle dressing station. A fragment hit the after distribution board entering on the port side, knocking out all the tie breakers which caused a loss of power to the after section of the ship. The board was still receiving power at this time from the after engine room as the indicator lights didn't fail.[300]

A third shell at 0837 came through the port side of the after engine room about ten feet below the ship's normal waterline at frame 124. The hole made by the shell was estimated to have had a diameter of one foot. This shell passed through the air casing around No. 3 boiler and entered the boiler. As far as it was known, it pierced the generating tubes and lodged in the boiler. This hit knocked the fuel oil quick-closing valve off the fuel oil line, and the fuel oil supply was cut off to the burners by closing the fuel oil throttle valve. The water flooded through the hole with such force that it spouted up against the casing of No. 3 boiler. This rendered it impossible to ascertain the damage to No. 3 boiler. At this time bilge pump two was pulling water from the forward engine room, and this was switched to pull from the after engine room. At 0840, radars went out of operation, and the skin of the ship had cracked along a ten foot vertical span about half an inch

---

[298] *Gambier Bay* Action Report.

[299] Ibid.

[300] Ibid.

wide, and this was also flooding the compartment. The lights went out, but emergency lights came on.[301]

ON BOARD THE *HAGURO*

Captain Sugiura gave the order to check fire at 0830. The *Haguro* was moving south at twenty-eight knots. By 0836, he received a signal from the *Yamato*, "Enemy is retreating in southeast direction." Then at 0842, Captain Sugiura observed one enemy aircraft carrier with a large list to starboard.[302] When the range closed to 7,672 yards, bearing 080° he ordered his guns to open fire. He observed her sinking a short time later.[303]

ON BOARD THE *GAMBIER BAY*

At 0843, a shell hit the after part of the engine room at frame 134 port side, first platform deck about where No. 4 ventilation fan was located. Damage and effects of this hit were not noted. This hit was probably below the waterline at this time due to the port list of the ship. At 0843 all boilers were ordered secured on order of the Engineering Officer. Due to the excessive flooding and the possible explosion of No. 4 boiler, this boiler and No. 2 engine were secured at 0845. As a result of the uncontrolled flooding of the forward engine room, machine shop, and after engine room, the ship's G.M. was rapidly becoming negative, and the ship's stability was in jeopardy. By 0845, the *Gambier Bay* sat dead in the water.[304]

Passing astern of the carrier, the crew of the *Heermann* then saw the *Johnston* swinging to the left at 0840 and again backed full emergency astern. The *Johnston*'s bow missed the *Heermann*'s bow by three inches. When the collision was avoided, a very loud spontaneous cheer rose up from all hands on the topside of both vessels. While backing away from the *Johnston* the *Heermann* made contact with an enemy cruiser on our port bow bearing 120° true, distance approximately 12,000 yards at 0841. This cruiser was firing full salvos into the *Gambier Bay* at the time.[305]

---

[301] *Ibid.* The size of the entry hole would indicate this hit was made by a heavy cruiser. It may have come from the *Tone* which had shifted fire to the *Gambier Bay* at 0828.

[302] *Gambier Bay* was the ship the *Haguro* engaged.

[303] *Haguro* Detailed Action Report.

[304] *Ibid.* A ship with a negative G.M. is at high risk of capsizing.

[305] Ibid.

Figure 74: The *Gambier Bay* as seen just after the previous photo while *Kalinin Bay's* firefighters perform their duties. The *Kalinin Bay* was the rearmost carrier in the formation at this time with the *Gambier Bay* just a bit forward on her port side. In this photo the *Kalinin Bay* has closed the distance between the two carriers.

Figure 75: Here the *Kalinin Bay* has pulled even with the *Gambier Bay*. The *Gambier Bay* has slowed significantly as the *Kalinin Bay* passes her. As she continued to fall back, the leading Japanese cruiser, *Tone,* took her under fire. This may have saved the *Kalinin Bay* by diverting gunfire from her.

Figure 76: The very tip of the stern of the *Gambier Bay* can be seen in the right side of the photo along the horizon as the *Kalinin Bay* passes her. Shell splashes continue to fall around the stricken carrier.

Figure 77: The *Kalinin Bay* was under concentrated cruiser fire at this time, and a close salvo prompts the men managing the hose to "hit the deck." Damage can be seen on her flight deck.

Figure 78: *Heermann* on the starboard quarter of the carrier formation after her torpedo attack, racing at flank speed to get back onto the port side of the formation. The *Dennis* and the *John C. Butler* are the two destroyer escorts on the horizon also racing south. The *Heermann* reported yellow splashes falling close to her, indicating *Haruna's* projectiles. Even in a black and white photo the splashes seem gray, not bright white, indicating they may be dyed.

Figure 79: *Heermann* backing away (note she has no bow wave) from *Kalinin Bay* after a near collision at approximately 0836. *Heermann's* action report incorrectly claims the carrier was the *Fanshaw Bay;* this photo was taken by *Kalinin Bay*.

Figure 80: *Heermann* **passes astern of** *Kalinin Bay* **at 0836-37.** *Kalinin Bay* **has passed** *Gambier Bay,* **in the background falling out of formation.** *Heermann* **was now on the port side of the formation. Past her port side, faintly in the distance, the** *Johnston* **is visible laying smoke.**

ON BOARD THE *JOHNSTON*

Lt. Hagen reported in the *Johnston*'s action report, "During this period the ship was heading in general to the southwestward several miles astern of our main body. As we headed southwesterly direction in general we had the Japanese cruiser and battleship force on our port quarter and the Japanese destroyers on our starboard quarter. This picture was clearly held in the mind of Cdr. Evans at all times. The range varied from 7,000 to 12,000 yards to all these Japanese units. At 0830, *Gambier Bay* came under heavy fire and was listing to port. She was being fired upon by a Japanese cruiser at this time. The *Johnston* closed this cruiser to 6,000 yards in an attempt to draw her fire away from the *Gambier Bay*. The maximum rate of fire was expended on this cruiser but she ignored our attempt and continued to fire into the carrier. By 0840, fire was checked as it became apparent to us that the Japanese destroyers were closing to starboard."[306]

Lt. Hagen later wrote, "The *Johnston* now headed south-west, several miles behind our main force. On our port quarter was the Jap cruiser and battleship force, and on our starboard were the Jap destroyers, pouring steel our way. At all times, the leading enemy ships were within 12,000 yards of us. At 8:30, we observed that the *Gambier Bay* was under heavy fire from a big Jap cruiser. Cdr. Evans then gave me the most courageous order I've ever heard. 'Commence firing on that cruiser, Hagen,' he said. 'Draw her fire on us and away from the *Gambier Bay*.' Again I said, 'Aye, aye! Sir,'

---

[306] *Johnston* Action Report.

and under my breath again I said, surely you jest. A crippled tin can engaging in a deliberate slugging match with a heavy cruiser. We closed to 6,000 yards and scored five hits. Reacting with monumental stupidity, the Jap commander ignored us completely and concentrated on sinking the *Gambier Bay*. He could have sunk us both. By permitting us to escape, he made it possible for us to interfere a few minutes later with a destroyer torpedo attack that might have annihilated our little carrier force. At 8:40, the captain broke off the futile battle with the cruiser when he saw seven Jap destroyers closing in rapidly on the carriers."[307]

Cdr. Evans ordered his ship toward the enemy destroyers. Suddenly through the smoke the *Heermann* appeared less than 200 yards off the starboard bow on a collision course. Cdr. Evans ordered emergency back full on all engines. The *Johnston* crew could see *Heermann* backing at full power, and the ships avoided a collision by the narrowest margin.[308]

According to Hagen, "We were coming out of a heavy smoke screen. Suddenly we saw the *Heermann*, only 200 yards away, headed straight at us on a collision course. The skipper bellowed, 'All engines back full!'—That meant one engine for us. With one engine, we couldn't do much more than slow down. I felt a curious, hopeless, detached sort of wrung-out unconcern as I looked over our bow and couldn't see water—only the *Heermann*. Hope we don't batter her up too much, I dreamily thought, for our bow was pointed straight at her bridge. Finally, the *Heermann*'s two engines backed her barely out of the collision course. We missed her by less than ten feet."[309]

ON BOARD THE *SAMUEL B. ROBERTS*

Lt. Cdr. Copeland maneuvered the *Samuel B. Roberts* from 0815 until 0855 south by southwest down the port side of the carrier formation. The range closed to 5,300 yards to a Japanese *Tone*-class heavy cruiser, which had been selected as the ship's target. The *Samuel B. Roberts* engaged this cruiser with the heaviest, fastest, and most accurate fire which the *Samuel B. Roberts*, with limited fire control installations, was capable. The range varied between 6,000 and 7,500 yards during this time. Occasionally, fire was directed momentarily to other vessels as the *Samuel B. Roberts* maneuvered to escape ladders of enemy fire, preventing her guns from bearing on this particular cruiser. At 0840, the *Samuel B. Roberts* got clear of a near collision between the *Johnston* and the *Heermann* (all ships were laying smoke and firing at Japanese cruisers to port) and changed course to the left to interpose between the Japanese cruisers and the carriers, as directed about five minutes previously by Clifton Sprague.[310]

---

[307] Hagen, "We Asked for the Jap Fleet—and Got It."

[308] *Johnston* Action Report.

[309] Hagen, "We Asked for the Jap Fleet—and Got It."

[310] *Samuel B. Roberts* Action Report.

ON BOARD THE *YAHAGI*

Captain Yoshimura at 0823 recognized the shape of an enemy aircraft carrier through the smoke bearing 210°. He remarked how the smoke screens were making it difficult to confirm. Then at 0825, the shape of a destroyer was seen along with the shape of an aircraft carrier. The *Yahagi* and the Tenth Squadron were almost directly astern of the carrier formation and closing rapidly. By 0830 the destroyer was bearing 190° true, slightly to starboard at a range of 12,056 yards. Yoshimura gave orders to open fire on the destroyer, and twenty-eight salvos were fired.[311] At 0845, the range on the destroyer was down to 11,508 yards, but the smoke screen made it difficult to see her. He recognized the shape of two carriers and shifted fire to the carriers, but the smoke soon enveloped them, forcing him to check fire, unable to see the results.[312]

ON BOARD THE *HARUNA*

At 0816, the *Haruna* fired a single salvo at the three destroyers in the rear of Taffy 2, and Rear Admiral Shigenaga observed the three destroyers were reversing course.[313] Shigenaga then ordered the main battery to shift to a new target. At 0824, the *Haruna* re-opened fire on a destroyer at a range of 34,743 yards.[314] The target was lost at 0828, and fire was stopped. The *Haruna*'s lookouts warned of a flight of dive bombers bearing 040° to port at 0836 and then sighted more masts bearing 037° to port. At 0842, she fired to port at the three U.S. destroyers, distance 35,072 yards. At 0843 and then again at 0845, two more salvos were fired. The shells come close, but no hits were scored.[315]

ON BOARD THE *HAGGARD*

Cdr. Harris on the *Haggard* reported, "Felix Stump ordered destroyers to close the carriers at 0836. On turning away from the enemy, the cruiser was plainly visible in its entirety and the main deck and superstructure of a battleship could be easily seen and identified with the aid of binoculars. Estimated range to the cruiser was at 25,000 yards. At 0837, speed was increased to twenty-five knots. At 0842, a four gun salvo presumably fired by the cruiser, sent up greenish yellow splashes about 250 yards astern of this vessel and close aboard the *Franks*. We commenced weaving immediately. At 0843, a second salvo of five or six guns fell short by about 300 yards. The splashes

---

[311] This was the *Johnston* who was coming across the carrier formation from port to starboard to interpose herself between the Japanese destroyer column and the U.S. carriers.

[312] *Yahagi* Detailed Action Report.

[313] *Haruna* opened fire on the *Franks* of Taffy 2.

[314] *Heermann* documents the *Haruna*'s yellow-dyed shell splashes falling around her at this time.

[315] *Haruna* Detailed Action Report. After she stopped firing on the *Heermann*, she re-opened fire on the *Franks*. The masts to port were the carriers of Taffy 2. The *Haruna* was the only Japanese ship to take Taffy 2 under fire. Times she fired on Taffy 2 are taken from U.S. reports.

of all salvos fired at this vessel were greenish yellow, with the emphasis on the green. At 0845, a seven gun salvo moved up to 200 yards astern. The pattern in range and deflection didn't exceed seventy-five yards."[316]

On Board the *Hailey*

Cdr. Brady of the *Hailey* reported, "At 0820, we formed column double distance. At 0821, the *Gambier Bay* reported her forward engine room flooded. At 0828, Clifton Sprague ordered an undetermined number of his escorts to intercept an enemy cruiser approaching the *Fanshaw Bay*. At 0833, Felix Stump steadied on course 115° true speed eighteen knots. At this time the enemy was bearing 322° true and under heavy air attack. At 0835, enemy appeared to change course toward the south. At 0837, destroyers of our task unit were ordered to close our own CVE's. We increased speed to twenty-five knots. At 0842, at a range of 34,000 yards one enemy heavy ship opened fire on our destroyers. This ship was definitely identified as a heavy cruiser of the *Mogami* class.[317] Our destroyers at this time were in column at double distance, 600 yards. The first enemy salvo landed midway between the *Hailey* and the *Franks* sharp on the starboard quarter. Destroyers increased speed to thirty knots, formed line of bearing 135° relative on the division leader and took 1,000 yards distance between ships. We commenced fishtailing to avoid enemy gunfire while closing our own CVE's. By this time the entire area where Taffy 3 was operating was hampered by heavy black smoke and nothing could be seen of the action taking place except for occasional gun flashes, splashes, and explosions."[318]

On Board the *Franks*

Cdr. Stephan of the *Franks* reported, "At 0819, received a report that the *Gambier Bay* had lost her forward engine room and was dropping out of formation. At 0837, changed speed to twenty-five knots. At 0842, a four gun salvo landed 100 yards on the starboard beam. We immediately commenced fishtailing on a course of 140° true. At 0844, another four gun salvo landed 200 yards astern. At 0845, we opened the distance between our own destroyers to 1,000 yards."[319]

On Board the *Natoma Bay*

At 0817, Rear Admiral Felix Stump got word that his three destroyers, he had positioned to his rear had come under fire. The enemy was still estimated to be twenty to twenty-five miles distant but

---

[316] *Haggard* Action Report.

[317] The Japanese cruisers were ahead of the *Haruna,* and the *Hailey*'s crew appeared to have thought the enemy gunfire was from the leading cruisers. It is also possible that the *Haruna* was mistaken for a cruiser which happened rather routinely within the various action reports.

[318] *Hailey* Action Report.

[319] *Franks* Action Report.

closing at a rate of 1,000 yards every ten minutes. He immediately gave orders for the three destroyers to close the formation. At 0833, he changed course to 037° true to launch a second strike and land six VT bombers from Taffy 3. This unfortunately caused Taffy 2 to close on the enemy position. Enemy cruisers were firing on Taffy 3 on their port quarter astern and two battleships were astern of Taffy 2. At 0841, the rear destroyers were taken under fire again. Felix Stump sent word to Kinkaid and Thomas Sprague that his ships were now under fire. After launching and landings were completed by 0844, he swung his task force back to the southeast to open the range and give time to prepare to launch a third strike.[320]

ON BOARD THE *TONE*

Captain Mayuzumi identified *Heermann* as a light cruiser, and at 0845 fired both guns and torpedoes at this ship. It was seen to explode, so the *Tone*'s crew also claimed this ship as being sunk.[321] *Tone* received 5-inch shells from one of the U.S. escorts. The captain's bed room took a hit. The windlass room was hit. The bridge was riddled from strafing.[322]

ON BOARD THE *HEERMANN*

Heermann's crew identified an enemy cruiser as a *Tone*-class cruiser and took it under fire. This ship was leading a column of six units with the first four being heavy cruisers. All enemy vessels were firing in the direction of the U.S. forces with at least four ships concentrating on the *Heermann*. Red, yellow, green, and no-color splashes were seen.[323] At 0845, a fragment struck the pilot house killing three men, fatally wounded a fourth, and destroying the ship's log from 0700-0845. The first 8-inch shell hit entered the spray shield at frame 72 on the port side, main deck, passed through the forward uptake space, B101E, No. 1 boiler uptake, the forward starboard corner of the vegetable preparation space, B103L, and exited through the main deck bulwark at frame 91 on the starboard side. A 4-foot hole was made in the port side of B-101E. The No. 2 boiler remote control for auxiliary steam stop was destroyed, and the searchlight power and control cables were damaged. Operation of No. 1 boiler was not impaired.[324]

---

[320] CTU 77.4.2 Action Report.

[321] The crew of the cruiser *Tone* witnessed the shell impacts from the *Kongo* at 0850 that flood her bow and made her appear to be sinking by the bow.

[322] *Tone* Detailed Action Report.

[323] These colors identify that *Kongo* and *Haruna* have both engaged *Heermann* along with the cruiser *Tone*.

[324] *Heermann* Action Report. This hit coming from forward and traveling aft through the ship lines up with the *Tone*'s position.

ON BOARD THE *FANSHAW BAY*

The fire had been extinguished on the forecastle by 0817. By 0823, the main enemy cruiser group was bearing 355° at a distance of 23,000 yards. Then at 0825, the *Gambier Bay* reported serious damage with one engine room lost. By 0827, Clifton Sprague changed course to 215°. By 0828, one enemy destroyer closed to 15,000 yards bearing 048°, and Clifton Sprague observed planes attacking the enemy destroyer at 0829. The main enemy group was now at a distance of 29,000 yards. By 0830, he changed course to 240°.[325] It was clear that the Japanese cruisers were closing from the port quarter. At 0833, Clifton Sprague ordered the destroyers to make a smoke screen between the CVE group and enemy cruisers to port. By 0838, the closest enemy destroyer was bearing 021°, distance 11,800 yards. The main body was bearing 021°, distance 21,600 yards. The enemy cruisers were at 075°, distance 18,600 yards. By 0845, the enemy main body apparently changed course to southeast, distance 19,000 yards, bearing 024°. In response Clifton Sprague changed course to 180°.[326]

ON BOARD THE *WHITE PLAINS*

At 0826, the screen reported all torpedoes expended. At 0830, *St. Lo* reported five ships closing her starboard quarter. Then at 0836, the *White Plains* changed course to 240°. A salvo of three or four splashes impacted close aboard on the port bow, and the *White Plains* began to maneuver violently. By 0837, another salvo landed close to port. Then at 0839, a third salvo landed close to starboard, and by 0840, two more salvos landed close aboard.[327]

ON BOARD THE *KALININ BAY*

The heavy cruisers continued their fire towards *Kalinin Bay*. A salvo exploded under the counter of the fantail on the carrier's port side, sending fragments into the hull at frame 203.5. The explosion under the bottom plating warped and distorted the deck and beams within compartment C-308-M (Pyrotechnic locker) which flooded to a depth of 6 feet. Another salvo exploded just off the fantail, and fragments penetrated the stern on the port side into C-204-16L (mess attendant's compartment) and continued and penetrated bulkhead 199.[328]

---

[325] Clifton Sprague was slowly turning the carriers to the southwest, which would open the range between him and Kurita on the *Yamato* as the *Yamato* sailed to the southeast and more toward Taffy 2.

[326] *Fanshaw Bay* Action Report. The *Yahagi* and her group of destroyers was bearing 21° at 11,800 yards. The Japanese battleships at this time were bearing 40° at roughly 30,000-31,000 yards. The *Chikuma* and the *Tone* were bearing roughly 75° at 18,000-19,000 yards, and they were followed by the *Haguro* and the *Chokai* which were approximately 21,000-22,000 yards away.

[327] *White Plains* Action Report.

[328] *Kalinin Bay* Action Report.

Kalinin Bay's crew reported, "At about 0825, at a range of approximately 16,000 yards a direct hit by this vessel was scored on the *Nachi* class cruiser's turret 2.[329] The 5" gun commenced rapid fire after observing the hit and another hit was scored just below the previous one. After the first hit the No. 2 turret was observed to be slowly enveloping in flames and the second hit caused a quick burst of flames which completely obscured the turret. The cruiser then turned hard to port and withdrew from the formation temporarily. Several hits were observed on the *Gambier Bay* at this time that was off our port bow. When the *Gambier Bay* had been severely damaged the enemy increased their rate of fire into this vessel and began to close range and deploy off the port quarter."[330]

ON BOARD THE *KITKUN BAY*

The bearing of the enemy force at 0820 was 056° with a range of 22,000 yards and continuing to close. The *Gambier Bay* was seen to receive several hits, one of which was reported by TBS transmission to be in her engine room. She lost speed and was observed to rapidly drop out of formation on a westerly course at 0825. By 0826, the leading enemy cruiser directed its fire at the *Kitkun Bay*. Evasive action was continued between 0826 and 0921 with at least eight salvos from an enemy cruiser falling within 1,000 yards of the ship, the closest landing fifty yards astern and causing superficial damage.[331]

During this phase the enemy closed to 10,800 yards. At 0833, Captain Whitney received word by radio transmission that friendly planes which had earlier attacked the enemy had refueled and rearmed at Leyte and were returning to attack. Captain Whitney observed approximately twenty-four planes attack the enemy at 0842.[332] The destroyers and destroyer escorts of the screen interposed themselves between the carriers and the enemy on the port side of the formation at this time.[333]

PILOTS OF VC-5, THE *KITKUN BAY*

Lt. Cdr. Fowler with the rest of VC-5 with no opportunity to attack from high altitude let down intending to make a low-altitude attack at 0840. As he came below the clouds, he observed the enemy battleships were in a staggered formation. The second and fourth battleship would fire a main-battery salvo and then turn to switch places with the first and third, who would then fire a

---

[329] This observation may have come around 0800 when the *Haguro*'s turret was hit by a bomb. It is also possible that at this later time a secondary explosion within the turret gave the crew of the *Kalinin Bay* the perception that they had scored a hit. The *Haguro* was the only *Nachi*-class cruiser that had her number two turret destroyed, and by her account this was by a bomb at 0800.

[330] Kalinin Bay Action Report.

[331] *Kitkun Bay* Action Report.

[332] These aircraft are from Taffy 2 and Taffy 3.

[333] *Kitkun Bay* Action Report.

salvo and exchange places again. Certain salvos would shoot up a yellowish-green spray on impact which seemed to be every third salvo.[334]

This same color range-spotting seemed to apply to AA firing, with a violet-colored burst at 8,000 feet, a green burst at 6,000 feet, and a yellow burst at 4,000 feet. These bursts appeared well ahead of the diving planes and apparently gave slant range spots for AA battery fire, either in local or in director control. In most cases the 5-inch AA seemed to be director-controlled as the patterns were well controlled and concentrated.[335] The heavy cruisers' 8-inch fire and AA seemed to employ this same scheme except they stayed in column. All fire was very deliberate, and at no time did he observe any battleship or cruiser go into rapid fire.[336]

The screening destroyers laid down smoke, seemingly quite effective, astern of the carriers. The destroyers turned to make a torpedo attack. Lt. Cdr. Fowler couldn't see the results as he climbed to make an attack the heavy cruisers on the port quarter of the task unit.[337]

As he reached 8,000 feet, a group of fighters and torpedo bombers attacked the battleships, and he noticed several hits and many misses. A couple of the torpedo bombers dropped bombs from 6,000 feet in practically a horizontal flight. In fact one torpedo was dropped from about 6,000 feet. Whether it fell out on opening the bomb bays is not known. He observed that most attacks made by planes from Taffy 3 were well executed, but in many cases, sufficient numbers and different load outs prevented a coordinated effort. This however was reasonable due to the strain the task unit was under from continued enemy surface bombardment.[338]

ON BOARD THE ST. LO

At about 0820, the St. Lo received a message that the Gambier Bay reported she had been hit hard and had lost her forward engine room. Gambier Bay rapidly dropped aft and was never seen again. At this time the screen was ordered to shift from the starboard quarter of the formation to the port side of the formation. Hoel was seen falling back and was never sighted again. The group of Japanese ships off the starboard quarter, believed to consist of one light cruiser and eight destroyers, was closing rapidly. By 0821 the St. Lo opened fire, but range was opening at this time and check fire was immediately ordered. By 0826 smoke generator had been completely expended, and stack smoke was begun. It was at this time that the John C. Butler came out into the clear, and the Dennis was located, and the John C. Butler headed for the Dennis in order to form up on her. Clifton Sprague

---

[334] Composite Squadron VC-5, Kitkun Bay, Commander R. L. Fowler.

[335] Ibid.

[336] Ibid.

[337] Ibid.

[338] Ibid.

ordered the two destroyer escorts on his starboard quarter to interpose between him and enemy heavy cruiser on his port quarter.[339]

Figure 81: The *Fanshaw Bay* as seen from the *White Plains* along with the *Dennis* and the *John C. Butler* on the horizon. The two destroyer escorts are closing the formation at flank speed to position themselves on the port side of the formation and interpose themselves between the carriers and the Japanese cruisers.

Captain McKenna observed the *Dennis* and the *John C. Butler* were the escorts referred to. The target angle at this time was about 070° true to the enemy cruisers at 22,000 yards on the port side. The enemy cruisers were on a parallel course to the carrier formation making thirty knots. The *John C. Butler* and the *Dennis* then came to a course to cross the carrier formation, and they prepared for a torpedo attack by the *John C. Butler* who still had three torpedoes. However, it was soon realized that unless the enemy cruiser changed to a closing course the *John C. Butler* couldn't close to effective torpedo range.[340]

Then the *Kalinin Bay* at 0830 swung sharply to the right and astern of the *St. Lo* and then pulled herself back on course taking up position off the starboard quarter instead of the port quarter. Japanese forces were reported at various ranges. The closest range was 6,900 yards off our starboard

---

[339] *St. Lo* Action Report.

[340] Ibid.

quarter at 0844. Other ranges were at target bearing 090° true 9,400 yards and at target bearing 115° true range 11,000 yards.[341]

ON BOARD THE *KALININ BAY*

At about 0830, five destroyers were sighted on the starboard quarter "head on view" approaching in column formation. These ships were initially thought to be friendly units coming to assist. It wasn't until they opened fire from a range of approximately 14,500 yards that they were known to be hostile.[342] At this time the heavy cruisers attacking from the port quarter were obscured from view by a smoke screen laid down by friendly escorts. The fire of the aft 5-inch gun immediately shifted to the Japanese destroyers from the starboard quarter. Fire was continued, and the Japanese closed the range to 10,500 yards at which time they were definitely recognized to be of the *Terutsuki* class, with high bow and two gun mounts forward and heavy tripod foremast and mainmast.[343] Many salvos from the destroyers exploded close aboard. A number of shells passed directly overhead. The *Kalinin Bay* continued to fire on the attacking destroyers with her aft 5-inch gun.[344]

Figure 82: At 0830 the *Kalinin Bay* turned to starboard, soon to cross the stern of the *St. Lo*. The *Dennis* and the *John C. Butler* crossed the carrier formation ahead of the *St. Lo*. This photo was taken from the *Kalinin Bay*.

---

[341] Ibid.

[342] This is the *Yahagi* and her destroyers closing on the carrier formation.

[343] This description matches the *Yahagi*.

[344] *Kalinin Bay* Action Report.

ON BOARD THE *DENNIS*

At 0817, Lt. Cdr. Hansen resumed firing at the enemy cruiser closing on the port side of the formation. At 0819, the *Gambier Bay* reported her forward engine room was flooded. By 0820, Lt. Cdr. Hansen noted that the *Dennis* was in formation with two destroyers and one destroyer escort on course 220° true.[345] At 0843, he recorded an observed 5-inch hit on a Japanese cruiser, bearing 090° true. By 0846 he changed course to 180° true. Her crew observed a bomb hit on an enemy cruiser, bearing 090° true.[346]

ON BOARD THE *JOHN C. BUTLER*

At 0834, she opened fire on an enemy heavy cruiser at about 17,000 yards. The *Dennis* and *John C. Butler* were at this time about 700 yards apart on a course converging with the enemy cruiser and were under steady enemy fire. The *Dennis* was just forward of the *John C. Butler*'s port beam toward the enemy. Many salvos fell between the two ships. At 0842, the leading enemy cruiser and destroyer turned away at a range of 14,000 yards, but another enemy cruiser and destroyer astern of the first two ships, maintained their course and kept up their fire. She shifted fire to the cruiser. Both destroyer escorts were laying smoke during this entire period.[347]

Figure 83: Japanese shells land within fifty feet of the *St. Lo* as the two carriers close on each other. This photo has been labeled by the National Archives as the critical hit on the *Gambier Bay* even though it correctly identifies the carrier taking the photo as the *Kalinin Bay*. In reality, the *Gambier Bay* was always to the *Kalinin Bay*'s port side and this ship was to starboard.

---

[345] The two destroyers are the *Hoel* and the *Heermann*, and the destroyer escort is the *John C. Butler*.

[346] *Dennis* Action Report. This may be the *Chokai* which was disabled at 0850.

[347] John C. Butler Action Report.

Figure 84: *The St. Lo, Fanshaw Bay, Dennis,* and *John C. Butler* seen from the *Kalinin Bay*, now on the starboard quarter of the *St. Lo*. This photo has also been miss-captioned as showing *Gambier Bay,* but *Gambier Bay* had fallen behind by the time *Dennis* and *John C. Butler* crossed the formation.

Figure 85: *Dennis* was taken under fire and would be hit by one of the Japanese cruisers as she attempted to shield the carriers with her smoke screen.

ON BOARD THE *RAYMOND*

At 0828, Lt. Cdr. Beyer received orders from Clifton Sprague to intercept an enemy cruiser approaching the formation on the port quarter. This target appeared to be the one the *Raymond* was firing at. At this time the last of the funnel smoke was exhausted, and she had no torpedoes left. The bearing of the enemy cruiser was 113° true, initial range 12,600 yards, closing rapidly to 5,700 yards; 414 rounds of 5-inch ammunition were expended.[348]

ON BOARD THE *YAMATO*

At 0830, the *Yamato* lost radio contact with #2 air scout aircraft. Then at 0834, the *Yamato* opened secondary-battery fire against an enemy cruiser bearing 230°. This was the *Hoel*. At 0839, the *Yamato* turned 10° to starboard and was on a course of 170°. By 0840, the *Yamato* observed the *Hoel* sinking.[349] By 0845, three enemy aircraft carriers were sighted, bearing 135°. The fact she couldn't see all six carriers was an indication that the smoke screens were still interfering with her ability to observe the entire U.S. formation.[350]

ON BOARD THE NAGATO

Nagato wasn't in the best position behind *Yamato* to engage the carriers. With the enemy now sailing to the southwest, she was furthest from the targets, and U.S. planes began to steadily attack her. At 0818, enemy dive bombers attacked from port bearing 10°, followed at 0823 by four torpedo bombers attacking bearing 30° to port. More torpedo planes attacked at 0827 bearing 045° and again from the port side. Rear Admiral Kobe maneuvered his ship to avoid being hit and to maintain station behind the *Yamato*. His AA guns fired continuously when an enemy dive bomber attacked from starboard resulting in a near-miss bomb off her starboard bow. By 0838, Kobe gave orders to check AA gun fire as the air attacks seemed to be over for the time being. He noted observing one enemy cruiser was sinking at this time.[351]

ON BOARD THE NOSHIRO

Captain Kajiwara decided to turn his destroyer division in a complete circle, and by 0822 his heading was 000° north, then by 0824 it was 046°, and *Noshiro* opened fire and shot six salvos. By 0825, she has turned to 090°, and Captain Kajiwara ordered a reduction in speed to twenty-four knots. He continued to turn the squadron until 0830 when he settled on a course of 180° due south, and by 0830.5 he gave the order to increase speed to twenty-eight knots. By 0832, his lookouts reported one enemy carrier was on fire, but then at 0833.5 the lookouts spotted a destroyer bearing 110°. This was the *Hoel*. Captain Kajiwara issued orders to open fire on the destroyer and reduced speed to twenty-four knots. By 0838 he confirmed two hits made on the *Hoel* and a minute later at

---

[348] *Raymond* Action Report.

[349] *Hoel* capsized to port, the side that took the majority of her damage, most likely from *Yamato*'s 6-inch battery.

[350] *Yamato* Detailed Action Report. In fact none of the Japanese records count more than four carriers after 0800, giving the Japanese the perception that two U.S. carriers had been sunk.

[351] *Nagato* Detailed Action Report. *Hoel* was the destroyer observed to be sinking.

0839 changed course to 200° true. His lookouts reported at 0841 three enemy aircraft to starboard at 5,480 yards. He spotted two carriers through the smoke at 0842, bearing 189° true. He then saw the *Hoel* bearing 130°, sinking, so he gave orders to increase speed to twenty-eight knots to pursue the aircraft carriers.[352]

ON BOARD THE *KISHINAMI*

Captain Fukuoka received a message from the *Yamato* at 0835, "Pursue in southeast direction, one enemy aircraft carrier was on fire." He gave orders at 0836 to increase speed to twenty-eight knots. At 0845, he observed one enemy aircraft carrier to be on fire. Both the *Noshiro* and the Second Destroyer Squadron opened fire on the burning aircraft carrier.[353]

ON BOARD THE *HOEL*

While slowing down between 0815 and 0840 and then while dead in the water, several more hits were received as follows: port side of navigation bridge between No. 2 and No. 4 lookout chairs, wardroom passage, port side mark 37 director rangefinder, No.1 magazine causing a small fire which failed to stop the firing of the forward guns, wardroom 202, No. 2 upper handling room, ship's office and the forward fire room rupturing the No.165 steam line. During these hits, she continued to list further to port and settled by the stern. By 0840, with a 20° list to port and with the stern awash, the orders to abandon ship were given.[354]

---

[352] *Noshiro* Detailed Action Report.

[353] *Kishinami* Destroyer Division 31 Detailed Action Report. The carrier was probably the *Gambier Bay* which did receive three small-caliber hits on the starboard side.

[354] *Hoel* Action Report.

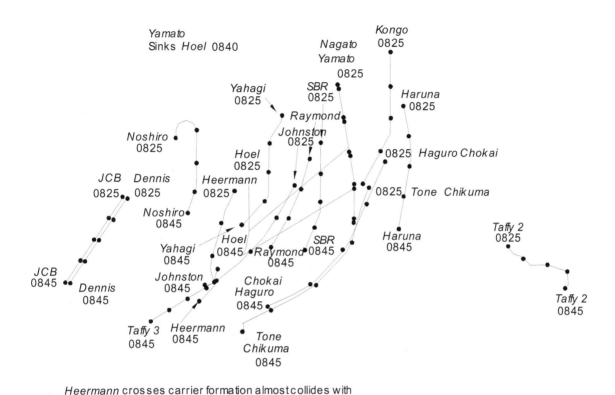

Figure 86: U.S. and Japanese track from 0825–0845.

ON BOARD THE *WASATCH*

Vice Admiral Kinkaid received reports from Rear Admiral Oldendorf at 0820 that TG 77.2 had formed a circle formation in preparation of Japanese air attacks as it sailed to the north. Oldendorf wanted to come to the assistance of the CVE's but was approximately sixty-five miles from gunfire range and this equated to about three hours' sailing time. His battleships didn't have a full load of AP ammunition but still had plenty of base-fuzed high-capacity rounds. Because of this perceived shortage of AP ammunition, his chief of staff insisted that the proper strategy was to keep his force concentrated and inside Leyte Gulf and let the Japanese force come to him. In this way he could set a similar trap that was successful in destroying the Japanese southern pincer by gaining the tactical advantage of maneuver. Kinkaid, still desperate for help, sent another plain language message to Halsey at 0829, "Situation critical, battleships and fast carrier strike wanted to prevent enemy penetrating Leyte Gulf." Up to now there had been no reply from Third Fleet.[355]

---

[355] CTU 77 Action Report.

ON BOARD THE *SANGAMON*

Rear Admiral Thomas Sprague received reports at 0815 from the *Santee* that her fires were under control. At 0820, the *Suwannee* reported that she had a hole in the flight deck and hangar deck, but that her first four arresting wires were in commission, the after elevator was in working order, and that her flight deck would be in commission again in one to one and a half hours. She had taken considerable casualties: 106 killed, 106 wounded, and 144 missing. The *Santee* had lost 21 men killed and 29 wounded. At 0825, enemy planes appeared overhead but didn't attack.[356]

ON BOARD THE *NEW JERSEY*

Halsey listened intently to the U.S. aircraft reports and the initial air strikes then being conducted on the Japanese northern force. Cdr. McCampbell assigned approximately eighty aircraft to attack the lead group and another sixty to attack the second group of ships. At 0817, the American planes attacked. Fighters went in first, then dive bombers, and this was followed by the torpedo planes.[357]

The first message of what was happening off Samar arrived on the *New Jersey* at 0822. This message read, "CTU 77.4.3 reports enemy battleships and cruisers fifteen miles astern of his unit and firing on him. Position eighty miles bearing 060° from Homonham Island." Then at 0830, a message from Kinkaid was received saying, "Fast battleships are urgently needed immediately at Leyte Gulf."[358]

At the same moment the first wave of air attacks was achieving some success. Pilots began reporting hits to Japanese aircraft carriers and various other ships, and this was what Halsey's true focus was on at the time. At 0834, Halsey ordered TF 34 to close on the Northern Group at a speed of twenty-five knots. With the Japanese carrier fleet disabled, he could now use his heavy ships to achieve Admiral Nimitz's strategic goal of sweeping the Japanese navy from the seas. Then Halsey received at 0838 another message from Clifton Sprague, "Under attack, 0722 Item in latitude 11-44, longitude 126-29. Enemy composed of four battleships, eight cruisers, and many destroyers split in two forces one bearing 286° eleven miles. Second bearing 307° at fifteen miles."[359]

---

[356] CTU 77.4 Action Report.

[357] CTU 38 Action Report.

[358] Ibid.

[359] Ibid.

CHAPTER 6. THE DECISION: 0845-0945

ON BOARD THE *YAMATO*

Cdr. Tonosuke Otani was a member of Kurita's staff attempting to gather all the confusing pieces of intelligence and make sense of what exactly they were up against. The first problem was identifying the type of ships they were fighting. In a postwar interrogation he said, "We found ourselves perplexed by your carriers because they didn't correspond to their photographs, and first we thought that they were regular carriers." Cdr. Otani believed at the time of the battle that the U.S. carriers were fleet aircraft carriers capable of thirty knots, and the men standing on *Yamato*'s bridge didn't perceive that they were closing on the enemy. After the battle when there was more time to consider what they had actually witnessed, Cdr. Otani decided that the carriers were auxiliary or converted carriers, but when the *Haruna* as well as the *Yamato*'s lookouts spotted Taffy 2, Cdr. Otani expressed, "We received word from the tops that there was another formation, and at that time we wondered if we were not confronted by twelve or thirteen carriers in all."[360]

Where were the U.S. battleships that normally accompany the U.S. carriers? Why had the U.S. only counter-attacked with a few cruisers and destroyers? Kurita had not received any information from Ozawa and didn't know his location. He had not received any reports from land-based air reconnaissance. Kurita and his staff remained effectively blind. They were attempting to match up the spotted American carrier groups to the intelligence Admiral Toyoda provided prior to the battle. At 0851 *Yamato* launched her #1 air scout in another attempt to gain real intelligence on the disposition of the U.S. fleet, but within thirteen minutes the air crew reported being chased by enemy fighters; at 0930, severe damage sent the plane heading for nearest land base.[361] The information available on *Yamato*'s bridge created a totally distorted perception of the battle.

Rear Admiral T. Koyanagi explained, "Our task had been to proceed south, regardless of opposition encountered or damage sustained on the way, and break into Leyte Gulf. But for the unexpected encounter with the enemy carrier group it would've been simple. We estimated that the enemy carrier task force that was east of San Bernardino Strait on 24 October had steamed south during the night and taken new dispositions the next day, separating into at least three groups so as to surround us, and that we had encountered the southernmost group."[362]

---

[360] Otani, Tonosuke, Commander IJN, Interrogation Nav. No 41, USSBS No. 170.
[361] *Yamato* Detailed Action Report.
[362] Evans David, *The Japanese Navy in World War II*, pp 355-384.

From Kurita's point of view, what was shaping in his mind was confirmation that the Third Fleet had not been lured away at all. With twelve fleet carriers in the immediate area, his original idea that the U.S. fleet was maneuvering to surround him and attack from the air was being reinforced. He believed the U.S. fleet was built around three carrier groups. He had run into one and attacked it. A second was just to his southeast. A third was maneuvering to his north to cut off his escape and surround him. Ever since they had spotted the U.S. forces, they had been under constant air attack, but these air strikes were made by only a few planes at a time and were not coordinated. This changed at 0845 when the *Yamato, Nagato,* and *Haruna* all came under intense air attack.[363]

At 0850, the *Yamato* turned onto a course of 220° true, and then at 0859, to 250° true to head for the enemy carriers, but this course was dramatically changed at 0901 to 130° which was toward Taffy 2. Kurita then observed many U.S. sailors in the water with large amounts of debris and oil where the *Gambier Bay* had sunk. This was definite confirmation that they had sunk at least one enemy aircraft carrier.[364]

From the bridge of the *Yamato,* they had lost sight of the leading Japanese cruisers. Then at 0906, two enemy torpedo bombers attacked from over the bow. The *Yamato* opened fire immediately with her AA guns. More planes attacked, and at 0908 four torpedo tracks were sighted bearing 040° port. The *Yamato* turned hard to port to evade. More planes attacked and new torpedo tracks were sighted bearing to starboard. Again, the helm was turned hard to starboard to avoid these torpedoes.[365]

Rear Admiral Koyanagi after the war wrote down his assessment of the situation at the time, "We pursued the enemy at top speed for over two hours but couldn't close the gap; in fact it actually appeared to be lengthening.[366] We estimated that the enemy's speed was nearly thirty knots that his carriers were of the regular type, that pursuit would be an endless seesaw, and that we would be unable to strike a decisive blow. Running at top speed, we were consuming fuel at an alarming rate."[367]

By 0911, Kurita felt his fleet was too spread out, and the number and coordination of the enemy air attacks had increased to the level he experienced on 24 October. Having chased thirty-knot carriers for two and a half hours, he suspected the enemy had already escaped while his own surviving units were extremely vulnerable to coordinated air strikes. The time had come to re-assemble his forces if he was going to attempt a break through into Leyte Gulf. At 0911, he issued a

---

[363] *Yamato* Detailed Action Report.

[364] Ibid.

[365] Ibid.

[366] At 0820 *Yamato* had logged a range of 21,920 yards to the carriers, but by 0850 the range had increased to 30,688 yards. This was due to Clifton Sprague's turning Taffy 3 west while *Yamato* steered southeast and more toward Taffy 2.

[367] Evans, *The Japanese Navy in World War II,* pp 355-384.

fleet order to assemble in sequence to the north, speed twenty knots. Even as the order was sent, two more torpedo bombers attacked from starboard. At 0915, one enemy aircraft was shot down. The *Yamato* turned to course 205°, then at 0917 two more torpedo bombers attacked, and she turned back to 120° and then the attacks seem to be over. At 0918, Kurita received a report from the *Chokai*, "Bomb hit forward engine room, trying to repair." Then at 0920, Kurita got word from the *Chikuma*, "One propeller, and eighteen knots, unable to steer." At 0922, the *Yamato* slowed to twenty knots and turned to a course of 040°. At 0925, she turned to course 000° north. In her only surface action of the war, she had expended one hundred 18.1-inch Type 1 AP rounds and at least six of the Type 3 AA rounds of the twenty-four she would expend that day in the surface battle. Her 6.1-inch secondary guns fired 127 Type 91 AP rounds and 174 Type 0 HC rounds during the surface action.[368]

As the message to re-group was received by the individual ship commanders, it was followed without question. This was part of their officer training at Etajima—never question the order of a superior officer. At Etajima severe disciplinary action would be carried out on any subordinate who didn't immediately follow the orders of a superior.[369] Therefore, the various ship captains didn't bother to inform Kurita that they had closed to within 10,000 yards of the enemy and were in a truly advantageous tactical position. They simply turned around as ordered. Therefore, Kurita's perception that the enemy had already escaped was allowed to continue.[370]

At 0932, battle rations were issued to the crew, and by 0937 the *Yamato* reduced speed to eighteen knots. At this point, Kurita's plan was to collect his forces into a proper formation and then continue towards Leyte Gulf. He retired to the north because he didn't want the U.S. forces to make another counterattack while his ships gathered. He would remain under constant air attack, and the time needed to re-group would also allow him and his staff to decide their next move.[371]

ON BOARD THE *NAGATO*

At 0847, Rear Admiral Kobe received the signal from the *Yamato* that she had observed an enemy aircraft carrier suffering explosions to port. The *Nagato*'s lookouts reported to Kobe a large group of aircraft bearing 030° to port at a distance of 38,360 yards at 0850. Kobe ordered the main battery and smaller guns to fire in anti-aircraft mode. He then received a signal from the *Yamato* on spotting three enemy aircraft carriers bearing 135°, distance 38,360 yards. This was followed by another

---

[368] *Yamato* Detailed Action Report.

[369] Marder, Arthur, J. *Old Friends and New Enemies.* Clarendon Press, 1981, pp 269-271.

[370] U.S. officer training allowed commanders to use their own initiative if they saw an opportunity to inflict damage on the enemy. This is shown by the actions of Commander Evans of the *Johnston* and Commander Kintberger of the *Hoel* making torpedo attacks even before such orders were given.

[371] *Yamato* Detailed Action Report.

signal from the *Yamato* at 0852 of an enemy aircraft carrier being sighted bearing 220°, distance 30,688 yards.[372] Two minutes later, a plane was spotted bearing 105° at a distance of 15,344 yards, and then at 0856 eight aircraft were spotted on the port side bearing 020 degree with three more aircraft approaching from 130°. Kobe gave orders to open fire on the aircraft at 0858. The AA guns began firing, but the planes passed by, so the order to check fire was quickly given. At 0900, Ugaki sends a signal from the *Yamato*, "First Battleship Division turn towards the port side enemy aircraft carriers." By 0901, Kobe observed the *Gambier Bay* sinking. She was bearing 075° relative to the starboard bow. The *Nagato* didn't open fire on the sinking carrier but continued to follow the *Yamato*.[373]

ON BOARD THE *GAMBIER BAY*

Captain Vieweg ordered all classified material jettisoned. By 0850, he gave the order to abandon ship. The navigator who was officer of the deck had remained with the captain on the open bridge until then and was directed to abandon ship and did so via the starboard bridge life lines just as another salvo pierced the island structure. Two more shells struck the ship at 0850 with the first entering the port side of the stores keeper's office. about frame 79. A large explosion was felt and heard, and the compartment's port hatch at the first platform deck was blown open. The CO_2 built-in system control was broken, causing the CO_2 to start flooding into stores keeper's office. Flooding had commenced, and no further action could be taken.[374]

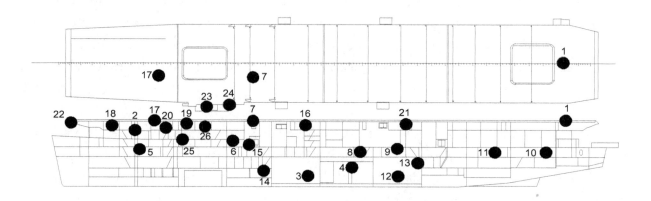

Figure 87: The *Gambier Bay's* battle damage.

---

[372] The ranges and bearings from *Yamato* documented within *Nagato*'s action report at 0850 are important; this is the third Japanese action report detailing this information, helping to establish the distance separating the Japanese battleships from Taffy 3 at the time *Heermann* was hit by two shells from *Kongo*.

[373] *Nagato* Detailed Action Report.

[374] *Gambier Bay* Action Report.

The second hit at 0850 stuck the TBM aircraft still on the hangar deck, causing it to explode and cause considerable damage to the forward part of the hangar deck. Large fires began, and Repair Two attempted to fight them, but by this time all water pressure had been lost. Many men attempting to abandon ship by way of the hangar deck were killed or wounded by this hit.[375]

By 0855, Captain Vieweg attempted to reach the interior of the ship via interior island structure ladders but was driven onto the flight deck then aft over the starboard side by hot, toxic, black smoke. The ship was now being hit repeatedly. Shells struck the conditioning room, the catapult track on the flight deck, and the gallery between guns 41 and 43, exploding on the outboard bulkhead of the radar room No. 1 and killing or wounding men at both gun mounts and within the radar room. Another shell made a large hole in the passage way near the executive officer's stateroom. A hit to the pilot house knocked down the SK radar, and the forward elevator machinery room was also hit. Before the ship capsized, there was a large explosion that blew the forward elevator overboard. The *Gambier Bay* capsized at 0907 and slipped beneath the waves at 0911.[376]

ON BOARD THE *NAGATO*

At 0908, the *Yamato* warned Kobe of an estimated thirty B-24 aircraft[377] and sixty enemy carrier aircraft coming to attack. Kobe then received a signal from the *Kongo* at 0913 of enemy aircraft bearing 160° true. At 0916, six U.S. aircraft began an attack run on the *Nagato* from 045° to port. Kobe immediately ordered his gunners to open fire. At 0920, Ugaki sent a signal for the *Nagato* to follow the *Yamato*. By 0920, the enemy aircraft were now bearing 090° to port with a 10° elevation, and then more aircraft attacked, diving on the port bow, elevation 40°, distance 14,248 yards at 0922. Kobe was able to maneuver the *Nagato* to avoid any damage to his ship. The *Yamato* was also under air attack at the same time. By 0922, the *Nagato* changed course to 000° true and fell back in behind the *Yamato* heading north. The chase was over, and by 0930 Kobe ordered all guns to check fire and rest from battle stations. In her only surface action of the war she had fired only forty-five 16.1-inch Type 1 AP rounds. She would expend fifty-two 16.1-inch Type 0 HC rounds and eighty-four 16.1-inch Type 3 AA rounds as well, but these figures cover all actions from October 24 through October 26. Her secondary battery expended ninety-two 5.5-inch 04 common projectiles normally used for surface action and forty-one Type 0 HC rounds which could be used in both surface and AA roles.[378]

---

[375] Ibid.

[376] Ibid.

[377] There were no B-24 aircraft present. This was a misidentification by the *Yamato*'s crew.

[378] *Nagato* Detailed Action Report.

ON BOARD THE *KONGO*

Rear Admiral Shimazaki was given a message from the *Chikuma* at 0845 that she was engaging enemy aircraft carriers bearing 230°. He then spotted a carrier bearing 135°, distance 38,360 yards at 0850. At the same time, he received a signal from the *Yamato* that she had sighted one carrier bearing 220° at 30,688 yards and three carriers bearing 135° to port, distance 38,360 yards.[379] He received a signal from the *Haruna* that she too had sighted an enemy aircraft carrier. Shimazaki received a warning at 0858 of enemy aircraft attacking his ship, but then he got some good news at 0900: the main rangefinder which had been disabled at 0725 was back in action. At the same time, a message from the Third Cruiser Squadron confirmed one enemy aircraft carrier was sinking, bearing 220°. Over the last few minutes *Kongo* had been engaging a U.S. destroyer which now appeared to be sinking. At 0902 Shimazaki logged into *Kongo*'s report that she had sunk one destroyer.[380] Her secondary battery continued to engage up to 0903, firing several salvos, but results were unclear.[381]

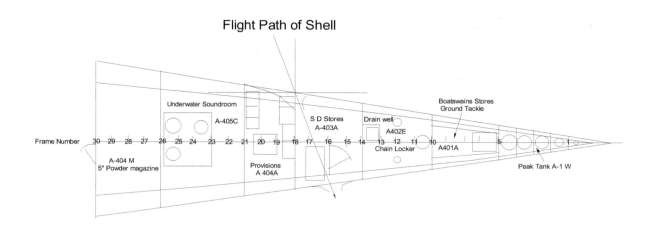

Figure 88: The *Heermann's* battle damage for Hit 2.

ON BOARD THE *HEERMANN*

At 0850, the *Heermann* received two heavy-caliber shells hits forward. Hit number two entered the port side three feet forward of frame 18, six inches below the second platform deck level, passed

---

[379] *Kongo* and *Yamato* are very close to each other at 0850. In fact they would have to be to document the same bearing and range to Taffy 2. This is consistent with the track chart. *Yamato* also documents the range to Taffy 3 at 30,688 yards, bearing 220 degrees. If *Yamato* and *Kongo* share the same range and bearing to Taffy 2 at 0850, then they also share the same range and bearing to Taffy 3.

[380] This destroyer observed to be sinking was the *Heermann* which was severely down by the bow after taking two 14-inch shells from the *Kongo*.

[381] *Kongo* Detailed Action Report. The fact she still can't observe her results may be due to the distance involved as well as effective smoke screens.

through provision storeroom A-403A, and left at frame 16 starboard fifteen inches below the second platform deck. The port side shell plating was ruptured from frame 17 to 21 and indented to four feet around the hole. Frames within this area were damaged and bent. On the starboard side the shell plating was ruptured two feet around the shell hole and the beams and frames were indented and bent for three feet around the hole. The forward loops of the degaussing cables were damaged, and connection box D-2 was rendered useless. Bulkheads from frame 17-21 on the third platform deck were wrinkled on both sides and pierced on the port side. This resulted in the solid flooding of the following compartments; A-404A, A-405C, and A-502A. Compartments A-301-3A, A-302L, and A-403A were partially flooded and in free communication with the sea.[382]

At the same time, a third shell exploded close to the keel at frame 32. The starboard A strake was holed between frames 29.5 and 34.5. A two-foot section of the vertical keel and the flat bottom was blown away. The vertical keel was bent slightly to port between frames 31 and 32. At these frames, the keel brackets were torn lose from the vertical keel at the welds. All frames in the holed area were damaged. The sound dome was pierced; damage to the sonar projector was undetermined. A-5031/2C, A-504M, and A-505M were flooded. It was believed at this time that the force of the explosion loosened manholes 4-31 and 4-39, causing flooding in A-407M and A-409M. Failure of the magazine crew to dog down doors 4-30 and 4-38 and hatches 3-30 and 3-38 led to the solid flooding of compartments A-406M and A-408M and partial flooding of A303L. Upon arriving, damage control parties found A303L had flooded to approximately two feet. Hatches 3-30 and 3-38 were dogged down tightly. Leaks continued around hatch 3-30. The flooding caused by these two hits increased the draft forward by seventeen and a half feet.[383]

All fully flooded compartments were left dogged down. With compartment A-302L in free communication with the sea, attempts to control the flooding by use of mattresses proved unsuccessful due to the size of the hole in the bow. Water would range from three feet to five feet within the compartment as it poured in and out. The forward bulkhead of A-303L was shored up.[384]

Fragments forward of frame 22 riddled the hull at and above the waterline, causing compartments A-1W, A-301-1T, and A-301-2A to flood to the level of the holes. A-1W was plugged

---

[382] *Heermann* Action Report. Based on *Yamato*'s and *Kongo*'s action reports and the bearings and range they give at 0850, the *Kongo* may be 30,688 yards away. This range does match the track chart and is consistent with the Japanese records.

[383] *Ibid.* An under-keel explosion would lift the hull up aft of the center of the explosion but hog the bow down forward in the location of Hit 2 as it pushed up her keel. This may have negated the angle of fall of the projectile that struck forward as it passed through the ship. *Heermann* may also have been heeling over on her starboard side at the moment of impact, for the hull plates around Hit 2 are crushed in around the hole, giving the impression that this hit was more like a deck hit than a projectile hitting a vertical surface. Unfortunately no photographs of *Heermann*'s battle damage could be located to confirm what the damage actually looked like.

[384] Ibid.

after the engagement and pumped dry raising the bow four inches. Fragments also entered the pilot house on the port side, killing four men. At 0855, fire-control radar was out of commission, and the *Heermann* began using search-radar ranges. By 0900, fire-control radar returned to operation, and the ship altered course to 200° true. Cdr. Hathaway noticed the *Heermann* was down by the bow. At 0902, the *Heermann* ceased firing at the *Tone*-class cruiser as it had turned away to the east. At 0905, Cdr. Hathaway changed course to lay a smoke screen between the rear of the carrier formation and enemy heavy units to the rear and starboard quarter. An enemy cruiser, identified by the gunnery officer as being *Maya*- or *Atago*-class, was sighted to starboard at 0907 and was taken under fire.[385]

At 0910, action with the enemy was broken off as range opened, and the *Heermann* attempted to rejoin the carrier formation, laying a smoke screen all the while. Just prior to the last firing, the gunnery officer believed that he observed the *Hoel* and the *Johnston*. The *Johnston*, about 2,000 yards off the port beam, was afire amidships. The *Hoel* was about 4,000 yards on the port quarter. Both of these ships had their masts hanging down over the superstructure decks, and both appeared to be underway although they were under constant enemy gunfire at this time. These vessels were not sighted again.[386]

Cdr. Hathaway later wrote, "The enemy splashes were consistently close, but not too close. The red splashes were closest. Then all at once a red salvo landed 1,000 yards short. The next red salvo was one-hundred yards closer.[387] Thus they walked up in steady one-hundred yard steps until they hit us squarely. Even then, the Nips didn't have sense enough to know they'd found the range. The next salvo landed over us, and we were never hit again.

---

[385] *Ibid. Kongo* probably could not see that she had hit *Heermann* at 0850. What she observed was *Heermann* severely down by the bow at 0900.

[386] *Ibid.* Since *Hoel* had already been sunk by this time, it is likely that Cdr. Hathaway saw the *Samuel B. Roberts*.

[387] Red-dye projectiles belonged to the *Kongo*. Only battleship-caliber shells used dye loads.

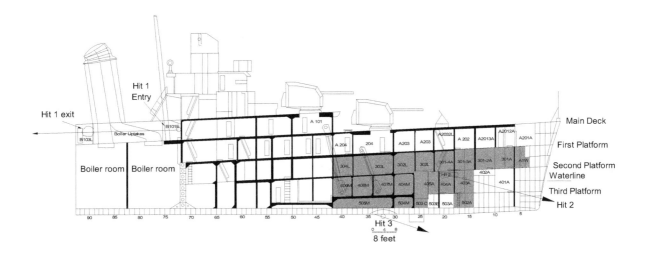

Figure 89: The *Heermann's* flooding.

"By all rules of naval warfare, that should have ended the battle. The sea rushed into the forward part of the ship and we began to go down rapidly by the bow. The ship felt as though, racing full speed, she were about to dive headfirst beneath the surface. We were so far down by the head that our anchors were dragging in the bow wave, throwing torrents of water on the deck. Yet, except for our number two gun, which had taken a piece of shrapnel, we were still firing.

"The whole ship had shuddered and pitched when the salvo hit. Now, although she was steady except for the forward pitch of the deck, a lot of thoughts raced through my mind.

"The one I couldn't forget was that the ships which had slowed down that day had continued to receive more and more damage. So I decided to keep going and take a chance. Thus, we raced along, firing rhythmically, wondering how long we could last."[388]

ON BOARD THE *HARUNA*

At 0850, Admiral Shigenaga counted thirty enemy aircraft headed toward his ship. At 0852, *Haruna* fired another salvo at the three U.S. destroyers in the rear of Taffy 2. The *Yamato* signaled the *Haruna* at 0854, "Attack enemy carriers to port, bearing 140°." Admiral Shigenaga ordered flank speed. Distance to the three enemy destroyers was 39,456 yards. Then his lookouts warned of ten planes approaching from starboard. The *Haruna* opened fire with her anti-aircraft guns at 0855. As this air battle with the ten aircraft was carried out, another twenty-five planes approached the *Haruna* gradually and split up, with torpedo bombers approaching off her bow. Shigenaga knew his ship was

---

[388] Hathaway, A. T. "The Story of the *Heermann.*" *The American Magazine*, April 1945.

about to face a well-structured and organized strike. This delayed any attack the *Haruna* could execute on the rearguard destroyers of Taffy 2.[389]

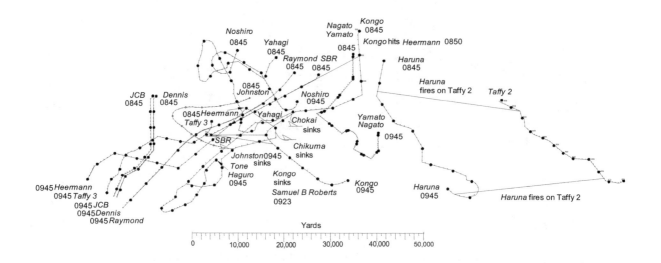

Figure 90: Japanese and U.S. track chart from 0845-0945.

At 0901, the *Haruna* opened fire on the next wave of U.S. aircraft. By 0912, three torpedo bombers approach off her port bow, and she engaged these aircraft and one was seen to explode and fall, but the other two were able to drop their torpedoes. Shigenaga ordered full port rudder. The *Haruna* heeled over in a turn, but no sooner had these two torpedoes been avoided than another plane dropped a torpedo to starboard. Shigenaga ordered full starboard rudder. The *Haruna* responded, heeling over at flank speed, and the torpedo was narrowly avoided—it may have even grazed the hull as it passed down the starboard side.[390]

At 0928, another torpedo attack developed as a single plane approached from the starboard bow. Once the pilot dropped his torpedo, Shigenaga ordered hard to starboard, and this time the torpedo passed down the port side of the ship.[391]

[389] *Haruna* Detailed Action Report.

[390] Ibid.

[391] Ibid.

Figure 91: The *Haruna* was under attack at 0930 from planes of Taffy 2. Smoke amidships came from her AA guns firing at the attacking aircraft. Her main battery was trained to port ready to engage the rear guard destroyers of Taffy 2. Her wake shows she has made several hard turns at flank speed.

PILOTS OF VC-5, THE *KITKUN BAY*

Lt. Comdr. Fowler circled the heavy cruisers for three turns to gain cirrus cloud cover and attacked through this cloud, from out of the sun, at 0905. He caught the second cruiser (*Mogami* class) in column completely by surprise as he received absolutely no AA fire. At this time he had only four bombers as the twelve fighters, and other bombers had fallen out of formation in the thick weather. He completed his dive in about thirty-five seconds. The attack scored five hits amidships on the stack, one hit and two near misses on the stern, and three hits on the bow. The third plane hitting the stern sent the cruiser into a sharp right turn.[392]

On rendezvous after the 0905 attack, he stayed close to the "*Fuso*"- and the "*Ise*"-class battleships just out of AA range.[393] Their course was 120° with a speed of twenty-seven knots, closing Taffy 2 which at the time was thirty miles distant to the southeast. Fowler radioed Taffy 2 and gave them this information about 0910. Taffy 2 at the time was launching a large strike group intended to attack these battleships. They struck at 0930 with strafing, bombing, and torpedo attacks. The battleships responded with their usual turn and almost immediately afterward reversed base course and headed northwest apparently to join the other units. The other units appeared to break off the

---

[392] Composite Squadron VC-5, *Kitkun Bay,* Commander R. L. Fowler.

[393] The ship identifications are incorrect, as there were no *Fuso*- or *Ise*-class battleships present.

attack on Taffy 3 about 0920. Just prior to the attack by Taffy 2, the *"Fuso"* fired on three destroyers astern of that unit, but the salvos fell short.[394]

ON BOARD THE *NOSHIRO*

Captain Kajiwara's lookouts reported a U.S. plane bearing 150°-180° approaching at 0848. He ordered his gunners to take aim and turned his ship onto a course of 345° true. He saw the Seventh Cruiser Squadron bearing 10° at a distance of 30,688 yards at 0856.5. At 0900, he turned his ship around to a new course of 130° true which was completed by 0903. At 0907, he saw what he believed was a U.S. cruiser (actually *Johnston*) at a distance of 16,440 yards and ordered his gunners to take aim and open fire. At 0910, he turned to a new course of 150° true. Then at 0912.5, he received *Yamato*'s message to re-group. Kajiwara had his gunners check fire at 0915. At 0917, he saw the *Chokai* dead in the water, bearing 200° at a distance of 8,768 yards. At 0919, he turned his ship away from the enemy with *Johnston* remaining at 16,440 yards. Then at 0922, he witnessed another U.S. ship explode and immediately sink. By 0929, his ship's course was 000° true and heading away from the battle.[395]

ON BOARD THE *KISHINAMI*

Captain Fukuoka noted an enemy destroyer sinking at 0853. This was the *Hoel*. By 0910, he gave the order to check fire. At 0925, he received the signal from the *Yamato* to assemble. By 0930, he signaled the rest of the destroyer division, "Assume line a head formation." The Battle off Samar was over.[396]

ON BOARD THE *YAHAGI*

Captain Yoshimura at 0846 gave word, "Prepare for port side torpedo battle." At 0848, he saw an enemy destroyer to port closing to attack.[397] He engaged his guns on the destroyer and noted that it sank at 0915.[398]

ON BOARD THE *HOEL*

The enemy fire continued until about 0850. At 0855, the ship rolled over on her port side and then sank stern first. No appreciable underwater explosions occurred. Her crew estimated that more than 300 two- and three-gun salvos were fired at the ship before she sank, many of which were

---

[394] Composite Squadron VC-5, *Kitkun Bay*, Commander R. L. Fowler.

[395] *Noshiro* Detailed Action Report. The ship that exploded at 0922 was the *Samuel B. Roberts*.

[396] *Kishinami* Destroyer Division 31 Detailed Action Report.

[397] This was *Hoel*.

[398] *Yahagi* Detailed Action Report.

major-caliber and dye-loaded. Practically all major-caliber ammunition was armor-piercing and penetrated both sides of the ship without exploding. Her crew estimated most of the minor-caliber shells were anti-personnel.[399]

ON BOARD THE *YAHAGI*

At 0855 *Yahagi* saw another enemy destroyer bearing 170°.[400] Captain Yoshimura ordered his gunners to open fire. At 0859, the destroyer hit *Yahagi* in the port side officer's stateroom with a 5-inch shell. Yoshimura sighted an enemy aircraft carrier at 0906 bearing 170° to the south. He gave the order to fire torpedoes and swung the light cruiser 090° to starboard to bring the torpedo mounts to bear. The *Yahagi* discharged seven torpedoes, speed No. 2, and depth 13 feet. At 0919, the lookouts report, "Enemy aircraft carrier hit by two torpedoes and sunk." However, by 0920 this was revised, "Two torpedo water spouts confirmed, can't confirm if carrier was sunk." Yoshimura turned his ships to the east so that the fleet could re-group by 0940. At 0953, he saw an enemy destroyer which was observed to be listing and immobile; the enemy from the 0855 gun battle was observed to be sinking.[401]

ON BOARD THE *JOHNSTON*

After the near collision with the *Heermann,* Cdr. Evans on board the *Johnston* gave the order to increase speed. Speed was immediately picked up, and the Japanese destroyers were sighted at 10,000 yards. The destroyer leader was immediately taken under fire. The *Johnston*'s gunfire seemed effective as the range closed to 7,000 yards with several hits observed. The *Johnston* was also being hit during this time period, but at approximately 0906, the crew was amazed to see the enemy destroyer leader turn 90° to starboard to break off the action. Fire was immediately shifted to the second destroyer which in turn also turned away to starboard. Amazingly, all six destroyers turned away, and the range began to open rapidly.[402]

Lt. Hagen in his own words, "First we pounded away at the destroyers; they were sleek, streamlined *Terutsuki*-class vessels,[403] our match in tonnage and weight of guns, but not our match in marksmanship, crippled as we were. We should have been duck soup for them, but, though we were taking hits, we were giving back better than we received. First, we scored twelve devastating hits on the destroyer leader. She quit cold and retired from the fight. Next we concentrated on the second destroyer and got in five hits. Then a most amazing thing happened. Instead of coming in for the

---

[399] *Hoel* Action Report.

[400] This was the *Johnston*.

[401] *Yahagi* Detailed Action Report.

[402] *Johnston* Action Report.

[403] *Yahagi* is consistently misidentified by the Americans as a *Terutsuki*-class destroyer.

kill, all six remaining destroyers broke off the battle and began following their vanishing leaders away from the scene. They waited until they were well out of our effective gun range before launching their torpedo attacks—this was about 9:20 A.M.—and all their fish went wild. We can only guess what happened, but apparently the Nip admiral got his wind up and decided he must retreat through San Bernardino Strait quickly or face annihilation. If the Nip had possessed one tenth the courage of our skipper, he would've fought his destroyers five minutes longer and scored some real victories. Cdr. Evans, feeling like the skipper of a battleship, was so elated he could hardly talk. He strutted across his bridge and chortled; 'Now I've seen everything!'"[404]

Prior to the duel with the destroyers, a TBS transmission had directed that the destroyer escorts interpose between the carriers and the Japanese cruisers to port. *Johnston* checked fire and made a turn to port to head for the cruisers. For the next half hour she engaged first the cruisers to port and then the destroyers to starboard, alternating frequently. By 0930, *Johnston*'s luck was running out as she found two heavy cruisers ahead of her, destroyers on her starboard quarter, and two cruisers on her port quarter. Numerous Japanese units had her under fire, and all of these ships were within 6,000 to 10,000 yards. An avalanche of shells knocked out her last engine and boiler room, communications, her main gun director, plot, and all gun mounts but No.4. At 0945, Cdr. Evans gave the command to abandon ship.[405]

Figure 92: *Johnston* crosses *Kalinin Bay's* stern after engaging Japanese destroyers on the formation's starboard side 0930-0935. This was the last photo of the *Johnston,* mislabeled by the National Archives as a Japanese cruiser, but no Japanese ships were laying down smoke.

Lt. Hagen wrote, "At 9:00 A.M., the *Gambier Bay* was lost, but we still were battling desperately to keep the destroyers and cruisers, which also were closing in, from reaching the five surviving carriers. At 9:10, we had taken a hit which knocked out one forward gun and damaged the other.

---

[404] Hagen, "We Asked For the Jap Fleet—and Got It."
[405] *Johnston* Action Report.

Fires had broken out. One of our 40-mm ready lockers was hit, and the exploding shells were causing as much damage as the Japs. The bridge was rendered untenable by the fires and explosions, and Cdr. Evans had been forced at 9:20 to shift his command to the fantail, where he yelled his steering orders through an open hatch at the men who were turning the rudder by hand.

"In the gun director, we were having our own troubles. The place was full of smoke; our eyes were streaming and we were coughing and choking as we carried out our duties. We now were in a position where all the gallantry and guts in the world couldn't save us. There were two cruisers on our port; another two cruisers ahead of us, and several destroyers on our starboard side; the battleships, well astern of us, fortunately had turned coy. We desperately traded shots first with one group and then the other. We knew we couldn't survive, but we figured that help for the carriers must be on the way, and every minute's delay might count.

"Down at one of my batteries, the gun captain, a Texan, kept exhorting, 'More shells! More shells!' and one of his gang, even while breaking his back at the task, grumbled, 'I'm sure glad there aren't no Japs from Texas!'[406]

"By 9:30, we were going dead in the water; even the Japs couldn't miss us. They made a sort of running semicircle around our ship, shooting at us like a bunch of Indians attacking a prairie schooner. Our lone engine and fire room was knocked out; we lost all power and even the indomitable skipper knew we were finished. At 9:45, he gave the saddest order a captain can give: 'Abandon ship.'"[407]

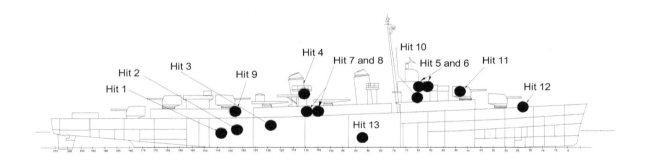

Figure 93: The *Johnston's* battle damage.

---

[406] Ibid.

[407] Ibid.

ON BOARD THE *ST. LO*

At 0851, Captain McKenna received a message over VHF that a Japanese cruiser had been hit by a torpedo in the bow. Two Japanese ships could be seen off the port beam bearing 134°, range 10,400 yards. The enemy ships off the starboard quarter had closed to 6,900 yards, and the *St. Lo* was receiving considerable fire from this direction though the *Kalinin Bay* seemed to be their main target. At approximately 0910 the Japanese ships reversed course but fired a torpedo spread during this run. At 0911 Captain McKenna received word that half of Japanese force was retiring westward. By 0913, the *St. Lo*'s course was 240° true. Japanese ships reported bearing 048° at 12,000 yards, 159° at 15,200 yards, 109° at 11,200 yards. Then at 0915 the range continued to open as targets were now at 163° at 15,500 yards, 108° at 12,500 yards, and 162° at 16,300 yards. At 0924, a *St. Lo* plane piloted by Lt. Waldrop sighted torpedoes astern of the formation. Several torpedoes were sighted from the ship, and they were porpoising out of the water near the end of their run. Lt. Waldrop strafed one of the torpedoes which exploded as it neared the *Kalinin Bay*.[408] The *Kalinin Bay* also took several other torpedoes under fire from 20 mm and 40 mm guns. All ships maneuvered to run parallel with the wakes, and no torpedo hits were scored during this phase. By 0943, the Japanese forces were definitely retiring to the northwest, and all fire had stopped.[409]

PILOTS OF VC -65, THE *ST. LO*

Lt. (jg) L. E. Waldrop after making his strafing runs, turned his badly damaged plane back towards the carriers. He circled the formation, and at 0924 he radioed the position and track of twelve or thirteen torpedoes approaching the carriers. Twice he strafed torpedoes that were getting dangerously close. At least one was exploded by his strafing.[410] During the time he acted as torpedo spotter, he flew at dangerously low altitudes while shells from enemy surface forces were still landing throughout the area.[411]

Most of VC-65 fighters after making their initial strafing attacks headed for Tacloban airfield. Several pilots still had some ammunition available, so Lt. J.T. Riley, LT. C. K. Maino, Lt. (jg) J. A. Hamman, and Lt. (jg) W. E. Hammett returned to the scene of the action and began strafing runs on a heavy cruiser and destroyer at approximately 0900. They watched as a Japanese light cruiser fired

---

[408] This torpedo explosion close to the *Kalinin Bay* was undoubtedly one of the plumes the crew of the *Yahagi* observed, giving them the perception a torpedo hit the carrier.

[409] *St. Lo* Action Report.

[410] The explosion was certainly spotted by the crew of *Yahagi* who counted it as a hit.

[411] Composite Squadron VC-65, *St. Lo*, Lt. (jg) L. E. Waldrop.

into the *Gambier Bay* at approximately 1,000 yards. This ship was chosen for their final strafing run as their ammunition was exhausted.[412]

ON BOARD THE *KALININ BAY*

By 0845, the leading Japanese cruiser was pulling even with the *Kalinin Bay*, the rearmost ship in the formation. It was during this time period that the Japanese began to hit her on a regular basis. Hits 4 and 5 were two 8-inch shells that entered the port side of A-301-L at frame 18 approximately 5 feet above deck level and exiting the starboard side of the hull at frame 19, one at deck level and one about 3 feet above deck level. A-301-L flooded to 5 feet and A-401-A flooded to 4 feet due to these hits, but the shells didn't detonate.[413]

The *Kalinin Bay* then took her most serious hit. Hit 6 was an 8-inch shell that landed at frame 77, port side on the officers' stateroom #316 one foot above deck level. The shell then passed through the platform deck about 4 feet inboard from the port side, through storeroom A-407-A and entered the forward port corner of the port aviation lube oil tank where it exploded. Fuel lines for tanks A-911-F, A-910-F, A-909-F, A-912-F, A-915-F, and B-903-F were ruptured. More importantly the forward bulkhead to the forward engine room was ruptured in ten places along the platform deck. The forward engine room began to flood up to 4 feet of water as the crew struggled to plug the holes. Fragments had peppered the bulkheads of compartment #318 and the passageway amidships to A407-A which also flooded to a depth of 4 feet before the holes were plugged and flooding controlled. This shell missed going through the bottom of the ship by a narrow margin.[414]

---

[412] Composite Squadron VC-65, *St. Lo,* Lt. J.T. Riley, LT. C. K. Maino, Lt. (jg) J. A. Hamman, and Lt. (jg) W. E. Hammett.

[413] *Kalinin Bay* Action Report. Note that the majority of the projectiles hit forward and then traveled aft into the ship, which indicates the firing ship was ahead of her at the time. This occurred only at the very end of the battle when the *Tone* and the *Haguro* had pulled to within 10,100 yards.

[414] *Kalinin Bay* Action Report.

Figure 94: Japanese shells land aft and to the *Kalinin Bay's* port side.

Hit 7, an 8-inch shell, hit the port side of frame 51.5 at deck level of A-0102-AL and the overhead of the carpenter shop, went across the elevator pit and into passageway A-204-1T, then out the starboard side of the ship at frame 53.5 one foot above the second deck.[415]

---

[415] Ibid.

Figure 95: A salvo of shells landed just aft of the *Kalinin Bay*. Note how tight the Japanese shell pattern was.

Hit 8, another 8-inch shell, struck the port side at A-301-4L (aviation armory) between frames 103-104, 4 feet above deck level, passing through after bulkhead and into B-301-6L (ship's armory), out the inboard bulkhead of the same compartment, and down into the first platform deck, into passageway B-301-2T at frame 107, through the machine shop, through B-404-F, across the athwartships passage and into 3-405-W where it exploded. Fuel oil tanks B-402-F, B904-F and bulkhead 118 (forward bulkhead to the aft engine room) were ruptured. The first platform deck was perforated at frames 106-108. B-301-6L flooded up to a level of 10 feet. Fires in the aviation armory, ship's armory, and machine shop were not brought under control for at least 1.5 hours after the hits. Hit 9 penetrated the port side of A-201-A between frames 8-9 about 3 feet above deck level and passed through the starboard side at frames 9 and 10, one foot above deck level without exploding. Hit 10 was an 8-inch shell that struck the flight deck at frame 55.5 just starboard of the forward elevator, passing through A-0207-2T and into forward elevator pit. The shell broke into three pieces, each passing through A-0102T and into officer's stateroom #0117. One piece exited between frames 58-59 creating a 2.5-foot by 5-foot hole in the starboard shell. The other two pieces left compartment #0117 at frames 55.5 and frame 54.[416]

Hit 11 was an 8-inch shell that hit the flight deck at frame 59.5 outboard of the forward elevator, passed through A-0207-2T into the elevator pit, and then went down to the base of the forward elevator where it exploded. The elevator pit and flight deck were holed between frames 59-61. The forward elevator itself was wrecked. Hit 12 was another 8-inch shell that struck the flight deck at frame 67 between the elevator and the island, then passing through the starboard radar transmitter room and into the radar control room. It tore large holes on its way through the radio direction finder and radio generator room. Hit 13 struck the forward starboard stack, and hit 14 struck the flight deck at frame 87 amidships, entering the forward uptakes. It passed to starboard through flight crew lockers and out the starboard side at frame 90.5 without detonating.[417]

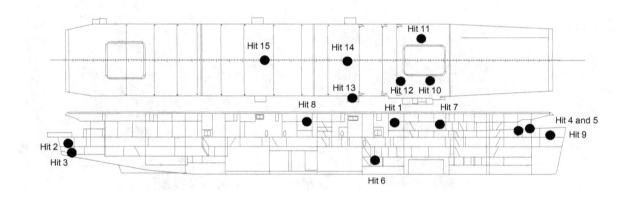

Figure 96: The *Kalinin Bay's* battle damage.

Hit 15 struck the flight deck at frame 119 amidships and entered the after uptakes, went through the gallery deck, and passed out the starboard side at frame 124. The flooding caused by these hits resulted in a 7° list to port. Damage control shifted ballast to compartments C-908-F and C907-F and then she suddenly took an 8° list to starboard. Due to the starboard list, they realized that there was a hole in compartment A-301-L and the ship was developing a negative GM. Damage control then pumped out compartments A-903-F and A-904-F, pumping the fuel into C-907-F and C-909-F, which raised her bow and allowed her to steady herself.[418]

---

[416] Ibid.

[417] Ibid.

[418] Ibid.

Figure 97: The little puffs of black smoke on the horizon to the left edge of the photo are salvos of gunfire coming from the *Yahagi* and her destroyers. The *Johnston* was now attempting to cross the U.S. formation heading towards the right edge of the photo.

On the *Kalinin Bay*'s stern, her 5-inch gun crew witnessed at 0930 a direct hit amidships on one of the Japanese destroyers, which was immediately enveloped in white smoke. The enemy destroyers made a radical maneuver and began to withdraw, but continued to fire on the American ships. A friendly destroyer crossed the *Kalinin Bay*'s stern at 500 yards and made smoke and closed the Japanese destroyers as she approached. Fire of the 5-inch gun was checked at 0935 due to the presence of this friendly destroyer and because the enemy destroyers were no longer visible due to the smoke screen.[419]

A TBM aircraft, believed to be from the *St. Lo*, had been circling the formation; it made a steep glide astern of the ship and strafed in the wake of the ship about a hundred yards astern, exploding two torpedoes which had been fired by the enemy destroyers. The explosion of the torpedoes, only a short while after the enemy had ceased surface shelling, was the first warning of a torpedo attack. Immediately after these torpedoes were exploded, another torpedo was sighted directly astern in the wake of the ship. It appeared to be broaching. The 5-inch gun on the fantail opened fire at a depressed elevation of 2°, and a shell exploded approximately 10 feet ahead of the approaching torpedo, which was next observed veering to port. At least twelve other torpedo wakes were

---

[419] *Ibid.* The friendly destroyer crossing astern is the *Johnston*.

observed on parallel course on both sides of the ship. After the torpedo attack the entire enemy surface force retired to the northward.[420]

Figure 98: A six-shell pattern falls short of the *Kalinin Bay* as the *Johnston* moves along the horizon toward the right edge of the photo.

ON BOARD THE *FANSHAW BAY*

Clifton Sprague changed course again at 0847 to 220°. By 0849, she was still under fire from enemy cruisers bearing 113°, distance 16,500 yards. The enemy main body was bearing 025°, distance 18,900 yards.[421] Salvos from battleships were infrequent and inaccurate. At 0850, the *Fanshaw Bay* changed course to 240°. At 0853, cruiser salvos scored close straddles. At 0855, a shell hit the forward end of flight deck.[422]

---

[420] Ibid.

[421] The ships bearing 025° at a distance of 18,900 yards were *Yahagi* and her destroyers, not the battleships which were bearing 40° true at 30,688 yards.

[422] *Fanshaw Bay* Action Report.

Figure 99: More puffs of smoke along the horizon to the left of the photo while a four-shell pattern falls short of the *Kalinin Bay*. The *Johnston* approaches the right edge of the photo with her white smoke blending into the color of the sky.

A fourth shell hit the flight deck at frame 13, about thirteen feet from the port edge, smashed the catapult track, and penetrated the deck tearing a 24-inch by 48-inch hole in the flight deck. The projectile then tore out a section 24 inches long along the top of No. 5 longitudinal flight deck stringer. It continued, tearing away sections of transverse deck beams No. 5, No. 4, No. 3, and No. 2. The large longitudinal flight deck support, located sixteen feet from the port side of the flight deck, suffered a penetration about eight inches down from the stiffener, while the No. 6 longitudinal beam was distorted for a distance of sixty inches. The No. 7 longitudinal beam was distorted in two places. The projectile then ripped through the lower half of the transverse flight deck beam frame 6, tearing a hole 24 inches by 36 inches, along with a section of the lower flange of the transverse flight deck beam at frame 3 about thirty-six inches long. One enlisted man was injured by fragments as a result of this hit. The shell didn't detonate.[423]

Hit 5 exploded below the waterline on the starboard side. An 18-inch by 18-inch hole opened in the hull about seven feet below the waterline between frames 9 and 10 with fragments entering A-1-W, then causing a 12-inch by 12-inch hole in the port hull plates at a point 5 feet below the waterline between frames 10-11. No change in list or trim was noticeable.[424]

---

[423] Ibid.

[424] Ibid.

Lastly, a near-miss explosion sent a fragment into the hull at second deck level on the port side at frame 15, tearing a 10-inch by 10-inch hole and expending itself in the crew's head in compartment A-209-L.[425]

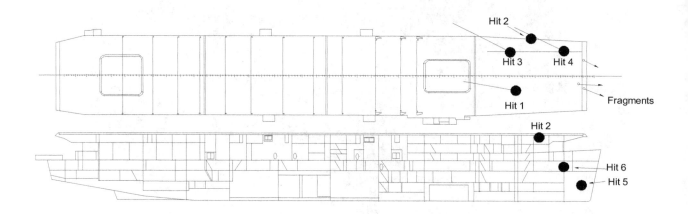

Figure 100: The *Fanshaw Bay*'s battle damage.

Figure 101: Crew members of the *Fanshaw Bay* inspect the battle damage she received from hit 4 at the forward end of her flight deck.

Clifton Sprague reported, "This ship under fire from two cruisers and two destroyers."[426] By 0856, he changed course to 280°.[427] At 0903, he observed his own destroyers between his carrier

---

[425] Ibid.

[426] Ibid.

[427] Clifton Sprague's turn west was critical in opening the range between him and Kurita, reinforcing Kurita's perception that he must be fighting fleet carriers capable of thirty knots.

group and the enemy making smoke and firing. At 0906, the enemy cruisers closed to 14,000 yards, bearing 142°, with the main body bearing 010°, distance 18,000 yards. He decided to change course to 240° by 0908. At 0910, he observed two enemy cruisers of the *Tone* and the *Nachi* classes with two destroyers closing on his port beam, bearing 092°, distance 13,600 yards. Then at 0911, a *Terutsuki*-class destroyer made a torpedo attack from astern. The main enemy group was bearing 028° distance 20,100 yards.[428] At 0916, he ordered another change in course to 260°. Clifton Sprague observed one enemy group bearing 070° at a distance of 19,600 yards. He gave another order to change course to 270° at 0917. One minute later, he change course to 240°. He then received a report from a pilot that one Japanese cruiser was smoking and retiring. He changed course to 230° by 0920 and flooded the gas pump room with CO_2. At 0922, he change course again to 200°.428F[429]

At 0924, the main Japanese fleet was reportedly breaking formation and maneuvering radically to evade air attack. By 0925, Clifton Sprague changed course to 210°. The bearing on the enemy ships was now 021° distance 21,000 yards. The Japanese DDs were making a torpedo attack as reported by the *St. Lo.* At 0927, the *St. Lo* reported torpedoes coming up on her stern and opened fire on them. Clifton Sprague ordered the formation to change course to 225°.[430]

By 0929, the Japanese force of cruisers was bearing 153°, distance 21,000 yards, seen turning away and heading north. Numerous torpedoes were seen to be porpoising parallel to the formation and expending themselves. By 0930, he changed course to 210°, and observed the Japanese fleet retiring to the north. By 0931, he gave orders and checked fire from the *Fanshaw Bay*'s 5-inch battery. He then changed course to 200°, coming under fire again from enemy cruisers. He continued to give orders for his destroyers to make smoke between the carriers and the enemy cruisers.[431]

Suddenly at 0934, a torpedo wake was reported at 180° relative. The *Fanshaw Bay* opened fire with her 40 mm guns. Clifton Sprague ordered, "Left full rudder." The torpedo wake was soon reported 090° relative. Clifton Sprague steadied the ship on a course of 190°. By 0940, the Japanese fleet continued retirement, bearing 075°, distance 28,000 yards.[432]

Clifton Sprague in his own words, "To me, it was a miracle that under such terrific fire for that length of time only one carrier had suffered a crippling hit. Two others had suffered several hits and three others none at all. And all of my six carriers, except the *Gambier Bay*, were able to make their maximum speed. But at 0920 the Japs, having given us everything they had in surface fire, opened up with a torpedo attack, launching from twelve to fourteen fish on our starboard quarter. Again

---

[428] This "main group" and the *Terutsuki*-class destroyer were in reality the *Yahagi* and her destroyer division.
[429] Ibid.
[430] Ibid.
[431] Ibid.
[432] Ibid.

they showed their timidity by striking from too far away—about 10,000 yards—so that when the torpedoes reached our formation they were near the end of their rope and, fortunately, parallel to our course. Several of our pilots, passing over our carriers between strikes, were quick-witted enough to strafe torpedoes which seemed about to hit ships, and exploded several of them in the water. At 0925, my mind was occupied with dodging torpedoes, when near the bridge I heard one of the signalmen yell, 'God damn it, boys, they're getting away!' I couldn't believe my eyes, but it looked as if the whole Japanese fleet was indeed retiring…."[433]

ON BOARD THE *KITKUN BAY*

With all but sixty rounds of 5-inch ammunition expended, the order was given to check fire from the stern 5-inch gun at 0901. By 0921, the enemy cruisers turned away and commenced retiring on a northerly course. This ended two hours and twenty-three minutes of continuous shelling of the ships of Taffy 3.[434]

ON BOARD THE *WHITE PLAINS*

At 0846, *White Plains* changed course to 200°. The *Gambier Bay*, which had disappeared from view, was requested to acknowledge this signal, but no answer was received. At 0849, the range had closed to 18,000 yards from the leading Japanese cruiser, so the order was given to open fire from the 5-inch gun battery. At 0854, the *Dennis* reported being hit astern below the waterline. At 0904, enemy cruisers to port reached a minimum range of 11,700 yards. At 0907 two *Nachi*-class cruisers were seen bearing 150° at about 25,000 yards. By 0905, the enemy ships extended from starboard quarter around aft to the port quarter, the cruisers had closed to 11,700 yards.[435]

Salvos were falling close aboard, but by numerous changes in course, the *White Plains* somehow avoided getting hit. Any enemy ship that closed within 18,000 yards was taken under fire by the ship's 5-inch gun. Her crew estimated at least six hits were observed on a cruiser, one of which appeared to disable a forward turret. At 0918, two returning destroyer escorts were ordered to take position on formation's port bow.[436]

By 0920, heavy cruisers on the port beam fired two salvos which fell very short. Then at 0932, the enemy launched torpedoes and retired to northwesterly course. The *White Plains* made an emergency turn to avoid the torpedoes reportedly approaching on port beam.[437]

---

[433] Sprague, "They Had Us on the Ropes."

[434] *Kitkun Bay* Action Report.

[435] White Plains Action Report.

[436] Ibid.

[437] Ibid.

Figure 102: The *Tone* (left) and probably the *Raymond* (right) on the horizon to the port side of the U.S. carrier formation. This photo was taken from the *White Plains*.

Figure 103: Puffs of smoke on the horizon mark the position of the Japanese cruisers as shell splashes fall close to the *White Plains*.

Figure 104: The final shells from the Japanese cruisers on the horizon land in the *White Plains's* wake.

ON BOARD THE *HAGURO*

At 0848, Capt. Sugiura sighted an enemy destroyer bearing 050° starboard and immediately ordered his main battery to open fire. At 0849, course was changed to 255°, and main battery salvos were checked. He noted that the First and Third Battleship Divisions were to port. At 0851, *Chokai* was 70° to port 1,644 yards ahead, and *Tone* was 040° to starboard. The enemy was within an expanding smoke screen when aircraft made a concentrated, well-coordinated air attack on *Chokai*. Capt. Sugiura ordered a 090° turn to starboard to avoid bombs, but the *Chokai* made no evasive turn and was hit on the starboard side. Sugiura noted that the *Chokai* made a mistake by not turning with the *Haguro*. The bomb hit the *Chokai*'s forward engine room, and she fell out of formation. Sugiura continued to pursue the enemy carriers and re-opened fire on one, bearing 077° to starboard at 0852. Eight salvos were fired at a carrier at 11,508 yards with the results unclear due to the smoke.[438] At 0901, an enemy torpedo bomber was engaged to starboard. Then at 0902, eight torpedo bombers approached and were immediately engaged, and the planes passed to port. At 0905, a destroyer bearing 055° relative was sighted, and he ordered the main battery to re-open fire on the enemy aircraft carriers, distance 12,604 yards. Seventeen salvos were fired, but again the results were unclear due to smoke.[439] At 0910, four torpedoes past aft across her stern to port. Then at 0911, he ordered *Haguro* to fall in behind *Tone*. The main battery fire was checked at 0912. By 0916, he received the signal from *Yamato* for all forces to re-assemble. By 0920, both *Tone* and *Haguro* turned around and headed north to re-join the *Yamato*. The *Tone* reported three torpedoes passing in front of her as they turned to port. At 0921, he noted in the *Haguro*'s logs that the enemy aircraft carriers were moving away, disappearing into the smoke screen. By 0922, all firing had stopped, and she reduced speed to

---

[438] At 0855 *Fanshaw Bay* was hit on her flight deck near the forward edge.

[439] *Haguro* probably hit *Kalinin Bay* at this time as she received the majority of her hits during this phase of the action.

twenty-six knots. The *Haguro* listed 345 8-inch rounds fired during the surface battle in 108 salvos during the surface battle.[440]

Figure 105: The heavy cruiser *Tone*, seen from the *White Plains*.

ON BOARD THE *TONE*

Captain Mayuzumi witnessed the attack on the *Chikuma* and described it as follows: "Four torpedo planes executed extremely low-level attack on the *Chikuma*, two from each side. Several enemy fighters simultaneously were over the ship. The *Chikuma* was seen firing with all of her guns at the enemy aircraft. The *Tone* was approximately 5,480 yards aft of her. One fighter and one torpedo plane were shot down off the *Chikuma*'s starboard side.[441]

"The *Chikuma* was maneuvering to evade the two torpedo planes which attacked first from starboard side by turning in the direction of the planes. Two other torpedo planes made an extremely low level attack from the port side. Shortly thereafter a torpedo hit the stern. There was a burst of flame and simultaneously a column of water almost as high as the length of the ship. The after-deck single mount machine guns and other gear were thrown up into the air by the explosion. The after half of the after-deck was apparently heavily damaged and settled in the water, but the ship continued to move at a reduced speed. Her guns kept firing and she circled around and signaled us her rudder has been knocked out. Other than the stern damage no other damage was observed."[442]

---

[440] *Haguro* Detailed Action Report.

[441] Hoyt, Edwin P. *The Battle of Leyte Gulf: The Death Knell of the Japanese Fleet.* Weybright and Talley, 1972, p 304.

[442] *Ibid.*

Figure 106: Bombs land close to *Tone* as seen from *White Plains*.

U.S. aircraft focused on *Tone*, now the lead Japanese ship. *Haguro* pulled in line by 0912, and Mayuzumi signaled her about launching torpedoes. He felt that continuing the pursuit of the enemy carrier group would be extremely effective and that they had finally achieved a favorable tactical position. Then at 0914, he got Kurita's message to reassemble. Mayuzumi didn't signal Kurita informing him of his tactical position. At 0920, he turned his ship around and headed north, away from the U.S. ships. *Tone* did not list her ammunition expenditure.[443]

PILOTS OF VC-10, *GAMBIER BAY*

Lt. Cdr. Huxtable flying above the carrier formation looked down to see the enemy cruisers maneuvering to box the carriers between themselves and the battleships. He radioed to *Fanshaw Bay* that the best course was now directly south. The enemy cruisers were now in the clear with the battleships still at the edge of the rain squall and smoke. He saw some fighters make a strafing run, so he decided to make a mock torpedo attack until he approached to about 3,000 yards, drawing enemy fire. He made four such runs and then, hearing flight leaders from other air groups, decided the situation was improving enough for him to head for Tacloban airfield at 0915. He radioed ahead to see if Tacloban airfield had any bombs available. They replied negative, so he decided to look for an escort carrier to land on. He asked permission and was denied and instructed to go back to Tacloban. When he arrived at 1030, Tacloban was full, and they directed him to Dulag airfield where he landed at 1130.[444]

Ensign Shroyer started to climb to gain altitude when at approximately 0900 he spotted a *Tone*-class cruiser. There were about ten to twelve fighters strafing the ship, so he followed them in. He released his two bombs and believed they both hit the fantail, which was confirmed by two fighter

---

[443] *Tone* Detailed Action Report.
[444] Composite Squadron VC-10, *Gambier Bay,* Lt. Cdr. Huxtable.

pilots, Lt. Paul Garrison of VC-5 and Ensign Lischer of VC-10. Half an hour later, this cruiser was seen dead in the water. He then departed for Tacloban airfield to re-arm but on arrival was directed to Dulag airfield where he safely landed. Ensign Lischer joined up with Cdr. Fowler to attack the Japanese heavy cruisers closing on the carrier formation. He made eight strafing attacks on a *Mogami*- and a *Tone*-class cruiser, encountering, heavy to moderate AA gunfire, but wasn't hit. He saw one cruiser get hit amidships which he couldn't identify and one *Tone*-class cruiser get hit on the stern leaving a large oil slick. At 0900, he departed for Tacloban airfield where he safely landed.[445]

PILOTS OF VC-27, THE *SAVO ISLAND*

On the morning of 25 October, VC 27 was slated to send ten TBM's on direct-support work at 0745. Just prior to launching time, word came through to cancel the sorties; the TBM's were to stand by for immediate take-off. Thirteen of the squadron's VF had already left on Combat Air Patrol.[446]

Then the order came to remove the bombs from the TBM's and replace them with torpedoes. The suspense in the ready room was obvious, and each pilot was tensely awaiting the word of what was up. The loading crews were scrambling like mad to remove the bombs and load the torpedoes. Finally the news came: there was a large enemy task force bearing down from the north, only twenty odd miles away, already firing on other escort carriers. Pilots were told to man their planes. A check of loaded torpedoes was made. Five planes were ready. At 0816, the first TBM was launched. Then an order from Captain Ekstrom on the bridge over the bull-horn, "Your mission is to cripple as many of the enemy's ships as possible, don't waste time for a kill." The four other bombers took off in rapid succession. All available TBM's with torpedoes from CTU 77.4 had been called out. A quick rendezvous was made overhead. Five planes from the *Marcus Island* joined up, with Lt Henry of VC-27 as flight leader. They circled to gain altitude as the enemy force was only a few miles away. As their angle increased, the pilots could see tall pagodas of the Japanese ships to the north, then the ships themselves, and finally the shell fire aimed at the carriers who were taking it on all sides and some of whom were aflame. At 9,000 feet, they proceeded to a point northwest of the enemy task force. The first count showed three battleships of *Kongo* class and *Ise* class, two heavy cruisers of *Mogami* and *Tone* class, and numerous destroyers.[447]

Lt. Henry divided his five bombers into two sections and directed other bombers to organize similarly. The enemy ships were in a rain squall. and the cloud coverage over them was about .7 broken cumulus. After a quick survey of the enemy forces disposition, Lt Henry led his planes

---

[445] Composite Squadron VC-10, *Gambier Bay*, Ensign Shroyer, Ensign Lischer. Composite Squadron VC-5, *Kitkun Bay*, Lt. Paul Garrison, Cdr. Fowler.

[446] *Savo Island* Action Report.

[447] Ibid.

across the force at 9,000 feet, and directed that the VC-27 division make an anvil attack and the VC-21 division from the *Marcus Island* to come in on a wave attack. The first division was to take the foremost of the cruisers or battleships as their target, and the *Marcus Island* the next cruiser or battleship in line.[448]

Figure 107: The *Chikuma,* crippled by a torpedo hit, desperately attempts to fight off further attacks. Ordnance from her AA guns impact the water, and she may have fired a salvo from one of her main gun batteries as a puff of smoke obscures her bridge.

At 0845, Lt. Henry, Lt. (jg) Yeaman, and Lt. (jg) Nathan were the first section of VC-27 to peel off at 8,000 feet, followed rapidly by Lt. Bitting and Ens. Wand of the second section. They moved over, down-sun, at 60-degree angle and broke through the clouds at 3,000 feet. Their target was a *Tone*-class cruiser which was steaming southwest, 2,000 yards to their starboard. The attack, being the first of all the torpedo planes and coming from cloud cover and down-sun was apparently a complete surprise to the Japanese as no AA fire was encountered until after the release of the torpedoes, and the cruiser made no evasive movements. The planes went in at 230 knots and leveled off. Five torpedoes were released, all aimed at the cruiser. Anti-aircraft fire of every sort had begun by this time, and it was difficult for the airmen to follow the course of the torpedoes. Three of them were observed to run straight and true; however, one was seen to pass astern of the cruiser and shortly thereafter an explosion was seen on the destroyer which had been flanking the cruiser to starboard. It was possible that the destroyer took this torpedo. Two other torpedoes were seen to hit the starboard side of the cruiser very near the stern. The whole stern seemed to blow up; huge columns of black smoke rose from the explosion, and debris filled the air above it. She was observed to be moving very slowly in a tight circle. The destroyer with several fires blazing aft seemed to be

---

[448] Composite Squadron VC-27, *Savo Island,* Lt. Henry.

dead in the water. As the TBM's passed over the cruiser for recovery in the west, they began violent maneuvers and maintained a low altitude at high speed to avoid AA fire, which was becoming more intense every moment. Yellow smoke bursts were very much in evidence. Only one plane was hit, under the port wing with minor damage to the wheel well and hydraulic system.[449]

Figure 108: The *Chikuma* seen from directly above as a U.S. aircraft passes over her.

PILOTS OF VC-21, THE *MARCUS ISLAND* TAFFY 2

Ten of the twelve torpedo bombers had taken off at 0530 for Leyte Gulf to make parachute drops of supplies to the 96th Infantry unit just west of Catmon Hills. At 0700 word was passed that six carriers of the northern group operating thirty-five miles to the north were under attack by a strong Japanese surface force. The two remaining TBM-1C planes were immediately loaded with torpedoes and piloted by Ens. Walker and Ens. Bankston who were launched with fifteen fighters. At approximately 0845 these two bombers along with approximately thirteen other TBM's made strafing and torpedo attacks on the leading Japanese cruisers. Both Ens. Walker and Ens. Bankston made their drops from 1,200 yards at 500 feet at an indicated air speed of 250 knots. Ens. Bankston's torpedo was believed to have passed under the target, but Walker's torpedo was believed

---

[449] Composite Squadron VC-27, *Savo Island*, Lt. Henry, Lt. (jg) Yeaman, Lt. (jg) Nathan, Lt. Bitting and Ens. Wand.

to have struck an *Atago*-class cruiser near the stern on the port side. The explosion was seen to take up the after third of the ship.[450]

Figure 109: The *Chikuma* with the destroyer *Nowaki* standing by as American planes pass overhead. The *Chikuma* was surrounded by oil and dead in the water. Eventually the *Nowaki* would take off the crew and sink her with torpedoes. Then the *Nowaki* would attempt to escape back through San Bernardino Strait alone.

ON BOARD THE *RAYMOND*

At 0920, the enemy cruisers veered to port and the range opened up rapidly. Fire was continued until the range opened to 18,000 yards at 0950. Gunnery officers observed that, during the interception period, the enemy cruiser was crossed at least five times with fifteen direct hits being obtained. During this period the enemy cruiser had shifted fire from the carriers to *Raymond*.[451]

ON BOARD THE *DENNIS*

At 0847, enemy salvos were falling close aboard to starboard. Eight enemy vessels, probably destroyers, reported closing on starboard quarter. At 0850, enemy salvos continue to approach. *Dennis* received a direct hit on port side three feet above platform deck at frame 35; it passed through the deck and out the starboard side at frame 31, three feet above water line. The ordnance storeroom and dry stores storeroom, compartment A0306A, flooded. One man in Repair I was

---

[450] Composite Squadron VC-21, *Marcus Island,* Ens. Walker and Ens. Bankston.

[451] *Raymond* Action Report.

fatally injured. Shell fragments entered the hull at frame 137 just below main deck, doing considerable damage.[452]

By 0900, she received another direct hit on after 40 mm director. The shell continued through superstructure deck into compartment A-102ACIM. Two men were killed, and two were fatally injured. She also received a hit on top of #1 5-inch gun shield. Both 5-inch guns reported inoperative, mount one because of personnel casualties and mount two because of broken breach operating spring. By 0902 she changed course to 220° true. Then at 0903 men were transferred from the aft 5-inch mount to the forward mount.[453]

The crew began bringing 5-inch ammunition forward from her after magazines as access passageways to her forward magazines were flooded via the ordnance storeroom. At 0907, not expecting the ship to last much longer, crew members threw overboard one weighted sack of registered publications. By 0910, she changed course to 240° true. Range commenced to open on the cruiser attacking from astern. Minimum range was about 7,500 yards. At this point her crew ceased disposing of registered publications. By 0920, No. 2 gun crew shifted aft, and the gun returned to service. At 0925 lookouts sighted land bearing 220° true, distance fifteen miles: Samar Island.[454]

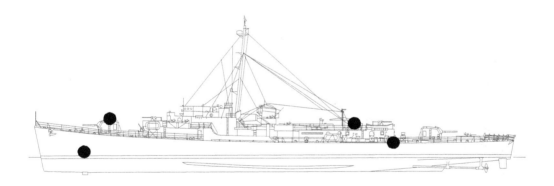

Figure 110: *Dennis's* battle damage.

ON BOARD THE *JOHN C. BUTLER*

At 0900, *Dennis* was observed to be hit by cruiser shells and retired behind *John C. Butler*'s smoke screen. It was at this time that both destroyer escorts had come out just abaft the port beam of their own formation. The enemy cruiser concentrated at first on *John C. Butler*, and four salvos landed

---

[452] *Dennis* Action Report.

[453] Ibid.

[454] Ibid.

close, one 100 yards astern and three 200 yards to port. With the salvos so close, *John C. Butler* radically zigged to starboard and then zagged back to the original course. Two hits on a *Nachi*-class cruiser were observed. At 0905, the cruiser shifted fire to a carrier, and although smoke screen covered the target, five or six salvos landed very close off the port bow. It was believed one salvo hit. At 0915 the cruiser shifted fire to the *Fanshaw Bay* which was on the *John C. Butler*'s starboard bow. By 0918 the *John C. Butler* checked fire since ammunition was getting very low. Clifton Sprague ordered the port-side destroyer escorts to get on port bow of formation. The *John C. Butler* was on the *Fanshaw Bay*'s port beam and was already moving up to her port bow and continued. By 0930 when the enemy turned away, range had closed to 13,200 yards. Formation speed was reduced to fifteen knots.[455]

ON BOARD THE *KONGO*

A message from the Tenth Squadron came in between 0900 and 0911 that one carrier had taken a torpedo hit, but no further details. At 0911, Shimazaki received Kurita's orders, "All ships in force head north speed twenty knots." Then at 0913, torpedoes were sighted, and the *Kongo* evaded them on her starboard side. At 0920, four more torpedoes were avoided and passed ahead of her. At the same time Shimazaki ordered gunfire shifted to a destroyer at a distance of 13,152 yards; her main and secondary guns opened fire. At 0923, the *Kongo* fired a salvo and scored four simultaneous hits on the U.S. destroyer which resulted in a huge explosion.[456] Shimazaki logged into the *Kongo*'s records that the target had been destroyed. Soon after this, another message from the Tenth Squadron arrived reporting that they had sunk one enemy carrier and another was on fire. At 0927, the *Yamato* re-sent her orders to head north at twenty knots. Shimazaki broke off the pursuit, and the *Kongo* headed north to join the flagship. *Kongo* had expended 211 14-inch Type 1 AP rounds during the surface battle. She also fired 48 of her 14-inch Type 3 AA rounds during the entire battle of Leyte Gulf, along with 175 of her 04 common projectiles and 97 of her Type 0 HC rounds from her secondary battery.[457]

ON BOARD THE *SAMUEL B. ROBERTS*

By 0851, the *Samuel B. Roberts* received her first hit, which put a hole below the waterline in No.1 lower handling room, and ruptured main steam line in No. 1 fire room, putting No. 1 fire room out of commission, and reducing maximum speed to seventeen knots. As the range closed to 4,000 yards at about 0900, hits were coming in rapid succession. No. 1 engine room was hit and knocked out, and a heavy shell, either 8- or 14-inch, hit the superstructure deck house aft and exploded,

---

[455] *John C. Butler* Action Report.

[456] This was the *Samuel B. Roberts*.

[457] *Kongo* Detailed Action Report.

completely obliterating the after twin 40 mm mount and after 40 mm director. No further trace of the mount, gun, shield, or director was ever seen. At about 0900[458] a tremendous explosion took place, believed to be hits from two or three 14-inch high-capacity shells, which tore a hole some thirty to forty feet long and about seven to ten feet high in the port side at the waterline. This salvo wiped out No. 2 engine room, ruptured the after fuel oil tanks, and started fires on the fantail. All power was lost.[459]

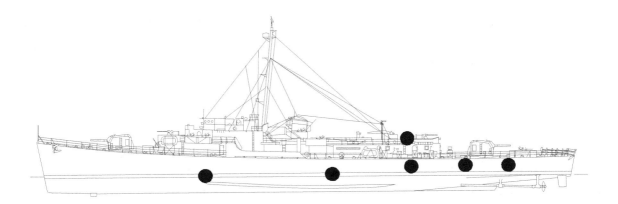

Figure 111: The *Samuel B. Roberts's* battle damage.

ON BOARD THE *HARUNA*

At 0930, Rear Admiral Shigenaga was handed the message from the *Yamato*, "Gradually reassemble." The *Haruna* had been headed for Taffy 2, and the range had closed to 31,126 yards; at 0933, the *Haruna* fired her last main-battery salvo at the U.S. ships and turned to starboard, heading for the assembly area as ordered. She expended ninety-five 14-inch Type 1 AP rounds during the surface battle. She also expended seventy-two Type 3 AA rounds and seven Type 0 HC rounds during the entire battle of Leyte Gulf. Her secondary battery fired ninety-eight of the 04 common projectiles normally used in surface battle and a total of 255 Type 0 HC rounds during the entire battle.[460]

---

[458] The Japanese documents have the *Kongo* hitting the *Samuel B. Roberts* at 0922-23 not at 0900. The Japanese account seems more accurate. *Noshiro* also documented seeing a U.S. warship explode at 0922. The *Heermann* saw *Samuel B. Roberts* after 0900 but misidentified her as the *Hoel* which had already sunk by that time.

[459] Samuel B. Roberts Action Report.

[460] *Haruna* Detailed Action Report.

ON BOARD THE *HAGGARD*

Cdr. Harris reported, "At 0849 destroyers increased speed to thirty knots. At 0852, a fourth and only three gun salvo arrived at 175 yards astern. The pattern was exceedingly small. At 0904 destroyers began to zigzag. It began to look as if this unit was temporarily out of range of the enemy. Some slight amount of tension was relaxed. At 0858, radar ranges showed the enemy to be distant 33,400 yards bearing 350°. Course and speed were not determined. Radar reports on the enemy were of no particular value. The operators couldn't differentiate between the enemy surface units, units of Taffy 3, and friendly aircraft. By 0925 the destroyers had closed to 4,500 yards of the carriers. From 0922-0936 when most of the valuable radar information was gathered. The enemy was tracked on a southerly course at twenty-five knots, range 31,800 yards, bearing 309° on a course of 250°. At 0932, the enemy forced turned right and at 0933 the last salvo directed at this vessel, a four gun salvo landed 150 yards astern."[461]

ON BOARD THE *HAILEY*

Cdr. Brady reported, "At 0902 our destroyers ceased fishtailing and steadied on course 140° true. The fourth and last salvo fell astern of us about 1,000 yards at 0900. Rate of fire was considered to be extremely slow. Enemy at this time was bearing 320° true, distance eighteen miles from *Hailey*. At 0908 we slowed to eighteen knots. Enemy was tracked on a westerly course at this time bearing 320° true at a distance of nineteen miles. At 0935 enemy disappeared from radar screens on a bearing of 320° true with a distance of twenty miles. The enemy fired four gun salvos near our formation that fell within a distance of 300 to 1,000 yards at a range of 32,000-35,000 yards. The pattern size was no more than 75-100 yards. The enemy used a green dye-loaded shell."[462]

ON BOARD THE *FRANKS*

Cdr. Stephan reported, "At 0846 a six shell pattern fell 300 yards astern. At 0848 increased speed to thirty knots. At 0852 range was 32,000 yards and opening when another 4 gun salvo landed dead ahead at 300 yards. Range to enemy opened to 36,000 yards and at 0903 we stopped fishtailing. At 0908 changed speed to eighteen knots. Carrier's torpedo attack groups reported attacking. At 0913 intercepted a pilots report that they scored a torpedo hit on a battleship. At this time enemy force was closing on a course of 120° true, twenty-five knots, and distance 33,000 yards. At 0925 we changed course to 095° true and changed speed to twenty-five knots. At 0934 a three gun salvo landed 250 yards on our starboard quarter but enemy then turned away apparently due to second torpedo attack by aircraft. Opening salvos were on in range even at fifteen miles. Enemy four and

---

[461] *Haggard* Action Report.
[462] *Hailey* Action Report.

six shell pattern was very tight. Estimated range pattern fifty yards and deflection of five yards even at a range of fifteen miles. Enemy appeared to be using direct spot, rather than any ladder doctrine. Enemy used bright yellow dye marker which showed as yellow on the splash and green on the flat water which suggests visual spot. Rounds fired at us detonated so deep that detonation didn't even ruffle the surface of the water. The only visual effect of the detonation was the appearance of a rapidly expanding compression ring, exactly the same as was seen with a depth charge. This suggests they were using (AP) ammunition."[463]

ON BOARD THE *NATOMA BAY*

Felix Stump listened to the pilots of his first strike as they attacked the enemy at 0855. This strike split in two, and the first group attacked two heavy cruisers and a light cruiser, which had Taffy 3 under intense fire. Based on pilot radio transmissions, this attack succeeded in scoring a single torpedo hit into each of the two heavy cruisers. The remaining balance of the first strike, which was supported by strike two, attacked the two heavy cruisers and a battleship directly astern of Taffy 2 which had briefly taken the rear guard destroyers under fire. His pilots reported scoring two more torpedo hits on one of the heavy cruisers.[464]

By 0924 the nearest enemy ship was sixteen miles off, and masts were reported on the horizon by his lookouts. Enemy shell salvos were coming closer, with one landing 1,700 yards from the stern of the carrier formation. Another pilot reported scoring a torpedo hit on a *Kongo*-class battleship. Felix Stump then witnessed the enemy immediately circling, and their gun fire on his units stopped. The enemy ships at this time were too close to his unit to risk turning into the wind, which at the moment was from 047° true at seven knots. Felix Stump decided to launch his third strike while on course 120° true. His catapult tables said he had to have twenty-two knots of wind for a fully loaded torpedo bomber to take off, and there was only twenty knots of wind coming over the flight deck on this course. It had to do, at 0935 Felix Stump's third strike of twelve torpedo bombers and eight fighters were ordered to launch despite the risk. All twenty planes took off without incident.[465]

Radar showed that by 0935 his force was opening range from the enemy which was turning away and heading back north. Messages from Clifton Sprague also reported that enemy had turned away for no apparent reason. Felix Stump was convinced that his first two strikes played a major role in forcing the Japanese commander's decision to retire at least temporarily. At 0945 he ordered his task force to change course to 050° true, into the wind, so he could land the aircraft from the first strike.

---

[463] *Franks* Action Report.

[464] CTU 77.4.2 Action Report

[465] Ibid.

Radar began to pick up bogeys, and two Betty bombers were sighted twelve miles to the northwest. Interception wasn't accomplished, but the sky began to fill with Japanese planes.[466]

ON BOARD THE *SANGAMON*

Thomas Sprague, with two carriers on fire and having already launched all available planes, could only listen to reports as they arrived. At 0853 he received good news from Kinkaid that he had directed one division of battleships and one division of cruisers from TG 77.2 to go to the assistance of Taffy 3. More good news at 0903 was received when the *Petrof Bay* and his own flagship reported that flight-deck operations could resume.[467]

Then at 0925 he received messages that Taffy 2 was under attack from enemy battleships. Another message at the same time reported that enemy cruisers and destroyers were in position to torpedo ships of Taffy 3. Then nothing: no further reports were received from either Taffy 3 or Taffy 2. At 0940 *Suwannee* reported all fires were out, but then at 0948 a report came in that the Japanese were landing troops on Leyte.[468]

ON BOARD THE *NEW JERSEY*

At 0848, Halsey issued orders to TG 38.1 and Rear Admiral McCain, "Proceed at best possible to southwest strike earliest possible enemy force reported to be four BB, eight CA plus DDs in vicinity 11-20 north, 127-00 east at 0800." Then at 0850 Halsey received a report his pilots attacking the Japanese northern force, "Preliminary report two carriers hit badly, one CL hit badly, one carrier untouched, one heavy ship; carrier or CVL sunk after tremendous explosion on fantail."[469]

Still concerned over the reports coming in that Kinkaid needed aid, Halsey sent another message to TG 38.1, "My 242348. TG 38.1 estimated position at 0700 lat 15-00 north long 130-00 east. CTG 38.1 advise CTF 77 and me earliest time of strike." Five minutes later another message arrived from Kinkaid, "Enemy force attacked our CVEs composed of four BB, eight CA and other ships. Request Lee proceed top speed cover Leyte. Request immediate strike by fast carriers." At 0901 another report from TG 38 pilots, "Attacking enemy force four carriers plus cruisers, destroyers who are in lat 20 north, 126-30 east, course northerly, speed twenty plus."[470]

By 0921 another message arrived from Kinkaid, "Still under attack at 0830/I in lat 11-35 long 126-29." One minute later another message arrived, "About 0700 CTU 77.4.3 reported under fire

---

[466] Ibid.

[467] CTU 77.4 Action Report.

[468] Ibid.

[469] CTU 38 Action Report.

[470] Ibid.

from enemy battleships and cruisers in position latitude 11-40 longitude 126-25. Evidently came through San Bernardino during the night. Request immediate air strike. Also request support from heavy ships. My OBBs low in ammunition."[471]

At 0927 Halsey sent a reply back to Kinkaid, "Your 242227. Am now engaging enemy carrier force. TG 38.1 with five carriers and four CAs has been ordered to assist you immediately x my position with other three carrier task groups 14-18 north long 126-11 east. Halsey." With these commands he felt that this would be sufficient and that he could now turn his attention to his own battle. By giving his position surely Kinkaid would realize that his forces were far too north to come to any assistance, but TG 38.1 could be within striking range by 11:00 am.[472]

CinCPAC Headquarters, Pearl Harbor, Hawaii

Admiral Nimitz received Kinkaid's report that his forces had won a great victory at Surigao Strait, but he was concerned that no reports had come from Lee engaging the Japanese Center force. Like Kinkaid, he too had made the assumption that TF 34 had been formed and was guarding San Bernardino Strait. Lee should have engaged the Japanese shortly after midnight, but no word had been received from him. He called his assistant chief of staff Captain Bernard Austin and asked him if there were any dispatches from TG 38 that he had missed. Captain Austin replied, "Will you tell me in particular what you are looking for?" Nimitz answered, "I am very concerned, because nothing I have seen indicates that Admiral Halsey has left San Bernardino guarded against Japanese units coming through there and getting our ships off Leyte." Captain Austin replied that some others had the same concern. Nimitz asked if anything came in to let him know immediately.[473]

The next signal came from Kinkaid in plain language, the message that Halsey received at 0922. Immediately thereafter, Nimitz was handed Kinkaid's previous request that "Lee proceed top speed cover Leyte."[474]

Captain Austin could tell Admiral Nimitz was deeply troubled as he paced the floor to his office. Nimitz still wanted to know where TF 34 was. At 0944, Captain Austin suggested, "Admiral, couldn't you just ask Admiral Halsey the simple question; 'Where is TF 34?'" Nimitz thought about it and then replied, "Go out and write it up. That's a good idea."[475]

---

[471] Ibid.

[472] Ibid.

[473] Potter, E. B. *Nimitz*. Naval Institute Press, 1976, pp 336-339.

[474] Ibid.

[475] Ibid.

CHAPTER 7. THE DIVINE WIND: 0945-MIDNIGHT

ON BOARD THE *NEW JERSEY*

At 1000, Halsey received a message from Admiral Nimitz who had been monitoring the radio transmissions from Pearl Harbor. Alarmed at the calls for help coming from Kinkaid and Clifton Sprague his message from Pearl Harbor read; "Turkey Trots to Water GG Where is Repeat Where is Task Force Thirty-Four RR, The World Wonders." The first and last phrase of the message, "Turkey Trots to Water" and "The World Wonders," were padding that were supposed to be removed after decoding. This padding was added to confuse Japanese attempts at decoding the message. The problem lay in the last phrase, "The World Wonders," which was interpreted by the staff on board the *New Jersey* as part of the message; so Halsey received, "Where is Repeat, Where is Task Force Thirty-Four RR, The World Wonders."[476]

Admiral Nimitz's orders to Halsey for the KING II operation had specific instructions, "Destroy enemy naval and air forces in or threatening the Philippine area. Protect air and sea communications along the Central Pacific axis." In addition, a late entry which was unnumbered and unlettered read, "In case opportunity for destruction of major portion of the enemy fleet offer or can be created, such destruction becomes the primary task."[477] Even more than this, though, Admiral Nimitz instructed Halsey, "Forces of the Pacific Ocean areas will cover and support forces of the Southwest Pacific in order to assist in the seizure and occupation of objectives in the Central Philippines."[478]

Halsey wrote Nimitz on his thoughts and how he interpreted his orders prior to the battle: "I intend, if possible, to deny the enemy a chance to out-range me in an air duel and also to deny him an opportunity to employ an air shuttle (carrier-to-target-to-land) against me.[479] If I am to prevent his gaining that advantage, I must have early information and I must move smartly. Insomuch as the destruction of the enemy fleet is the principle task, every weapon must be brought into play and the general coordination of these weapons should be in the hands of the tactical commander responsible

---

[476] CTU 38, Action Report.

[477] Commander in Chief, U.S. Pacific Fleet, Action Report.

[478] Ibid.

[479] The Japanese had used this strategy in the June Battle of the Marianas to out-range U.S. carrier aircraft and the U.S. officers believed this strategy would be repeated for the Leyte operation.

for the outcome of the battle. My goal is the same as yours – to completely annihilate the Jap fleet if the opportunity offers."[480]

Halsey in his own words of what he felt upon reading the "World Wonders" message, "I was stunned as if I had been struck in the face. The paper rattled in my hands. I snatched off my cap, threw it on the deck, and shouted something that I am ashamed to remember. Mick Carney [his chief of staff] rushed over and grabbed my arm; "Stop it! What the hell's the matter with you? Pull yourself together!"[481]

An enraged Halsey walked off the bridge with his chief of staff and retired to the admiral's quarters on the 01 level. It was of course the last three words of the message that Halsey perceived his superior officer was mocking him, humiliating him in front of his entire command, having no faith in his command ability, not coming to the aid of a fellow officer, and placing doubt in his own decision-making, just as he was about to carry out Admiral Nimitz's strategic vision outlined in Operation Granite.

Halsey's decisions[482] took shape within the two major objectives of this strategy: to maintain "unremitting pressure" against Japan and to totally destroy the Japanese Fleet. Halsey had maintained unremitting pressure on Japan when he moved up the entire KING II operation to October which had the effect of ruining the Japanese plans who hoped the U.S. would not invade until November.[483]

The enemy's total destruction would be accomplished by a major fleet action using all of the firepower provided by every type of naval platform available. This was the goal prompting him to take all of Third Fleet to attack the Northern force. This fleet action had its roots in Battle Plan 1-44 of 9 September 1944, which called for TF 34 to be deployed initially in the most probable direction of the enemy fleet and provided with adequate air cover, coordinating surface and air forces to intercept the enemy from the favorable position thus gained. This plan was in turn based on CINCPOA's operational plan 6-44 of 21 July 1944 drafted for Operation Stalemate II. This information shows that a plan for a fleet action using both battleships and carrier aircraft in a coordinated effort had been established well before Leyte.[484]

Halsey felt the Japanese carriers represented the primary threat; it was fresh and not previously under attack. However, as he reviewed reports on the air attacks against the Northern force

---

[480] Potter, E. B. *Bull Halsey*. Naval Institute Press, 1985, p 279.

[481] *Ibid.*, p 303.

[482] This is not a critique of his decision but an explanation of his priorities.

[483] Hone, Trent. "U.S. Navy Surface Battle Doctrine and Victory in the Pacific." *Naval War College Review*, Winter 2009, Vol. 62, No. 1.

[484] Vego, Milan. *The Battle for Leyte 1944*. Naval Institute Press, 2006, p 261.

something was not quite right. Halsey in his own words, "The Northern Force was caught by surprise, but Commander Third Fleet was puzzled by the fact that there were scarcely any planes on the decks of, or in the air near, the enemy force, and no sign of bogies around our own force. Later in the morning large bogies were picked up on the screen approaching from the south; they did not attack, and it is believed that they were planes of the enemy carrier groups ferrying out to the carriers unarmed and arriving too late."[485]

ON BOARD THE *WASATCH*

Kinkaid at 0953 ordered Oldendorf to take half of TG 77.2 and proceed north and come to the assistance of Taffy 3. When he gave this order he wasn't yet aware that the Japanese had retired. At 1000, he sent another message to Halsey, "We are still being attacked."[486]

ON BOARD THE *SANGAMON*

The first message from his other task units to arrive was a message at 1002 that Taffy 2 was under air attack. Then to cause alarm for his task group's safety, the *Santee* reported a submarine astern at 1016. Thomas Sprague immediately dispatched the *Rowell* to investigate the contact report.[487]

Finally at 1032 a plane reported Taffy 2 position at latitude 11° 07' north and longitude 126° 58' east. His own task unit was at this time fifty-nine miles from Point Fin, off Samar Island. The first message received from Taffy 3 since 0925 came at 1039 and reported that two battleships and a heavy cruiser had turned away at 0925 and that one battleship or heavy cruiser was dead in the water and another heavy cruiser was on fire. This had to have greatly relieved Thomas Sprague who for the last hour had heard nothing on the fate of Taffy 3. The good news didn't last long, for at 1040 the *Suwannee* reported her ammunition hoists and cherry picker were out of commission.[488]

ON BOARD THE *YAMATO*

Rear Admiral Nobuei Morishita spotted nine enemy planes bearing 150° approaching the *Yamato* at 0945. He ordered her speed increased to twenty-four knots. At 0948, lookouts reported what looked like a carrier bearing 280°. At 0950, Morishita ordered a change in course to 240°. He received a damage report at 0955 that *Yamato* had been hit twice by an enemy destroyer, but damage

---

[485] CTU 38 Action Report.
[486] CTU 77 Action Report.
[487] CTU 77.4 Action Report.
[488] Ibid.

was minimal. As he was receiving this report six torpedoes were sighted, and he ordered a turn to 280° to evade them, and by 0959 he gave orders to increase speed to twenty-six knots.[489]

At 1000, when Halsey was reading the message from Nimitz, Kurita sent a report to Combined Fleet Headquarters, "SMS251000, 1YB action spot report No. 1 25 October known results obtained to present; definitely sunk two aircraft carriers of which one was regular large type carrier, two heavy cruisers and some destroyers. Definitely hit, one or two carriers. Enemy carrier-based aircraft continue to attack us. The remaining enemy including six or seven carriers was making use of squalls and smoke screens to make good its retirement to the southeast. Friendly units heavily damaged; *Chokai, Chikuma, Kumano*. Others are being checked. We are at present proceeding northward."[490]

Admiral Kurita sent out orders at 1014 to the rest of the fleet, "All squadrons under the command of 1YB are ordered to assume #30 alert dispositions, course 000°, and speed twenty-two knots."[491] At 1018, Kurita instructed the destroyer *Fujinami* to assist the *Chokai* and, if she was unmaneuverable, to take off her crew and sink her with torpedoes. This was what eventually happened, and the *Fujinami* then attempted to withdraw alone through San Bernardino Strait. Kurita instructed the destroyer *Nowaki* to aid the *Chikuma*. Eventually she too took the crew off the *Chikuma* and sank the crippled ship with torpedoes. By the time this was completed, she was far behind the rest of the Japanese fleet but she made her way towards San Bernardino Strait alone.[492]

Meanwhile twenty-five enemy aircraft were sighted bearing 180°. Morishita ordered an increase in speed to all out flank speed or # 5 battle speed which due to her damaged bow remained at twenty-six knots at 1015.[493] At 1017, the *Yamato* opened fire with her AA guns. The enemy dive bombers attacked at 1019, and the *Yamato* heeled over to starboard in a tight turn to evade them. As this maneuver was completed at 1023, Morishita ordered a hard turn to port and two near-miss bombs exploded off her port bow. By 1026, he turned the ship back onto the course 000° north and at 1029 reduced speed to twenty-four knots.[494]

ON BOARD THE *NAGATO*

Rear Admiral Kobe received a report that enemy aircraft had been detected at 43,840 yards, bearing 81° to port at 1007. The *Nagato*'s current course at this time was 80° true. Kobe immediately ordered a speed increase to twenty-five knots and preparation for air attacks. At 1014, *Nagato*'s

---

[489] *Yamato* Detailed Action Report.

[490] Combined Fleet Headquarters Detailed Action Report and *Yamato* Detailed Action Report.

[491] *Yamato* Detailed Action Report.

[492] Ibid.

[493] At #5 battle speed, if undamaged, she should have produced a speed of 27-28 knots.

[494] *Yamato* Detailed Action Report.

lookouts reported sighting one enemy aircraft carrier that was obviously listing at a distance of 18,632 yards bearing 32° to starboard. The *Nagato* wasn't attacked by the American aircraft, and at 1016 Kobe ordered her speed reduced to twenty-two knots.[495]

The lull didn't last long, for at 1021 more American planes approached from starboard 15°, distance 15,344 yards. *Nagato*'s anti-aircraft guns opened fire. At 1026, two torpedo bombers attacked on the starboard bow bearing 30°. Kobe ordered a hard turn to port, and the torpedoes passed aft by 110 yards. He ordered his gunners to check fire at 1032.[496]

ON BOARD THE *KONGO*

At 1012, Rear Admiral Shimazaki received a flag signal from the *Yamato*, "aircraft bearing 170°." One minute later, the *Kongo*'s lookouts report sighting twenty dive bombers to port bearing 60°, and the *Kongo*'s anti-aircraft guns opened fire at 1015. The *Kongo* herself wasn't attacked, and she checked fire at 1021. Shimazaki received flag signals from the *Yamato* to stay in line relative to old position after the attack.[497]

ON BOARD THE *HAGURO*

Capt. Sugiura at 0947 reduced speed to twenty-six knots. His ships course was 032° true. By 0952, he reduced speed to twenty-four knots. At 1009, his lookouts reported sighting two carriers and seven surface warships bearing 160° true distance sixteen miles. No action was taken to pursue these ships. At 1010, two aircraft approached from astern, and Capt. Sugiura increased speed to twenty-six knots and opened fire. By 1012, he ordered his gunners to check fire. Ten aircraft bearing 170° were detected at 1013, but these aircraft bypassed the *Haguro*, so by 1025 Capt. Sugiura reduced speed to twenty-four knots and at 1026 set a course of 350° true.[498]

ON BOARD THE *YAHAGI*

Captain Yoshimura's detailed action report didn't give a time line after the surface battle. During the action she was strafed heavily by U.S. fighters, and her anti-aircraft gunners and crew topside took heavy casualties. She suffered 80 men killed or wounded. A near-miss bomb during the afternoon caused a fire within the number one torpedo mount similar to what occurred on *Suzuya*. Fortunately for the *Yahagi*, her crew quickly extinguished the fire before any explosion occurred.

---

[495] *Nagato* Detailed Action Report.

[496] Ibid.

[497] *Kongo* Detailed Action Report.

[498] *Haguro* Detailed Action Report.

Overall, she wasn't the focus of U.S. attention during her withdrawal as they attempted to sink or cripple the larger ships in the Japanese fleet.[499]

ON BOARD THE *NOSHIRO*

Captain Kajiwara's ship at 0953 was making eighteen knots. The 7th Squadron appeared to starboard at 0958. Capt. Sugiura then witnessed the *Yamato* open fire at 1005 with her AA guns. Capt. Kajiwara immediately alerted his ship and prepared for AA action. His lookouts sighted an enemy cruiser at 1008 bearing 220° distance 16,440 yards.[500] At 1010, eight U.S. aircraft approached but ignored the *Noshiro*. At 1014 her lookouts reported the enemy cruiser was on fire, and at 1018.5 she has sunk.[501]

His ship changed course several times so that at 1019 he was on a course of 160°; then at 1023 he was on course 240°, and by 1026 was on a course of 040° with a speed of twenty-four knots.

At this time an enemy formation of twenty aircraft bearing 350° was sighted, and at 1028 Captain Kajiwara ordered her main guns to open fire. Two planes dropped torpedoes, and Captain Kajiwara turned hard to port to avoid them and then brought the ship onto a course of 000° true.[502]

ON BOARD THE *JOHNSTON*

Lt. Hagen recorded the last minutes of the *Johnston*. "Up in the gun director, what with the smoke and lack of communications, we were a little slow in getting the word. The five stalwart men in there with me—Himelright, Buzbee, Powell, Gringeri and Thompson—were standing by quietly. There was nothing more we could do, I peered out and couldn't see a living soul on the foc'sle.[503]

"'What the hell are we doing here?' I said. 'Let's abandon ship.' The last word hardly was out of my mouth when the five men as one were out of the director and racing for the rail. I was so surprised that I stood stock-still a moment, then lit out myself. I made my way to the foc'sle—I couldn't get aft without walking over piles of bodies and, like a man in a dream, very carefully and leisurely took off my shoes and dived in. Taking off my shoes, incidentally, was the worst mistake I could make; my feet got so sunburned in the water that I limped for days after. When I got into the water, one of those utterly mad things that you wouldn't believe if it hadn't happened to you, occurred. My torpedo man, Jim O'Gorek, swam over to me and, as brightly as if he were meeting me on the street corner, said, 'Mr. Hagen, we got off all ten of them torpedoes, and they ran hot,

---

[499] *Yahagi* Detailed Action Report.

[500] This was the *Johnston*.

[501] *Noshiro* Detailed Action Report.

[502] Ibid.

[503] Hagen. "We Asked for the Jap Fleet—and Got It."

straight and normal!' At 10:10, the *Johnston* rolled over and began to sink. A Jap destroyer came up to 1,000 yards and pumped a final shot into her to make sure she went down. A survivor saw the Japanese captain salute her as she went down. That was the end of the *Johnston*."[504]

By 0955, all personnel capable to do so had left the ship. The crew successfully launched the gig and four rafts, but the gig had been hit by fragments and sank soon after it was in the water. The crew had difficulty in getting two floater nets over the side, and the ones they were unable to get off went down with the ship.[505]

ON BOARD THE *FANSHAW BAY*

Clifton Sprague continued to receive good news, for the distance between him and the enemy fleet continued to open. By 0940, the enemy was bearing 075° distance 28,000 yards. By 0945, the enemy was bearing 040° distance 31,000 yards, and he ordered his fleet to discontinue making smoke. By 0950, he ordered the fleet to slow to fifteen knots, and this was also welcome news to the engine room crews who reported that the stacks were overheating causing a fire hazard. By 0951, he received word that a Japanese heavy cruiser had its forecastle under water but was then handed a message reporting Taffy 1 was under air attack. One minute later the enemy surface units disappeared from radar, and the battle appeared to be over.[506]

ON BOARD THE *ST. LO*

At 1000, *St. Lo* launched one torpedo bomber armed with a torpedo to join up with aircraft of the *Kitkun Bay* on direction from Clifton Sprague. Since the *Fanshaw Bay*'s and the *Kalinin Bay*'s flight decks were out of operation she was instructed to take in any aircraft that needed to land. At 1002, she received confirmation that the enemy force was retiring, and by 1010 she secured from General Quarters. By 1020, Captain McKenna set condition watches into effect so crew members could get some coffee and begin to relax.[507]

ON BOARD THE *KITKUN BAY*

At 1013, five TBMs had been loaded with torpedoes and one with bombs, and the ship changed course to 010° so that these aircraft could be launched. At 1021, this was completed, and course was changed to 045° and speed reduced to sixteen knots. The ship took a new course of 135° at 1028 but at 1035 turned back into the wind on a course of 010° in order to land three TBMs and two FM-

---

[504] Ibid.

[505] *Johnston* Action Report.

[506] *Fanshaw Bay* Action Report and CTU 77.4.3, Action Report.

[507] *St. Lo* Action Report.

2 fighters. The returning pilots reported six 500 lb. bomb hits on an enemy cruiser which had started fires and explosions. The pilots reported watching this cruiser sink.[508]

ON BOARD THE *WHITE PLAINS*

Two TBM torpedo bombers had been loaded with torpedoes during the surface battle but were not launched due to the inability to turn into the wind. These two aircraft were launched at 1020, and then four TBM and one FM-2 fighter were landed, a task which was completed at 1026. At 1041 two more TBM aircraft were landed.[509]

ON BOARD THE *HEERMANN*

At 1000, Cdr. Hathaway slowed and stopped to shore up bulkheads in the forward part of the ship and inspected the ship for additional damage. By 1044 he picked up speed to ten knots to re-join with carrier formation.[510]

ON BOARD THE *DENNIS*

At 1000, the formation consisted of four carriers, one destroyer, and three destroyer escorts. At 1021 formation turned into the wind to land aircraft, and this was completed by 1030 when course was changed to 135° true. Repair 1 reported the ordnance store room taking water through a hole about three feet above the waterline. Compartment A-306A was flooded; pumping was under way in an attempt to make repairs.[511]

ON BOARD THE *JOHN C. BUTLER*

At 0950, the *John C. Butler* was ordered to assume formation 5R which called for the four remaining screening vessels to form ahead of the five remaining carriers. The carriers turned into the wind for flight operations which were completed by 1029.[512]

ON BOARD THE *NEW JERSEY*

At 1055, Halsey returned to the bridge and ordered Task Force 34 to turn around and head south, destroying his entire plan of fighting a battle of annihilation. He ordered TG 38.2 to also turn south and support Task Force 34. Mitscher would take TG 38.3 and TG 38.4 and pursue the Japanese Northern force. At 1115, the orders were carried out. Task Force 34 had reached a position

---

[508] *Kitkun Bay* Action Report.
[509] *White Plains* Action Report.
[510] *Heermann* Action Report.
[511] *Dennis* Action Report.
[512] John C. Butler Action Report.

only forty-two miles from being able to engage the Japanese, or approximately within two hours. His forces were so far north he couldn't arrive to block San Bernardino Strait until 0100, approximately fourteen hours later. Due to the time delay in which messages were sent, received, decoded, and then given to the respective commanders, he was completely unaware that the Battle off Samar was already over and the threat to Leyte Gulf had ended. Halsey later wrote, "I turned my back on an opportunity I had dreamed about since my first days as a cadet." The only response his mind could offer was to obey what he perceived as a direct order from his commanding officer, to turn back south, and go to the aid of Seventh Fleet.[513]

ON BOARD THE *NATOMA BAY*

Combat Air Patrol pursued numerous targets and at 1045 shot down a Jill twenty miles to the southwest. At 1051 Felix Stump received word from Clifton Sprague that he was under heavy suicidal air attacks and that elements of the Japanese fleet were closing again. Soon after another message from Clifton Sprague reported three of his carriers had been hit, but there was no further word on the Japanese fleet elements closing him. At 1115, the fourth strike was ready. This was a rather large strike made up of thirty-seven torpedo bombers and nineteen fighters. They reported the enemy task force at 11° 43' north, 126° 13' east at 1140, placing the force approximately forty-five to fifty-five miles from Taffy 2 at the time. This information was immediately transmitted to Kinkaid and Taffy 1. The enemy base course was reported as 225°, which may indicate he had begun a second run to the south, or was simply engaged in evasive maneuvers.[514]

The results of the fourth strike, based on his pilot reports, were several bomb hits on a heavy cruiser, a bomb hit and torpedo hit on a battleship, and continued strafing attacks on the enemy destroyers. After this attack around 1200 the Japanese were definitely heading north. At 1230 Felix Stump received pilot reports of several hundreds of men in the water in the vicinity of 11° 12' north, 126° 30' east. These men were survivors from Taffy 3. Felix Stump immediately sent the information to Kinkaid. At the same time around 1230 a large group of friendly planes were approaching Taffy 2. Subsequent voice communications established over VHF that these planes came from TG 38.1. The flight leader was asking for the latest position of the enemy and CIC of the *Natoma Bay* vectored these planes onto the target. At 1302 the flight leader "Tallyhoed" and began his attack on the enemy. Results were unknown.[515]

At 1331, strike five was launched, eleven torpedo bombers and eight fighters. CTU 77.4.1 ordered Felix Stump, "Keep striking, enemy appears to be badly weakened." Overall Felix Stump

---

[513] Potter, *Halsey*, p 304.

[514] CTU 77.4.2 Action Report.

[515] Ibid.

maintained a course of 120° true but when launching or recovering aircraft would turn into the wind with a course between 040°-055°. The resulting mean course was directly east, and as his force went farther out to sea, it reduced the chance of it coming under air attack from Japanese land-based aircraft.[516]

At 1508, the sixth and final strike consisting of twenty-six torpedo bombers and twenty-four fighters was launched. Upon completion of this launch, planes from TG 38.1 as well as planes from strike five were landed. Reports from strike five appeared to be mainly harassing with no major damage on the enemy due to the small number of aircraft involved. They executed their strike at 1420 and noted one cruiser was lagging behind the rest of the fleet. At 1538 another wave of aircraft from TG 38.1 was picked up on radar. They reported one battleship or heavy cruiser dead in the water in the vicinity of the previously reported cripples and confirmed the CVE reports. Some of the aircraft of this second wave from TG 38.1 attacked the crippled ship at 1550 with the balance proceeding toward the rest of the Japanese fleet.[517]

At this same time Felix Stump changed course to the west to render aid in the recovery of personnel in the water and, if practicable, attack with destroyers at night on the cripples. At 1549, Taffy 2 was on course of 290° true and at 1617 changed course to 250° true. Then the situation changed at 1632 when a large group of enemy aircraft were picked up on radar bearing 310°, distance seventy miles, on course of 130°. He also received word that the enemy fleet was at position 12° 30' north and 125° 25' east. Felix Stump immediately transmitted these coordinates to Kinkaid and Thomas Sprague. CIC reported the incoming raid was made up of at least thirty aircraft. Felix Stump immediately ordered the task unit to change course to 050° true and into the wind to launch additional fighters. By 1650 twenty-eight fighters had been launched, and this would be followed by twelve more by 1705. At this time he changed course to 120° true and formed disposition 5V for defense against air attack.[518]

At 1700 the lead fighters engaged the incoming strike while still at a distance of thirty-five miles from Taffy 2. Sixteen enemy aircraft were confirmed as shot down with ten others damaged, and the attack was completely repulsed with no enemy aircraft coming closer than seventeen miles from the task unit. Felix Stump had been very concerned since the other two task units had reported suicide attacks on carriers and was greatly relieved when this attack was completely repulsed. At 1723 strike six reported the position of the enemy fleet and attacked. They reported the enemy fleet as four battleships, three heavy cruisers, two light cruisers, and seven destroyers.[519]

---

[516] Ibid.

[517] Ibid.

[518] Ibid.

[519] Ibid.

By 1808 his strike was returning, so he changed course to 080° true to recover his aircraft. The last of the planes, including the dusk CAP, landed at 1831, and course was set at 210°, speed fifteen knots, zigzagging using plan #6. Felix Stump had received word that a rescue group had left Leyte Gulf to pick up survivors and that the heavy units of TF 38 were heading south to destroy any cripples. In light of this information, he abandoned his earlier plan to assist with picking up survivors and attacking the cripples with his destroyers and changed course to the west and then eventually to the southwest. The fighting for Taffy 2 for 25 October 1944 was finally over.[520]

ON BOARD THE *YAMATO*

The next wave of U.S. aircraft approached at 1035 when six U.S. torpedo bombers were seen charging in bearing 000°. Two torpedo wakes were sighted off the port bow at 1036, and Morishita ordered a port turn to evade them. At 1040, three torpedoes were sighted off the bow, and Morishita ordered a starboard turn and set course to 330°. The last torpedo plane launched its torpedo from a bearing of 020° starboard at 1041 and then was shot down at 1042. The torpedo passed by the bow at 1043, and all gunfire was checked by 1045.[521]

Figure 112: The *Yamato* was approached by a low-flying U.S. aircraft at approximately 1030.

At 1040, Kurita was handed a message sent by the *Yahagi* which had been sent at 1030. It read, "SMS 251030, from Flag 10 Division to the *Yamato* results obtained by us; one carrier of the *Enterprise* class sunk and one seriously damaged (its sinking was almost certain) three destroyers. Damage sustained the *Yahagi* hit but battle cruising not hindered." Kurita's staff took this as an

---

[520] Ibid.

[521] *Yamato* Detailed Action Report.

addition to what the *Yamato* and the heavy cruisers had accomplished and didn't consider that the Tenth Division had witnessed the same ships sinking. After digesting the news from the *Yahagi* at 1100 Kurita sent a new message to Combined Fleet Headquarters correcting his original report. It read, "SMS 251100, correct 1YB's action spot report No. 1 as follows: Three or four carriers including one of the *Enterprise* class have been sunk."[522]

The fleet was ordered to set course of 270° at 1055 and at 1100 the course was set to 255° heading back to Leyte Gulf. At 1115, Kurita and his staff received a message informing them that enemy carrier-based aircraft were using the airfield at Tacloban base, including those from the damaged enemy carriers. This information was based on enemy voice transmissions. At 1118, three enemy planes were sighted bearing 130°, and the fleet was turned to a new course of 180° at 1119. At 1120, a new enemy intercept was received. "Being attacked by an enemy force consisting of four battleships, eight cruisers, and other units. Vice Admiral Lee? will proceed to and from? Leyte area. Request that high speed carriers go to the attack immediately 0727." This message was sent by Owada Communication Unit. Kurita was well aware that Vice Admiral Lee commanded the U.S. fast battleships, and from this broken intercept it gave the perception that Lee was being sent to Leyte Gulf to come to the rescue.[523]

At 1120, Kurita sent a message to Combined Fleet Headquarters informing Admiral Toyoda of the fleet's position and that he was proceeding to the Leyte anchorage. He also informed Admiral Toyoda that he believed an enemy task force was in position thirty miles to the northeast, with another large force sixty miles to southeast. At 1123, Kurita ordered the fleet to a new course of 225°. At 1144, another U.S. intercept was sent to Kurita from Takao Communication Unit and it read, "Our force was being attacked by a force composed of four battleships, eight cruisers, and others. Proceed to Leyte at top speed." This message had been sent by Rear Admiral Clifton Sprague.[524]

At 1145 Kurita ordered the *Yamato* to launch the *Nagato's* #1 scout plane, which she had taken aboard before the battle, in hopes of gaining intelligence on the enemy disposition. This was his last plane available for search operations. The transfer of thirty-six aircraft to shore and the loss of several aircraft when the *Musashi* was sunk meant that the *Yamato* was the only ship with aircraft remaining on board by 25 October. At 1148, the fleet was ordered to a new course of 270° west. Then a message from Combined Fleet Headquarters which had been sent to First Air Fleet and Southwest Area Fleet to attack the enemy task force reported at 0945. This placed a U.S. carrier

---

[522] Combined Fleet Headquarters Detailed Action Report and *Yamato* Detailed Action Report.

[523] Combined Fleet Headquarters Detailed Action Report. In fact at this time Vice Admiral Lee with TF 34 was heading back south to confront Vice Admiral Kurita, but the distance between the two forces was much greater than Vice Admiral Kurita knew at the time he made his decision to turn north.

[524] Combined Fleet Headquarters Detailed Action Report.

striking task force in a position bearing 5° distance 130 miles from Suluan light. This position placed this task force to his north and again confirmed in his mind he was surrounded. At 1151, five masts bearing 173°, distance 41,648 yards were sighted, but no action was taken. At 1157, speed was reduced to eighteen knots. At 1201, Kurita issued this order to the fleet, "All squadrons under the command of 1YB are ordered to take the specified position."[525]

At 1206, Kurita requested information from Combined Fleet headquarters as to the targets of the aircraft and the results obtained. At 1230, he received another message sent from Owada Communication Unit which read, "Kinkaid cancels present orders and ordered addressee to proceed to point 300? miles southwest of Leyte Gulf in a plain text message."[526]

Kurita had to make the biggest decision of his life. From the enemy intercepts he concluded that U.S. forces were concentrating to block any attempt to penetrate the Gulf. In addition carrier-based aircraft were also concentrating at Tacloban airfield. It had been five days since the beginning of the invasion. How many transports were left and how much material had already been landed? It was obvious to him that U.S. forces had sufficient power to destroy Nishimura's forces as well as Shima's. There were no friendly units to the south to support or offer aid. However, all these details couldn't answer the burning question in his mind. What was the strategic gain for Japan? He could fight the battle for the sake of fighting a battle, but what would the nation of Japan gain for the sacrifice? Surprise was lost. The enemy was fully aware of every move he made and now had time to recover.[527]

General MacArthur planned the KING II operation believing that the Japanese would react quickly and decisively to any Philippine invasion. Therefore, KING II relied upon the quick unloading of supplies once the beachheads were established. From 20-24 October, the Northern Attack Force unloaded 114,900 tons of supplies and disembarked 80,900 men, while the Southern Attack Force unloaded 85,000 tons of supplies and 51,500 men;314 ships had already unloaded their supplies and left Leyte Gulf. By the evening of 24 October, only thirty-six of the Seventh Fleet's supply ships remained waiting to unload. Kurita and his staff were right to question the strategic value of SHO 1's target.[528]

Kurita estimated the situation, "The wiser course was deemed to be to cross the enemy's anticipation by striking at his task force which had been reported in position bearing 5°, distance 130 miles from Suluan Light at 0945.We believed that to turnabout and proceed northward in search of

---

[525] Combined Fleet Headquarters Detailed Action Report, the specified positions were a circle AA pattern.

[526] Combined Fleet Headquarters Detailed Action Report.

[527] Robertson, D. C. *Operational Analysis for the Battle of Leyte Gulf.* Naval War College, 10 March 1993.

[528] Morison, *Leyte*, pp 155-156.

this element would prove to be to our advantage in subsequent operations."[529] The key to this decision was the absence of TF 34 within the carrier groups he had attacked to the south. The southern forces would simply flee, and given the perceived greater speed, striking a decisive blow would be difficult. However, due to the intercepted messages TF 34 must be with the carrier group to the north, and the intercepted messages were calling for Vice Admiral Lee in command of the fast U.S. battleships to head south and attack his force. This U.S. task force to his north would accept battle where a decisive blow could be achieved in the open ocean. If friendly land-based aircraft attacked in coordination, a strategic victory may still be possible.

Rear Admiral Koyanagi wrote postwar on the turn to the north. "The enemy situation was confused, intercepted fragments of plain-text radio messages indicate that a hastily constructed air strip on Leyte was ready to launch planes in an attack on us, that Kinkaid was requesting the early dispatch of a powerful striking unit, and that the U.S. Seventh Fleet was operating nearby. At the same time we heard from Southwest Area Fleet Headquarters that a U.S. carrier striking task force was located in a position bearing 5° distance one hundred and thirty miles from Suluan light at 0945.

"Under these circumstances, it was presumed that if our force did succeed in entering Leyte Gulf, we would find that the transports had already withdrawn under escort of the Seventh Fleet. Even if they remained, they would've completed unloading in the five days since making port and any success we might achieve would be very minor at best. On the other hand, if we proceeded into the narrow gulf, we would be the target of attacks by the enemy's carrier and Leyte based planes. We were prepared to fight to the last man, but we wanted to die gloriously.

"We were convinced that several enemy carrier groups were disposed nearby and that we were surrounded. Our shore based air force had been rather inactive, but now the two air fleets would surely fight all-out in coordination with the First Striking Force. If they could only strike a successful blow, we might still achieve a decisive fleet engagement, and even if we were destroyed in such a battle, death would be glorious."[530]

While Kurita was making his decision, Morishita was trying to keep the *Yamato* safe. At 1212, more enemy planes began to attack. By 1217, the *Yamato* opened fire with her AA guns. At 1220, thirty enemy aircraft were approaching from a bearing of 210°. All vessels were ordered to turn to a new course of 320°. By 1230, forty-nine aircraft were observed approaching from 230°.[531]

Kurita made his decision at 1236 and sends the following message to Combined Fleet Headquarters, "First Diversion Attack Force abandoning plan to break through to Leyte Gulf.

---

[529] Combined Fleet Headquarters Detailed Action Report and *Yamato* Detailed Action Report.

[530] Evans David, *The Japanese Navy in World War II*, pp 355-384.

[531] *Yamato* Detailed Action Report.

Turning about and will proceed northward along the east coast of Samar in search of an enemy task force. After decisively engaging same, plan to go through San Bernardino Strait."[532]

At 1237, four planes made an attack on the *Yamato* herself, and Morishita ordered her to come to a course of 270°. A torpedo was launched, and he ordered her to make a 90° turn to starboard. By 1254, he turned her back onto a course of 320° and reduced speed to twenty-four knots and checked fire. At 1257 a new course of 010° to the north was set. By 1310, due to the delays caused by the air battle, Kurita transmitted his decision to the rest of the fleet.[533]

The next wave of U.S. aircraft arrived at 1314 which numbered about seventy aircraft. Morishita increased speed to twenty-six knots. The *Yamato* opened fire at 1322 and took a near-miss bomb on her port side at 1338, and fire was checked at 1339. Speed was reduced to twenty knots at 1345, but this didn't last long, for at 1353 sixteen U.S. aircraft were spotted, and speed was increased back up to twenty-six knots. Fire was opened at 1400 and checked by 1408, and the *Yamato* wasn't damaged in this attack.[534]

Morishita received reports of picking up aircraft formations on radar beginning at 1415 but the next attack did not occur until 1551 when four enemy aircraft approached her from a bearing of 220°, and *Yamato* opened fire. An enemy torpedo was sighted at 1552, and Morishita ordered a hard turn to starboard and eventually set a course of 100°. At 1600, sixteen more aircraft attacked, and *Yamato* suffered a near-miss bomb at 1608. At 1612, this attack was over, and she checked fire. Her speed was reduced to twenty knots. Forty more aircraft approach at 1640, and she opened fire once again. Speed increased to twenty-six knots, and she avoided an enemy torpedo to starboard and checked fire at 1647. Then at 1656 a single U.S. aircraft came within range of her guns, so she opened fire again, and this was checked at 1705.[535]

ON BOARD THE *NAGATO*

The next attack came at 1047, made by two torpedo aircraft bearing 70° to port. This time Kobe ordered a hard turn to port and avoided the torpedoes, and her guns checked fire by 1054. At 1056 a flag signal from the *Yamato* instructed the fleet to turn to a course of 270°. At 1110, three TBF aircraft were sighted bearing 80° to port with an altitude angle of only 1° at a range of 10,960 yards. Air alerts were sounded, and her anti-aircraft guns opened fire. The enemy planes passed the *Nagato*. At 1113, her lookouts sighted what appeared to be an enemy surface ship to starboard bearing 25°,

---

[532] Combined Fleet Headquarters Detailed Action Report and *Yamato* Detailed Action Report.

[533] *Yamato* Detailed Action Report.

[534] Ibid.

[535] Ibid.

distance 38,360 yards. No action was taken concerning the surface contact. By 1124, all her guns were quiet again, and by 1206 her speed was reduced to eighteen knots.[536]

Just when Kobe may have thought the relentless air attacks would be over, more planes arrived at 1211 bearing 132° with an altitude angle of 18°. At 1212, air alerts were again sounded. By 1215, the number of aircraft was determined as eight to ten enemy planes bearing 125° to starboard. At 1218, Kobe ordered her main guns to open fire.[537]

The American aircraft separated into attack groups and circled the Japanese formation. Signals from the *Yamato* turned the fleet onto a new course of 320° true at 1227. At least twenty aircraft came within range of her anti-aircraft guns at 1231, and she opened fire. At 1239 she fired another salvo from her main battery. At 1240 two SB2C aircraft attacked from port bearing 100° with an altitude angle of 7°. Kobe ordered a hard turn to port, and two bombs landed off her starboard bow.[538]

The next wave of U.S. aircraft approached at 1315, an estimated number of eighty aircraft. The *Nagato*'s main battery opened fire at 1323, and by 1325 her anti-aircraft guns opened fire. Dive bombers attacked from astern, and at 1334 a bomb penetrated her bow at frame seven, hitting her forecastle deck and passing through the carpenter's shop into the No. 3 storage compartment, creating a 16-inch hole in the upper deck. It then exited the starboard side of the ship and detonated at the waterline creating a hole sixteen feet wide in the bow at the waterline. The No.3 storage room on the upper deck and the paint locker on the middle deck were flooded. Overall damage was considered light. By 1343 she checked fire.[539]

At 1351 the *Yamato* signaled she had detected more U.S. aircraft approaching at 76,720 yards bearing 30°. By 1404 the *Nagato* opened fire on sixteen aircraft approaching her from astern. Kobe ordered a course change of 10° to port, and the planes passed by. By 1412 she checked fire again, and at 1413 her speed was reduced to number three battle speed.[540]

---

[536] *Nagato* Detailed Action Report.

[537] Ibid.

[538] Ibid.

[539] Ibid.

[540] Ibid.

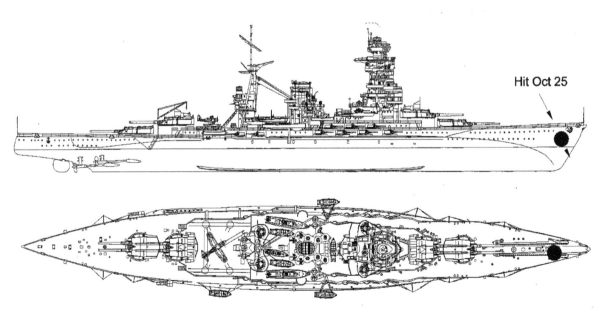

Figure 113 (top): The *Nagato* fires her aft 5-inch anti-aircraft guns as two bombs explode off her starboard bow at approximately 1240 pm. (bottom) *Nagato's* battle damage on October 25.

Her exhausted gun crews finally got a break in the action, for the next U.S. attack wave did not appear until 1545. This time planes approached from 210° and at 255° on the compass. The *Yamato* ordered a turn to 270°. At 1554 the *Nagato* opened fire from her anti-aircraft guns. At 1557 she suffered two near misses to starboard, and at 1608 two near misses fell astern. By 1616 this attack was over, the final attack on the *Nagato* for 25 October 1944.[541]

ON BOARD THE *KONGO*

The fleet changed course to 270° at 1054, then 225° at 1100, and 130° at 1115.At 1116, three enemy aircraft were sighted to port. Shimazaki prepared his ship for an air battle and to stand by at 1132. The three planes bypassed the *Kongo*, but a new threat materialized at 1146 when the *Yamato* sent word that she had picked up more enemy aircraft on her radar, distance thirty-eight miles and approaching. The fleet turned west to course 270° by 1148, and by 1213 the incoming planes become visible on the horizon. Shimazaki ordered the *Kongo*'s speed to twenty-four knots and prepare for AA action at 1221.[542]

Shimazaki observed the *Yamato* open fire at 1228, and his lookouts reported as many as fifty aircraft approaching 80° to port at 1230. They focused on the *Yamato*, and she was covered in smoke from her own guns by 1240. At 1241, the *Kongo* opened fire with her anti-aircraft guns and fired on several U.S. aircraft without hitting any. By 1255, Shimazaki ordered her guns to check fire. So far the *Kongo* had been lucky and was not the subject of attack during these raids. Speed was reduced to twenty-two knots by 1300.[543]

At 1318, the *Yamato* by flag signal reported detecting seventy aircraft bearing 50°. At 1322, the *Yamato* ordered the fleet to turn to course 290°, and the *Yamato* opened fire. This raid also ignored the *Kongo* and was seen to retire by 1347, but another wave appeared at 1402, and the *Yamato* was observed to open fire again. At 1404, the *Yamato* was observed from the *Kongo* to shoot down one enemy plane.[544]

The next wave was detected at 1541 when the *Yamato*'s radar picked up enemy aircraft at thirty-five miles. At 1552, the *Yamato* opened fire, and at 1555 one enemy plane was seen to fall. Admiral Shimazaki had his own gunners to standby for AA action at 1558. At 1609, Shimazaki saw two more U.S. aircraft fall, and then at 1610 another two aircraft went down. The fleet turned to course 310°, and at 1638 twenty dive bombers approached the *Kongo* bearing 120° to port. At 1640, her main guns opened fire, and by 1641 her anti-aircraft guns joined in. Her speed was twenty-four knots as

---

[541] Ibid.

[542] *Kongo* Detailed Action Report.

[543] Ibid.

[544] Ibid.

she fired on U.S. aircraft. At 1711, the *Kongo* fired another salvo from her main guns. At 1735, five torpedo bombers attacked her, but the torpedoes passed astern. By 1759, she reduced speed to twenty knots, and by 1800she checked fire.[545]

ON BOARD THE *HARUNA*

Rear Admiral Shigenaga's experience would be quite the opposite of Shimazaki's as the *Haruna* will be the focus of many of the U.S. attacks. At 1001, the *Haruna* was ready for anti-aircraft action. She witnessed the initial attacks on other ships of the fleet, but by 1049 four enemy aircraft picked her out. Three attacked from the port quarter, and one attacked from the starboard bow. Shigenaga ordered a hard turn to port, and one of the three planes attacking from astern was hit and seen to splash into the sea at 1050. She suffered three near-miss bombs to port and one near-miss bomb to starboard.[546]

At 1235, the next wave attacked, and the *Haruna* opened fire with her anti-aircraft guns at 1237. At 1240, two enemy aircraft attacked, and Shigenaga ordered a hard turn to starboard. She was bracketed by two bombs, one to port and the other to starboard, as the planes passed overhead. At 1250, three torpedoes were sighted to starboard, and Shigenaga ordered her to turn toward the torpedoes, and they were seen to pass close to her starboard side. By 1255, she reduced speed to twenty knots and checked fire by 1254.[547]

At 1314, an estimated seventy aircraft approached the fleet. At 1325, one enemy aircraft attacked from 130° starboard, and three attacked from 90° starboard. Shigenaga ordered a hard turn to starboard, and the ship suffered two near misses to starboard and four near misses to port. However, as soon as this attack was over, two more planes attacked from the bow. This time Shigenaga ordered a hard turn to port and five near-miss bombs exploded by her port side. As the planes passed overhead, both were hit and were seen to crash on her starboard side. At 1355, a group of ten aircraft bearing 30°, altitude angle 5° were detected, and at 1405 Shigenaga ordered main guns and anti-aircraft guns to engage these aircraft. None were hit, and the ten aircraft passed her at 1415.[548]

At 1550, another wave of U.S. aircraft was detected, and the crew was alerted for another AA action. By 1552 the *Haruna* opened fire, and by 1600 eight enemy planes attacked from her starboard side. Shigenaga ordered a hard turn to port, and as the *Haruna* heeled over, two bombs exploded off

---

[545] Ibid.

[546] *Haruna* Detailed Action Report.

[547] Ibid.

[548] Ibid.

her starboard side, and three bombs exploded off her port side. None of the attackers were hit, and by 1611 she checked fire.[549]

By 1639, however, another attack was forming up on her, and she opened fire again at 1640. Six dive bombers attacked from 70° starboard, and Shigenaga ordered a hard turn to starboard. Ten near-miss bombs fell to port at 1643. Then at 1649, four enemy aircraft attacked her from her port side. Shigenaga ordered a hard turn to port, and three near-miss bombs fell to starboard. By 1658 she checked fire. At 1703, there was another attack but not directly on the *Haruna,*and she checked fire at 1712. This was repeated at 1730 when she opened fire on U.S. aircraft and checked fire at 1734. This was the last attack on 25 October the *Haruna* took part in.[550]

ON BOARD THE *HAGURO*

At 1047, the *Haguro* was on course 000° at a speed of twenty-two knots. At 1052, the *Yamato* signaled to change course to 270°. At 1053, U.S. aircraft attacked, and Capt. Sugiura ordered her guns to open fire and increased speed to twenty-six knots. Fire was checked at 1057, but another group of aircraft was sighted at 1058. At 1105 this group was taken under fire as it passed by, and fire was checked at 1107. At 1118, course was set at 080°, but at 1122 this was changed to 225°, and speed was reduced to twenty-two knots.[551]

Another U.S. wave of aircraft was detected, and *Yamato* ordered a course change to 270° at 1148. The aircraft ignored the *Haguro*, but she changed course to 245° at 1156 and then back to 270° and slowed to eighteen knots at 1200. At 1212 the fleet turned north onto a course of 000°. Capt. Sugiura received multiple reports on U.S. aircraft and engaged several aircraft beginning at 1239 and ending at 1257, but his ship wasn't directly attacked. This was repeated from 1324 to 1348, 1402 to 1413, 1550 to 1628, 1643 to 1652, 1653 to 1703, and 1725 to 1758. *Haguro* didn't suffer any damage in the afternoon attacks.[552]

ON BOARD THE *SUZUYA*

Captain Teraoka's ship came under attack at 1050 and suffered a near miss on the starboard side amidships outboard of the number one torpedo mount. This blast then detonated one of the torpedoes which in turn detonated the remaining three. The explosions immediately destroyed the aft 5-inch gun mounts (port and starboard) and disabled the starboard engine rooms and No. 7 boiler room. Fires raged amidships, and the ship slowed to a stop. Captain Teraoka signaled *Tone* to

---

[549] Ibid.

[550] Ibid.

[551] *Haguro* Detailed Action Report.

[552] Ibid.

transfer Vice Admiral Shiraishi at 1130. The crew was attempting to fight the fires when more explosions occurred at 1200; the fires had cooked off ammunition from the forward 5-inch guns and the port side torpedo mounts. These explosions set the whole ship on fire. Captain Teraoka, seeing his ship was lost, ordered his surviving crew to abandon ship at 1300. The destroyer *Okinami* rescued 620 men, but Captain Teraoka decided to remain with his ship. At 1320 *Suzuya* slipped beneath the surface.[553]

ON BOARD THE *TONE*

Captain Haruo Mayuzumi ordered his ship to come alongside the burning *Suzuya* so that Vice Admiral Shiraishi could transfer his flag for a second time. This was completed by 1157. The *Tone* was the last surviving cruiser from the Seventh Cruiser Division. Her luck wouldn't last long, for soon after the Admiral was safely aboard the *Tone* came under air attack. At 1240 an estimated 500-lb. bomb struck her stern on the starboard side. The bomb exploded, making a hole 13 feet by 16 feet in the upper deck and destroying the 6th, 7th, and 8th officer's quarters below. The meat locker and freezer room were also damaged. The electric motors to aft steering were shorted out, and her rudders jammed. Three hundred tons of water entered her stern. Manual steering was soon applied so she could stay with the formation, but she had difficulty steering for the remainder of the battle.[554]

ON BOARD THE *KUMANO*

The *Kumano* was making her way back to San Bernardino Strait alone at fifteen knots. Near the entrance to the strait, she was attacked by U.S. aircraft and took a near-miss bomb on her port side which flooded her No. 6 boiler room. The planes came from TF 38.1.[555]

ON BOARD THE *NOSHIRO*

From 1040 to 1050 the *Noshiro* assumed several course changes to bring her back into proper position within the formation. At 1052 two fighter bombers were sighted, and then at 1056 Captain Kajiwara noted that the *Suzuya* was on fire. By 1100, speed was reduced to twenty knots, and then at 1101 the *Suzuya* suffered an explosion.[556]

Captain Kajiwara noted the *Yamato* came under attack at 1145, and then at 1212 fifty aircraft were detected bearing 040° at a distance of 29,592 yards. The fleet was ordered to turn to 250° at 1217 and then 240° by 1224 and finally 320° at 1226. By 1241, the aircraft were in range, and Kajiwara

---

[553] *Suzuya* Detailed Action Report.

[554] *Tone* Detailed Action Report.

[555] Lacroix, Eric and Linton Wells II. *Japanese Cruisers of the Pacific War.* Naval Institute Press, 1997, pp 498-501.

[556] *Noshiro* Detailed Action Report.

ordered his main battery to open fire. At 1242, aircraft approached from the bow, and the anti-aircraft guns opened fire. At 1242.5, the *Noshiro* took two near-miss bombs aft on the port side, opening No. 2 and No. 4 fuel oil tanks to the sea. The port outboard shaft was damaged, but she could still make thirty-two knots if needed. At 1245.5 an enemy aircraft dropped a torpedo which was avoided. By 1250, the U.S. aircraft retired.[557]

At 1313, a large formation estimated to be seventy aircraft approached, and Kajiwara alerted his ship to standby for AA action. By 1326 he ordered his main battery to open fire, but despite the heavy raid, the *Noshiro* wasn't attacked, and at 1342 she checked fire. The next wave of U.S. aircraft approached at 1549, and by 1555 Kajiwara ordered her main and secondary guns to re-open fire. At 1556, he saw one U.S. aircraft fall. At 1613, another U.S. aircraft was seen to go down. By 1628, the *Noshiro* checked fire.[558]

Another wave of U.S. aircraft appeared at 1640 bearing 020° at a distance of 10,960 yards. Speed was increased to twenty-four knots, and by 1642.5 the *Noshiro*'s guns were back in action. At 1643, four U.S. aircraft attacked, resulting in one near-miss bomb, and one U.S. aircraft was shot down. By 1648, the aircraft retired, and the *Noshiro* checked fire at 1651. Kajiwara resumed a course of 080° at 1654. Then at 1656, six aircraft approached from the bow, and Kajiwara immediately ordered his gunners to engage the aircraft. Two aircraft were shot down at 1657. The *Noshiro* wasn't attacked again on October 25; attempts to engage aircraft at 1752 to 1757 were her last actions of the day.[559]

ON BOARD THE *FANSHAW BAY*

For almost an hour, Taffy 3 sailed south and was able to land several planes returning from air strikes on the enemy, when at 1049 four enemy fighters appeared overhead. Anti-aircraft guns opened fire at 1050 as the four enemy planes dove on the carriers. Thirty seconds later, the *St. Lo* was hit by a suicide attack. One of the planes headed directly for the *Fanshaw Bay* but was hit by her AA guns and crashed alongside the ship resulting in no damage. The *Kalinin Bay* was then hit on her flight deck, and the *White Planes* took a hit alongside her flight deck resulting in minor damage. At 1055, the *St. Lo* suffered a massive explosion as her own planes exploded within her hangar deck. More explosions soon followed, and it became apparent she would be lost.[560]

Clifton Sprague ordered all his remaining escorts to pick up survivors from the *St. Lo*, leaving his four remaining carriers completely without escort. By 1105, the *St. Lo* sank. She had not suffered any

[557] Ibid.

[558] Ibid.

[559] Ibid.

[560] *Fanshaw Bay* Action Report and CTU 77.4.3 Action Report.

hits during the surface battle, and now in just fifteen minutes she was gone. He reported his situation to the rest of the American forces and requested additional fighter support.

Then at 1108, another Japanese plane made an attack on the *Kitkun Bay*, the only surviving carrier that had not suffered any damage. The *Fanshaw Bay*'s anti-aircraft guns along with the *Kitkun Bay's* opened fire and succeeded in hitting the plane and shooting it down before it could damage the *Kitkun Bay*. By 1115, still sailing southward, his four remaining carriers left the area, and his destroyers and destroyer escorts remained to pick up survivors from the *St. Lo*.[561]

Figure 114: Japanese aircraft appear above Taffy 3 at approximately 1050, 25 October 1944.

ON BOARD THE *ST. LO*

At 1040, she took on board one fighter from the *Kalinin Bay*'s air wing, two torpedo bombers from the *White Planes* air wing, and two torpedo bombers from her own air wing and lowered them all to the hangar deck so that they could be refueled and rearmed and keep the flight deck open for any other aircraft that needed to land.[562]

At 1051, AA fire was seen and heard coming from forward, and General Quarters was immediately sounded. The aircraft, spotted between 1,000-3,000 feet off the starboard bow, were thought to include both enemy and friendly aircraft. These planes started to pass by, but one plane as it came alongside of the *St. Lo* made a hard turn toward the carrier. The starboard AA guns opened fire but with no effect. The enemy aircraft was identified as a Zeke, with a bomb under each wing. It continued its right turn coming over the ramp at very high speed. After crossing the ramp he pushed over to strike the flight deck at the number five wire, fifteen feet to the port side from the center line of the flight deck. There was an explosion as one or both bombs struck the flight deck.

---

[561] Ibid.

[562] *St. Lo* Action Report.

The plane itself shattered with debris and fragments thrown across the flight deck, and the remnants of the plane went over the bow.[563]

At first Captain McKenna didn't feel that his ship had been seriously damaged. There was a hole in the flight deck with the edges smoldering which did burst into flames. Water hoses were immediately placed into action against the fire. Then he noticed that the smoke was coming up through the hole from the hangar deck, and smoke began to rise on both sides of the ship escaping from the hangar deck. He attempted to contact the hangar deck for a report, but communications were out. Within one and a half minutes after the enemy aircraft had crashed into the ship, a second explosion occurred which bulged up the flight deck aft of the original hole. Seconds later, a third and more violent explosion took place which peeled the flight deck open. This was followed by two more explosions which enveloped the aft part of the ship in flames and blew the forward elevator out of its shaft.[564]

Figure 115: The *St. Lo* was hit by a kamikaze.

By 1100, Captain McKenna couldn't even determine if the rear section of his ship was still attached and knew his ship couldn't be saved; he gave word to stand by to abandon ship. He next ordered all engines to stop. Once the ship had slowed to a stop, he ordered the crew to abandon ship. A fifth explosion caused the ship to list to port. Then more explosions occurred as the crew attempted to get the wounded men off the ship. A total of eight explosions were counted.[565]

---

[563] Ibid.

[564] Ibid.

[565] Ibid.

Figure 116: The *St. Lo* on fire after the kamikaze struck her flight deck and began fires within her hangar deck.

When Captain McKenna left the ship, she still had a port list but possibly due to explosion number six, seven, or eight, the starboard hull near the bottom was blown out and the *St. Lo* rapidly shifted to starboard. Her momentum overwhelmed her stability, and she capsized and eventually plunged by the stern at 1125. Three underwater explosions were noted once the ship left the surface with one being heavy, and the other two being moderate. Captain McKenna was in the water approximately ten minutes when the remaining escorts of Taffy 3 came to their rescue being picked up by the *Heermann*.[566]

---

[566] Ibid.

Figure 117: Secondary explosions rock the *St. Lo*.

ON BOARD THE *KALININ BAY*

At 1050, escorts on the starboard bow and beam commenced anti-aircraft fire, and three Zekes were sighted over the *White Plains*. A Zeke was picked up by the lookouts on the starboard bow at an altitude of five or six thousand feet. The Zeke was making high speed on an opposite course. The Zeke started a twisting spiral toward the ship, in about a sixty-degree dive. All guns which could be brought to bear commenced firing, and the Zeke was hit several times, but didn't appear to be damaged or out of control. The Zeke was still in a twisting dive when it crossed the starboard quarter and hit the flight deck at frames 120-132. There was a large burst of flame with intense heat, but it wasn't believed that there was a bomb explosion. A large hole was torn in the flight deck and a fire was started. The major portion of the Zeke skidded forward along the flight deck and went over the port bow at frame 10.[567]

---

[567] *Kalinin Bay* Action Report.

Figure 118: Damage to the flight deck of the *Kalinin Bay* due to the first kamikaze aircraft.

A second Zeke was then seen on the starboard quarter at an altitude of six to eight thousand feet. The plane was already in its dive when sighted. The dive was across the fore and aft line of the ship and the angle of the dive was about 70°. This Zeke was smoking from numerous AA hits. Whether or not these caused the pilot to lose control and the plane to pull up slightly wasn't known, but the plane struck the after port stack, catwalk, and 20 mm mount in the vicinity of frames 110-120. The plane crashed into the water near the port side, and there was a large column of water with considerable shaking of the ship. It was believed that the aircraft carried a small bomb.[568]

A third Zeke was close behind the second, and this attack wasn't subjected to AA fire. It wasn't known if the pilot made a poor dive or if he was distracted by the plane just ahead of him, but the third Zeke crashed into the water about fifty yards on the port quarter. The size of the explosion which followed was believed to be from a small bomb. No strafing was done by the attacking planes.[569]

---

[568] Ibid.

[569] Ibid.

Figure 119: A second kamikaze lands in the water off the port bow of the *Kalinin Bay* as a third begins his dive.

Figure 120: The third kamikaze to attack *Kalinin Bay* landed off her port quarter.

ON BOARD THE *KITKUN BAY*

At 1049, a group of five Zekes were sighted at 6,000 yards on the port bow. The ship's anti-aircraft guns opened fire. One Zeke was crossing ahead of the ship from port to starboard. Upon being brought under fire, it climbed rapidly, rolled and made a suicide dive directly at the bridge strafing as it came down. The plane passed over the island, crashed into the port catwalk, and fell into the sea about twenty-five yards on the port bow. Its fragmentation bomb exploded as the plane crashed, causing fires and damage to the ship.[570]

---

[570] *Kitkun Bay* Action Report.

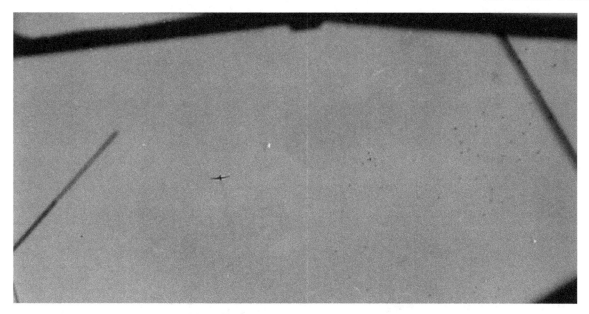

Figure 121: A Japanese plane, beginning to smoke from being hit by AA fire, attempts to crash into the *Kitkun Bay*. The plane would strike the port catwalk causing minimal damage.

At 1117, fifteen Judys were sighted approaching the formation from astern, distance five miles. At this time the *Kitkun Bay* launched two FM-2 fighters for CAP. The remaining carriers without any screen increased speed to seventeen knots and set a course of 210° by 1123. At this time a single Judy made a suicide attack on the *Kitkun Bay* from astern. The plane was brought under intense AA fire, and both wings were shot off. Part of the plane struck the water about fifty yards off the port bow, its bomb struck the water twenty-five yards off the starboard bow, and other parts of the plane hit the forecastle. Only minor damage was sustained. One man was killed and twenty wounded from both air attacks on the ship. By 1129 speed was reduced to fifteen knots.[571]

At 1301, five TBMs and six FM-2 fighters were landed. The pilots reported two torpedo hits on a *Tone*-class cruiser. At 1320, unidentified aircraft were reported approaching the formation at a distance of twenty-two miles, bearing 105°. No attacks from these planes were made. The *Kitkun Bay* launched four FM-2 aircraft for a CAP at 1423. At 1437, five planes from other carriers were landed. All S.A.P. bombs on board had been expended. Four TBMs were loaded with the last torpedoes and launched at 1539. When the planes returned at 1825 they reported a single torpedo hit on a *Nachi*-class heavy cruiser.[572]

---

[571] Ibid.

[572] Ibid.

Figure 122: Damage to the catwalk of the *Kitkun Bay* after the plane hit.

At 1930, the last plane was landed aboard the *Kitkun Bay*. Nine planes and pilots from the *Kitkun Bay* had landed at Leyte. Fourteen pilots and planes from other ships had chosen the *Kitkun Bay* to land on. During the late afternoon and early evening, the four carriers without any escort proceeded to rendezvous with Taffy 1. At 2002 a radar contact was made bearing 339°, distance 19,400 yards with the range closing. The 5-inch gun crews were ordered to man battle stations. The formation was within TBS range of Taffy 1, and Clifton Sprague requested screen of Taffy 1 to investigate the contact. At 2050 three destroyers were assigned, but when they approached, it disappeared. One destroyer reported seeing a conning tower and made a depth-charge attack. Thereafter this contact didn't reappear.[573]

---

[573] Ibid.

Figure 123: A kamikaze attempts to crash into the *White Plains.* **Note: The arresting wires are up on the flight deck as** *White Plains* **was in the process of landing U.S. aircraft when this attack began.**

ON BOARD THE *WHITE PLAINS*

At 1047, three enemy aircraft later identified as Zekes were sighted approaching from 140° at an altitude of 5,000 feet. One minute later, three more Zekes were spotted, and all six aircraft soon made diving attacks on the carrier formation. Two planes dove on the *White Plains*, and the bow 40mm guns took them under fire as soon as they were within range. When the Japanese planes had descended to 500 feet, distance 2,000 yards, they pulled out of their dive and headed down the *White Plains*'s port side. One plane was smoking, and the carrier's port side guns took it under fire. It came alongside the *St. Lo* and suddenly dove into *St. Lo*'s deck, starting a fire aft visible through the hangar-deck doors. The other plane circled the formation on the port side. When astern it turned and started a run on the *White Plains*. The plane's approach gave the impression that the pilot at the end of his shallow dive expected to land on the after end of the flight deck and crash down the entire length of the ship.[574]

Captain Sullivan ordered hard left rudder to avoid this attack, and as the plane came in, it veered from side to side to avoid incoming AA fire from the aft guns. When only a few yards astern the plane suddenly rolled over on its port side and dove towards the water. It missed the port catwalk just aft of stack two by inches, exploding on impact with the water. The catwalk, flight deck, after

---

[574] *White Plains* Action Report.

stack, and skin of the ship were showered with fragments and debris. Eleven men received injuries from these fragments.[575]

Figure 124: U.S. crewmen, realizing the pilot's intentions, begin to take cover; 20 mm cannon on her starboard side open fire on the Japanese plane.

ON BOARD THE *HEERMANN*

At 1050 Cdr. Hathaway observed an enemy Val dive into the flight deck of the *St. Lo*. At 1051 *Heermann*'s gunners opened fire on three enemy planes as they approached the *Heermann*, but fire was checked at 0753. At 1103, her AA guns re-opened fire, scoring two hits on a Japanese Val. At 1104 she shifted fire to another high-flying Japanese dive bomber and checked fire at 1108.[576]

At 1112, Clifton Sprague ordered all screening vessels to pick up survivors from the *St. Lo*. At 1123 the *St. Lo* was observed to sink. By 1130 commenced picking up survivors and at 1137 took on board Captain McKenna, commanding officer of the *St. Lo*. Then at 1140 a motor whaleboat was placed into the water to pick up survivors. The *Heermann* picked up seventy-two men and eight officers from the crew of the *St. Lo*.[577]

---

[575] Ibid.

[576] *Heermann* Action Report.

[577] Ibid.

Figure 125: The Japanese plane, only feet from the carrier with its engine dead and propeller stopped. Gunfire destroyed a second plane that crashed into the sea on the horizon.

Figure 126: The kamikaze plane crashes into the water spraying the *White Plains's* port catwalk, aft stack, and sides with fragments.

By 1300 she picked up a radar contact believed to be an enemy cruiser dead in the water, distance ten miles bearing 050° true. At 1355, Cdr. Hathaway established a scouting line with the *Raymond*, *John C. Butler*, and the *Dennis* to search for additional survivors. The *Heermann* had to stop to continue damage repairs forward at 1405. The remaining ships continued search operations. At 1445 the contact report of the enemy cruiser was delivered to OTC via VHF. At 1510 the enemy cruiser came in sight and was identified as *Tone*-class by the gunnery officer, bearing 050° true, distance 20,000 yards with smoke rising from her fantail.[578]

Figure 127: A view from *White Plains* of the site of the *St. Lo*'s sinking.

Then at 1513, fifty SB2C aircraft appeared and seemed to be about to attack. All ships were ordered by the *Heermann* to make proper identification by light. By 1518, the planes received our identification and proceeded northward. At 1533, intercepted VHF message from OTC stating enemy was retiring towards San Bernardino Strait. At 1534, the *Heermann* got underway at fifteen knots, course 120° in an attempt to re-join carrier formation.[579]

At 1621 secured from General Quarters. At 1625, Cdr. Hathaway ordered the *Raymond* and the *John C. Butler* to proceed ahead in order to re-join carrier formation. The *Heermann* and the *Dennis* could make only fifteen knots due to damage forward. At 1919 Cdr. Hathaway intercepted a TBS message from Clifton Sprague to the *Raymond* and the *John C. Butler* ordering these vessels to head for Leyte Gulf. At 1932, Cdr. Hathaway asked the *Raymond* and the *John C. Butler* to inform Clifton Sprague that the *Heermann* and the *Dennis* were headed to Kossol Passage, near the Palau Islands.[580]

ON BOARD THE *DENNIS*

At 1050, eight enemy planes attacked the formation. The *Dennis* opened fire with her after 40 mm gun at 1052 on the enemy aircraft bearing 045° relative. At 1054, her crew observed an enemy aircraft crash into the sea at about 5,000 yards, bearing 190° relative, having passed abeam of the ship. At 1055, Lt. Cdr. Hansen observed a plane crash into the *St. Lo*. By 1057, violent explosions were observed on board the *St. Lo*, and the carrier's crew began to abandon ship. By 1101, the

---

[578] Ibid.

[579] Ibid.

[580] Ibid.

remaining carriers began to zigzag on base course 120°, speed seventeen knots, unescorted, leaving behind the *St. Lo*.

Lt. Cdr. Hansen began closing on the *St. Lo* by 1102. Then at 1105, two more violent explosions rocked the carrier. At 1107, three more enemy aircraft dived on the carrier formation. Lt. Cdr. Hansen observed that one carrier was hit and damaged but was able to maintain her speed. He also saw three enemy planes shot down by the formation. At 1109 another explosion occurred on board the *St. Lo*. The *Dennis* began to take on board survivors beginning at 1110. Sixteen minutes later, the *St. Lo* sank. Three underwater explosions occurred at 1130 in the position where the *St. Lo* was observed to have gone down.[581]

Rescue operations continued to 1350 with the *Dennis* picking up 431 survivors. The *Dennis* continued to search for survivors in company with the *Heermann*, *Raymond*, and *John C. Butler*. By 1432 Lt. Cdr. Hansen secured the ship from General Quarters. At 1530 three men in a raft were spotted, so Lt. Cdr. Hansen stopped to pick them up by 1540. With 434 survivors on board, the *Dennis* formed screen 53 from USF 10A, as the *Heermann* as guide. Together the *Dennis* and *Heermann* headed for Kossal Passage, Palau Islands.[582]

ON BOARD THE *JOHN C. BUTLER*

At 1040 the crew of the *John C. Butler* sighted a group of six to eight enemy aircraft milling around off her port bow, distance approximately seven miles. Radar indicated friendly, but one plane closed and was identified as enemy when it came within four miles of the formation. Anti-aircraft guns opened fire immediately. This plane, identified as a Tony fighter, passed astern at about 2,000 yards, altitude 3,000 feet, position bearing 040°. When the plane reached the port side of a CVE, it started a slight climb and right bank. AA shells, 20 mm and 40 mm, appeared to be hitting it. The plane started to smoke and went into a dive on the carrier. Fire was checked at this point. The plane dove straight for the carrier and crashed into the water off the port bow. At about 1052, another enemy aircraft was making a run on the *Fanshaw Bay*. Lt. Cdr. Pace notified the carrier by TBS. The *Fanshaw Bay* succeeded in shooting down the plane. At 1112, Lt. Cdr. Pace received orders from Clifton Sprague to stand by and pick up survivors of *St. Lo*. The remaining carriers retired to the southeast. The *John C. Butler* picked up *St. Lo* 129 survivors, of which thirty-nine required serious medical attention. One man later died due to loss of blood. There were no casualties suffered by the *John C. Butler* during the battle.[583]

---

[581] *Dennis* Action Report.

[582] Ibid.

[583] *John C. Butler* Action Report.

On Board the *Raymond*

At 1050, Lt. Cdr. Beyer reported that enemy planes identified as Vals made suicide attacks on the carrier formation. This happened so suddenly the *Raymond* wasn't in a position where her anti-aircraft guns could be effective. Only one plane came within range of her 5-inch and 40 mm guns. Lt. Cdr. Beyer observed two planes miss the carriers and plunge into the sea, but one crashed into the carrier *St. Lo*. Another carrier was hit, but damage couldn't be ascertained through observation. The *St. Lo* suffered internal explosions, and it became clear she was sinking.[584]

Clifton Sprague ordered all screen units to stand by and pick up survivors from the *St. Lo*. The remaining carriers left the area on a southeasterly course. Lt. Cdr. Beyer ordered the whaleboat lowered to expedite rescue of the sailors in the water. By 1340, the whaleboat was hoisted, having recovered 109 survivors. Lt. Cdr. Beyer began to search the area for additional survivors, but at 1700 was ordered by the *Heermann* to sail in company with the *John C. Butler* and re-join carrier force. At 1900, TBS contact with Clifton Sprague was made and he ordered *John C. Butler* to proceed to Leyte Gulf.[585]

On Board the *Wasatch*

Kinkaid finally received good news at 1039 that the enemy had turned away. He canceled the orders to send half of TG 77.2 forward still concerned that if the remnants of the Japanese southern force should return he would need to shift his forces back to the south. His relief didn't last long, for at 1104 he received news that Taffy 3 had come under air attack, and three carriers had been hit. Reports from carrier aircraft soon plotted the enemy course heading back towards Leyte Gulf so that at 1127 Kinkaid renewed his orders to TG 77.2 to send one half his forces forward and engage the enemy.[586]

At 1230, Kinkaid received Felix Stump's pilot report of several hundreds of men in the water in the vicinity of 11° 12' north, 126° 30' east. This information was incorrect and represented a twenty- to forty-mile error. By 1300, enough reports on the enemy position and course showed that the Japanese were definitely retiring to the north, so once again Kinkaid canceled Oldendorf's orders to take half his force north to engage the enemy. His only available assets were the carrier planes of Taffy 1 and Taffy 2 which continued to attack until dusk. Kinkaid's primary responsibility was the protection of General MacArthur's forces, and he had to consider the remaining Japanese ships to

---

[584] *Raymond* Action Report.

[585] Ibid.

[586] Ibid.

the south. As long as TF 77.2 controlled the seas of Leyte Gulf, no Japanese force, whether it was air power or a surface fleet, was likely to break that control.[587]

ON BOARD THE *SANGAMON*

At 1045, Japanese aircraft activity began to pick up, and the CAP of Taffy 1 shot down a Japanese Nick aircraft. Ten minutes later at 1055, Taffy 3 reported being under air attack and requested additional CAP screen. Concerning Sprague's own task unit, the *Richard S. Bull* had pulled alongside his flagship to receive a doctor and medical supplies and take them to the *Suwannee* to assist that ship with her many casualties. As he was seeing to this, he was handed another message reporting that three carriers of Taffy 3 had been hit by suicide dive bombers. The Japanese had obviously organized a new kind of tactic. At 1104, Taffy 3 reported three carriers badly damaged. By 1115 Thomas Sprague launched all remaining available fighters to assist Taffy 3.[588]

At 1130, planes reported that the enemy was seventy-eight miles from Point Fin at 1055 on course 150° true, but at 1145 additional planes reported the same ships on course 225° true with a speed of twenty knots. Returning aircraft began to arrive, and one TBM crashed in the water on the starboard side of the formation, and Thomas Sprague sent the *Coolbaugh* to rescue the crew. Then at 1154, three or four Japanese single-seat aircraft attacked his formation. His anti-aircraft guns opened an intense amount of gunfire and drove off the attackers but not before they seriously strafed the *Richard M. Rowell* and attempted to drop bombs on the *Petrof Bay*. Luckily they missed, and no damage was done to the carrier, but *Richard M. Rowell* had one man killed and three wounded due to the strafing.[589]

By 1200 enough planes had returned to re-arm a third strike against the Japanese consisting of fifteen fighters and seventeen torpedo bombers. At 1203 another returning aircraft crashed into the sea, and this time the *Richard S. Bull* was sent to the rescue. At 1210 Destroyer Division 97, the *Sproston*, *Hale*, and the *Picking* were sighted approaching TU 77.4.1 headed to join TG 77.2. Thomas Sprague contacted Kinkaid and requested these three destroyers stay with his force. This was granted when at 1220 another enemy suicide air attack was made on the *Santee* which failed due to being driven off by the ships' gunfire.[590]

Soon after this attack at 1232 another wave of Japanese planes was picked up on radar, distance fifty-five miles from Taffy 1. Thomas Sprague was relieved when this enemy force didn't close on his formation. He received a message from the beach that additional planes were headed to Taffy 3

---

[587] Ibid.

[588] CTU 77.4 Action Report.

[589] Ibid.

[590] Ibid.

to provide CAP. Another returning plane landed in the water alongside his flagship, which promptly rescued the crew at 1312. The *Richard M. Rowell* came alongside the *Petrof Bay*, and the *Richard S. Bull* came alongside the flagship to transfer stretcher cases at 1330. At 1339 he received a message from Taffy 3 that contact with the enemy had been lost now for two hours. They believed one battleship, one heavy cruiser, and one destroyer were dead in the water with only a single escort destroyer. The remainder of the enemy fleet was heading for San Bernardino Strait. By 1420 the *Eversole* abandoned her search for the submarine and re-joined the task force. Another fighter crashed near the formation as it attempted to return at 1505. By 1527 planes from the *Hancock* were reported attacking the crippled Japanese ships; indicating that TG 38.1 was now within strike range. At 1550 more enemy planes were picked up, but they didn't close the formation. Thomas Sprague focused on the damaged *Suwannee*, and more casualties from her transferred to his flagship via the *Coolbaugh* at 1604.

Then at 1620 came land-based reports of at least twenty-five enemy bombers heading for the escort carriers. Thomas Sprague ordered the task unit to assume formation 5-V and prepare to defend itself against air attack. The bombers however didn't close Taffy 1. At 1700 the fourth strike from Taffy 1 was launched with all remaining available planes. This late launch meant that their return would have the added risk of night landings. Many pilots upon returning chose to land at Tacloban airfield instead of attempting to land on the carriers, but the field was in poor condition. Many planes crashed but fortunately without personnel casualties. As dusk approached the chances of further air attacks diminished, and at 1708 the formation assumed 5-R again to better protect themselves from submarine attack.[591]

ON BOARD THE *NEW JERSEY*

Task Force 34 made its way south at twenty knots but, unprepared for a high-speed run over the distance required, slowed to twelve knots at 1345 to refuel the destroyers. The battleships *Iowa* and the *New Jersey* were the fastest battleships at his command, so when refueling was completed at 1622, he divided his forces again creating TG 34.5 under the command of Rear Admiral Badger in the *Iowa* along with three light cruisers and eight destroyers. They left Lee and the remainder of TF 34 behind, traveling at twenty-eight knots.[592]

ON BOARD THE *YAMATO*

By 1710, the South West Area Force reported that, with exception of one regular carrier being damaged, results obtained were undetermined. At 1744, a group of Japanese bombers arrived over the fleet. Two Japanese dive bombers made an attack on the *Yamato* before the aircrews properly

---

[591] Ibid.

[592] CTU 38 Action Report.

identified the fleet below as friendly. Luckily, for the *Yamato*, no damage was sustained. The air crews asked for directions to the enemy, and the *Yamato*'s staff gave them their best estimate to the north. These aircraft returned thirty minutes later reporting they couldn't find the enemy.[593]

By 1830, Kurita had found nothing and decided to end the operation and return to Brunei. He had expected to find the enemy within two hours of turning north, but after six hours, nothing had appeared. Where was TF 34? Effectively blind with no way to ascertain where the enemy was, Kurita shifted his his main concern to fuel. Did he have enough to return home?

Exhaustion was also having an impact. Kurita had not slept since leaving Brunei on 22 October. By 1917, Kurita issued orders to all damaged units to make every possible effort to proceed alone but, where this was impossible, to dispose of any damaged warships and transfer the crew to its screening vessel and proceed to Coron.[594]

At 1925, Kurita and his staff were handed a message from Combined Fleet Headquarters in response to Kurita's message that they had abandoned the penetration into Leyte Gulf. It read, "Combined Fleet DesOpOrd No. 374: If there is an opportunity to do so, the First Diversion Attack Force will contact and destroy what is left of the enemy tonight. The other forces will coordinate their action with the above. If there is no chance of engaging the enemy in a night engagement tonight, the Main Body of the Mobile Force and First Diversion Attack Force will proceed to their refueling points as ordered by their respective commanders."[595]

With its focus on attack, the SHO 1 operation suffered for its flaws in reconnaissance and communication. Kurita, unable to conduct his own searches, depended on reports from either the First or Second Air Fleet, and these failed him as it became clear that the report of a U.S. task force to his north had been false. When he might have gainfully conducted a night battle, he had to count on the enemy's conveniently coming to engage him.[596] He had the option of resuming his mission to enter Leyte Gulf, but nothing had changed concerning the strategic significance of such a battle, a battle fought solely for its own sake. To fight a major engagement without a strategic objective was a concept without precedent in sound naval doctrine. Kurita admitted postwar that he never considered a return to Leyte Gulf.[597]

At 2130, his fleet passed through San Bernardino Strait. At this time he sent a message to First and Second Air Fleets, "In view of the one-sidedness of the decisive action carried out today, the 25th, there is much likelihood of the enemy's attempting to carry out revenge attacks against us with

---

[593] *Yamato* Detailed Action Report.

[594] Ibid.

[595] Combined Fleet Headquarters Detailed Action Report.

[596] Robertson, *Operational Analysis for the Battle of Leyte Gulf.*

[597] Ito, *The End of the Japanese Navy,* p 167.

the entire strength of the remainder of his task force. It is probable that such contact would be made in an area in the vicinity to the east or north of Legaspi on the 26th. We are of the opinion that the situation may offer an excellent opportunity for the shore-based air force units to strike the first blow against the enemy and gain control of the air."[598]

On Board the *Sangamon*

At 1730 Thomas Sprague was aware that the *Gambier Bay* and the *St. Lo* had been sunk, so he dispatched the *Richard S. Bull* and the *Eversole* to look for survivors. A returning pilot reported shooting down an enemy Kate torpedo bomber at 1428 and seeing two parachutes. It wouldn't be until 1945 that some aircraft of the final flight made it back to the formation. Thomas Sprague turned on the landing lights, and night landing operations began on the *Petrof Bay* and the *Santee*. All pilots made it back on board safely. At 1950 Admiral Thomas Sprague detached Destroyer Division 97 and ordered them to escort the four surviving carriers of Taffy 3, which was closing his own force at the time. As Destroyer Division 97 approached, they detected an unidentified vessel following Taffy 3 which was immediately challenged by *Sproston*, and the contact disappeared. At 2020 the four surviving carriers of Taffy 3 joined up with Taffy 1. *Sproston* closed the location, thinking an enemy submarine was attempting to close on the carriers. Pinging with her sonar, she gained a contact and attacked at 2049, but no conclusive results were obtained.[599]

Then at 2148 enemy aircraft were picked up at seventeen miles which sent the task unit to general quarters, but they didn't close the formation. Forty-four minutes later a periscope was sighted by *Coolbaugh* which immediately attacked with hedgehogs. Thomas Sprague ordered the carriers to make a 090° turn towards the sub immediately. Just as this turn was completed, two torpedoes straddled the *Petrof Bay*. The *Coolbaugh* reported heavy underwater explosions followed by debris, which Thomas Sprague considered a certain kill, and the enemy submarine that had been tormenting his task force the entire day was finally sunk. At 2300 Thomas Sprague instructed Taffy 3 to head for Woendi escorted by *Picking* and *Hale*.[600]

On Board the *Fanshaw Bay*

No further contact with the enemy ensued, but Clifton Sprague force was completely open to submarine and air attack. The *Kalinin Bay* was able to keep her fires under control but was heavily damaged due to gunfire and the kamikaze hit. Clifton Sprague set course for Taffy 1 and requested additional escorts. At 1948, a surface contact was made on radar bearing 272°, distance 22,700 yards—a possible submarine when his force was exposed. He was now fast approaching Taffy 1 and

---

[598] Combined Fleet Headquarters Detailed Action Report and *Yamato* Detailed Action Report.

[599] Ibid.

[600] Ibid.

joined with it at 2020. Escorts from Taffy 1 attacked the submarine at 2136 and reported a probable hit. Now safe with Taffy 1, he received orders from Thomas Sprague at 2300 to withdraw to Woendi to refuel and make repairs.[601]

ON BOARD THE *WASATCH*

As dusk approached and Kinkaid anxiety subsided, rescue of the men from the sunken ships began to take priority. Initially he ordered Thomas Sprague to send all available escorts for search and rescue operations at 1531. He then had Rear Admiral Barbey who commanded the amphibious force to set up a rescue plan. Rear Admiral Barbey placed Lt. Cdr. J.A. Baxter of *PC-623* in command of the operation. Six LCI, *PC-1119*, and *PC-623* headed for the reported position of the men leaving San Pedro Bay at 1835 on 25 October at their best speed of nine and a half knots. The destroyers *Richard S. Bull* and the *Eversole* of Taffy 1 reached the reported position at 2330 to find no one. They continued search operations until 1725 on 26 October but were always too far to the south to find any of the men in the water.[602]

WITH THE CREW OF *GAMBIER BAY*

After the *Gambier Bay* had sunk, her surviving crew assembled into seven or eight groups. They lashed life rafts and floater nets together and collected sections of flight-deck planking and any other floating debris with sufficient positive buoyancy to support those for whom there was no room on or around the rafts. At least three attacks before noon by groups of four to six TBMs each with escorting FMs were observed on enemy ships to the northeast. The men couldn't make out the ships being attacked except for one large ship with an attending destroyer to the southeast. At 1530 a group of forty U.S. aircraft approached at 10-12,000 feet. They circled around to the south and then to the northeast. Occasional bursts of AA fire could be seen. By 1800 the large enemy ship with a destroyer was still visible on the horizon. The crew believed the ship was a *Kongo*-class battleship but this was either *Chikuma* or *Chokai*. Night fell without any sign of rescue.[603]

WITH THE CREW OF *HOEL*

As the *Hoel* sank, men gathered onto rafts, and six Japanese ships passed close by. Cdr. Kintberger noted there was no attempt by the Japanese ships to open fire on his men. They watched the remainder of the battle from the sea, and as the enemy ships passed, Cdr. Kintberger noted how the *Yamato* class had radar on top of her main rangefinder, but the destroyers had no radar. Most of the crew expected an early rescue. The area that they had fought in was relatively small, and it was

---

[601] *Fanshaw Bay* Action Report.

[602] CTU 77 Action Report.

[603] *Gambier Bay* Action Report.

clear that at least three groups of U.S. aircraft had spotted them. The morning turned to afternoon, and then night fell, and the quick rescue expected didn't occur. Fifteen men perished during the first night.[604]

WITH THE CREW OF *SAMUEL B. ROBERTS*

The men of the *Samuel B. Roberts* formed into two groups. One group had one raft and one floater net, and the second had two rafts and one floater net. There were some men adrift in twos and threes using shoring or empty powder cans to help stay afloat. During the afternoon, a single aircraft buzzed the men in the water to let them know they had been sighted. Morale climbed as they were sure rescue was on the way, but as night fell there was no sign of rescue.[605]

WITH THE CREW OF *JOHNSTON*

Of the crew—about 326 officers and men—sixty had died in the surface battle. Commander Evans was seen with other officers and men in a small boat. This small boat would later sink due to fragment damage. An estimated 266 men clung to four life rafts. Within two hours of the ship's sinking, three U.S. planes flew overhead. Lt. Hagen believed they would be picked up in a few hours. As night approached his optimism was beginning to wane.[606]

---

[604] *Hoel* Action Report.

[605] *Samuel B. Roberts* Action Report.

[606] Hagen, "We Asked for the Jap Fleet—and Got It."

CHAPTER 8. WITHDRAWAL: 26 OCTOBER

ON BOARD THE *VINCENNES*

At 0026 on 26 October, Rear Admiral Francis Eliot Maynard Whiting was in command of Cruiser Division 14 in his flagship *Vincennes* as part of TG 34.5. Approaching San Bernardino Strait while on course of 135° true at a speed of twenty-eight knots, *Vincennes* detected a target by her after SG radar at 41,000 yards, bearing 142°. Four minutes later the forward SG radar made contact bearing 147° at a distance of 35,000 yards. Whiting was ordered by Rear Admiral Badger in the *Iowa* to close and engage the target. The range was reduced to 29,800 yards by 0036; the range-keeper had a solution, the main battery was loaded and matched in automatic on the target. Speed was ordered reduced to twenty-five knots by 0039.[607]

The range to the target fell to 20,500 yards by 0047, and the secondary battery was ready. Whiting changed course to 195° and then at 0053 to 250° true. With a target course of 269° and a speed of 20.5 knots, the range had decreased to 17,475 yards when Whiting gave the order to open fire at 0054. Main and secondary batteries engaged the target. After the initial salvo, the main guns were spotted up 200 yards, and the secondary guns were spotted down 100 yards. Continuous fire continued for three minutes when Whiting ordered the guns to check fire. The target had slowed and turned to 230°. A dull red glow was visible. At 0058, Whiting ordered the guns to resume fire from both the main and secondary batteries. The range had decreased to 16,850 yards, and the targets speed had been reduced to 11.5 knots. Flames burst from stem to stern with several heavy explosions. By 0101, the range was down to 14,870 yards, and the targets speed was seven knots. A minute later, the targets speed was down to 4.5 knots. Whiting checked fire at 0106 with the range at 13,650 yards. He then ordered Destroyer Division 103 to send two destroyers and finish her off.[608]

ON BOARD THE *OWENS*

Cdr. Carlton Benton Jones received the order to advance and finish the target off at 0106 in company with the destroyer *Miller*. Jones set course to 205° with the *Miller* forming a column on the *Owens*. At 1113, Jones informed the *Miller* that she had set a new course of 220° but was getting ready to come about sharply to 280°. The range was down to 4,900 yards, and the target was aflame and dead in the water. Believing the target was a cruiser and the only way to finisher her off would

---

[607] *Vincennes* Action Report.
[608] Ibid.

require torpedoes, Jones ordered his crew to prepare a half salvo fired at high speed. At 0117, five Mk 15 torpedoes were fired at the target.[609]

Now that the torpedoes were on their way, Jones ordered his guns to resume fire at 0119. The range at the time was 5,300 yards. Jones maneuvered around the target, slowly closing the range to 3,400 yards with both the *Owens* and the *Miller* raking the target with gunfire. Several eyewitnesses saw a small flash and a column of water when the torpedoes were timed to hit, but there were no conclusive visual or aural indications of a torpedo hit. The *Miller* had not been ordered to fire any torpedoes, and her captain recommended that she not fire any due to the obviously sinking condition of the target at 0124. Jones agreed. By 0132, the target suffered a huge explosion and a second explosion at 0135. She then disappeared at 0136. Fire was checked by 0137.[610]

Then radar picked up another contact, and fire was resumed at 0138. Star-shells were fired at 0142 to illuminate the area and see if the target was still afloat. Nothing was observed but some sailors on board the *Owens* felt they saw small arms fire from the target area. As they passed through the target area, the *Miller* reported that she had struck something, and then she felt an underwater explosion at 0145. At 0147, the crew of the *Owens* felt two more underwater explosions. Cdr. Jones, having passed through the target area and confident the target was sunk headed back to re-join TG 34.5 by 0148.[611]

ON BOARD THE *NEW JERSEY*

Halsey watched from the bridge of the *New Jersey* as his screening forces destroyed the one contact in the area. The Battle off San Bernardino Strait was the only surface engagement he would ever witness with his own eyes for his entire career. His flagship didn't even take part in it. It was more a massacre than a battle. The only enemy ship present was the Japanese destroyer *Nowaki*, which had escaped the *New Jersey* at Truk in February but was now caught with over 1,230 men on board as she attempted to rescue the crew of the heavy cruiser *Chikuma*. There would be no survivors.[612]

---

[609] *Owens* Action Report.

[610] Ibid.

[611] Ibid.

[612] *New Jersey* Action Report.

Figure 128: The *Yamato* was hit by two bombs at 0845 on 26 October.

ON BOARD THE *YAMATO*

During the night of 25 October and early morning hours of 26 October, what remained of Admiral Kurita's fleet retreated west in hopes they could put enough distance between themselves and the American carrier aircraft. They had passed through the Sibuyan Sea and had turned south at 0533 onto a course of 180° true. The fleet was northwest of the Island of Panay and it was Kurita's decision to head for Coron to refuel. At 0750, the first American plane was detected. By 0759, thirty aircraft were observed closing the formation. The fleet's course was changed to 210°. Rear Admiral Morishita increased speed to twenty-six knots. At 0834, the *Yamato* opened fire. Morishita swung his ship to port and settled onto a course of 170°. One U.S. aircraft was shot down at 0835. Four more U.S. planes dove on the battleship, and at 0845 two bombs struck her forward. By 0857, the attack was over, and she checked fire.[613]

Kurita received word that the *Noshiro* had taken a torpedo hit at 0852, flooding her No. 3 boiler room and stopping her dead in the water. Rear Admiral Mikio Hayakawa transferred his flag to the destroyer *Hamanami*.[614]

Morishita received damage reports for the two bomb hits forward. The first bomb hit at frame 63 along the center line, penetrated the forecastle deck and exploded on the upper deck. The second bomb struck at frame 72, 5.5 yards to starboard of the center line just ahead of the number one main-gun barbette. It too penetrated the forecastle deck and detonated on the upper deck. A large

[613] *Yamato* Detailed Action Report.
[614] Ibid.

hole was blasted up through the forecastle deck, the Starboard Divisional Officer's room was damaged, and the first heavy oil transfer pump and air vents on the upper deck were destroyed. Fragments had scarred the barbette armor around the base of turret one. No flooding was caused by the hits, and overall damage was considered light.[615]

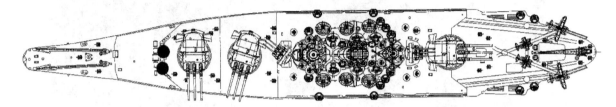

Figure 62. Location of bomb hits October 26, 1944 on the *Yamato*

By 1041, the *Yamato* spotted twenty-seven B-24 bombers bearing 220°. At 1053, the *Yamato* swung to a new course of 170° and opened fire. Then at 1055, bombs dropped close to the battleship's starboard side. Fragments wounded Rear Admiral Koyanagi in his waist and caused casualties to exposed crewmen topside. The ship was shaken by the shock waves from the bombs and suffered severe vibrations; however, no bombs hit the ship.[616]

The forward 6.1-inch turret's thermal insulation panel was penetrated by eighteen fragments, and the turret's gun shield by fourteen fragments; the starboard barrel was scarred by nine fragments, and barbette structure by twelve fragments. The aft 6.1-inch gun shield suffered three fragment penetrations. The first searchlight and mirror was destroyed. The outer hull was penetrated on the starboard side in six places above the waterline.[617]

ON BOARD THE *NAGATO*

Rear Admiral Kobe ordered a speed increase to twenty-five knots at 0757, and at 0812 his lookouts reported five dive bombers to port bearing 50° relative, distance 21,920 yards. Then at 0832, more U.S. aircraft appeared to starboard at 80° relative and a distance of 38,360 yards. By 0835, Kobe ordered his main battery to open fire, and by 0836 his secondary battery joined the action. Then at 0840, three dive bombers approached, and her light machine guns opened fire. Two aircraft attacked from the starboard bow, resulting in two near-miss bombs off the port bow. At 0850, five more bombers approached which resulted in two near-miss bombs off her starboard quarter. By 0910, the attack was over, and she checked fire. At 1033, a flight of thirty-seven B-24 bombers was

---

[615] Ibid.

[616] Ibid.

[617] Ibid.

detected bearing 40° to starboard. Kobe ordered speed increased to twenty-five knots at 1035 and prepared for AA action by 1040. At 1041, the fleet turned to a course of 150°, and Kobe ordered his main battery to open fire on the bomber formation. The U.S. formation split, and a group of nineteen aircraft approached the *Nagato*. At 1058, the *Nagato*'s anti-aircraft battery opened fire, and at 1104 her main battery fired another salvo. The *Nagato* herself did not come under attack from the B-24 bombers which concentrated on the *Yamato* and the *Haruna*. At 1105, he ordered his gunners to check fire. For the *Nagato*, the Battle of Leyte Gulf was over.[618]

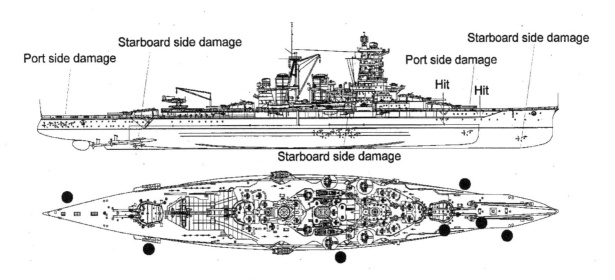

Figure 63. Battle damage to the *Kongo* after three days' fighting.

ON BOARD THE *KONGO*

Rear Admiral Shimazaki reported sighting two U.S. aircraft bearing 090° at 0756. By 0757, the ship's course was 200° with a speed of twenty-four knots. Air alerts were sounded, and at 0758, he gave word to open fire. The *Kongo* wasn't directly attacked, but she witnessed U.S. aircraft falling at 0810, 0834, and 0855. Shimazaki had increased speed during the action to twenty-six knots. By 1047, a group of B-24 bombers was sighted, and the *Kongo* opened fire at 1053. Shimazaki ordered flank speed, and the *Kongo* reached twenty-nine knots at 1100. His ship didn't become a target of the heavy bombers, and by 1145 he reduced speed to twenty-four knots. After three days fighting she had taken two direct hits on the starboard bow and severe fragmentation of her outer hull which flooded several void tanks within her torpedo defense system.[619]

---

[618] *Nagato* Detailed Action Report.

[619] *Kongo* Detailed Action Report.

ON BOARD THE *HARUNA*

Rear Admiral Shigenaga reported spotting five U.S. aircraft at 0753, and air alerts were sounded. He ordered the main guns to open fire at 0800, but then the fleet was ordered to make a turn to 030° true, so the main battery was then ordered to stand by. Shigenaga increased speed to twenty-seven knots. By 0812, her main battery opened fire. As the fleet turned, speed was reduced to twenty-six knots and then twenty knots by 0825. Thirty enemy aircraft approached bearing 68° with an altitude angle of 10° by 0830. At 0835, speed was increased to twenty-seven knots and at 0836 another salvo was unleashed from her main battery, and speed was then reduced to twenty-six knots.[620]

By 0854, ten U.S. aircraft attacked bearing 70° to port. Three of these planes dropped torpedoes, and Shigenaga ordered a hard turn to port. The three torpedoes passed down the starboard side of the ship, and one of the attacking aircraft was hit. By 0913 *Haruna* checked fire.[621]

At 1030, another large U.S. formation was sighted bearing 028°, and air alerts were sounded again. Shigenaga ordered her absolute maximum speed or No. 6 battle speed which would normally be twenty-nine to thirty knots.[622] At 1034, his lookouts reported twenty-two aircraft bearing 50° with an altitude angle of 4°. The *Haruna* engaged the aircraft at this time. The fleet turned to 140° at 1040, and by 1045 the anti-aircraft guns opened fire. Her lookouts now recognized the planes as B-24 bombers, and they split into several groups by 1056. Seven bombers led a second group of six bombers, and these headed for the *Haruna*. Shigenaga ordered a hard turn to starboard, and the B-24 bombers released their bombs at an altitude of 11,500 feet. Six of the bombs landed close on her port side, but none scored a direct hit. At 1118, Shigenaga ordered his guns to stand by, and by 1153 she checked fire. The *Haruna*, despite many near misses, came through the battle relatively unscathed.[623]

ON BOARD THE *HAGURO*

Captain Sugiura sounded air alerts at 0758 and by 0800 opened fire on the incoming U.S. air raid. Initially, the *Haguro* wasn't attacked, but at 0855 a single U.S. plane launched an attack that resulted in a near-miss bomb on her port side. By 0912, she checked fire. From 1035 to 1107, she engaged the B-24 aircraft, but she herself wasn't a target for these aircraft.[624]

---

[620] *Haruna* Detailed Action Report.

[621] Ibid.

[622] The actual speed she attained at this moment was not listed in her report.

[623] *Haruna* Detailed Action Report.

[624] *Haguro* Detailed Action Report.

ON BOARD THE *KUMANO*

The *Kumano* attempted to withdraw and was attacked at 0810 by twelve F6F, four SB2C, and seven TBM-1c aircraft, suffering three additional bomb hits. One bomb exploded near the base of the bridge on the port side. Two bombs detonated amidships near her funnel, placing seven out of eight boiler rooms out of commission. She slowed to a dead stop. Three more air attacks were repelled by using every gun she had, including her main battery. By 1000, she could make ten knots and arrived at Coron Bay at 1627 on 27 October. The destroyer *Okinami* with the rescued crew of the *Suzuya* on board made it safely to Coron Bay also arriving on 27 October.[625]

Figure 129: The *Kumano* under attack 26 October 1944.

ON BOARD THE *NOSHIRO*

Captain Kajiwara's ship was on course 220° with a speed of twenty knots at 0725 on the morning of October 26. At 0750, he prepared his ship for AA action. The first enemy aircraft were detected, bearing 020° at a distance of 16,440 yards. He ordered an increase in speed to twenty-four knots at 0759. Additional, U.S. aircraft were detected, bearing 350° at a distance of 32,880 yards at 0817. By 0845, the battle was joined, and both her main and anti-aircraft guns opened fire. At 0846, she took a direct hit from a bomb near turret two that set the ship on fire. At 0847, her lookouts sighted incoming torpedoes on the port bow. At 0852, one torpedo scored, immediately flooding No.1 and No. 3 boiler rooms, and by 0857 she had taken a 16° list to port.[626]

---

[625] Lacroix and Wells, *Japanese Cruisers of the Pacific War,* pp 498-501.
[626] *Noshiro* Detailed Action Report.

The crew attempted to control the flooding, but No. 2 boiler room progressively flooded by 0920, and then by 0937 the port engine room flooded, and the list grew to 29° by 1004. All power was lost at this time. Captain Kajiwara called for the destroyer *Hamanami* to come alongside and transfer Rear Admiral Hayakawa. As this was occurring he ordered counter-flooding of starboard compartments which corrected the list to 8° by 1030.[627]

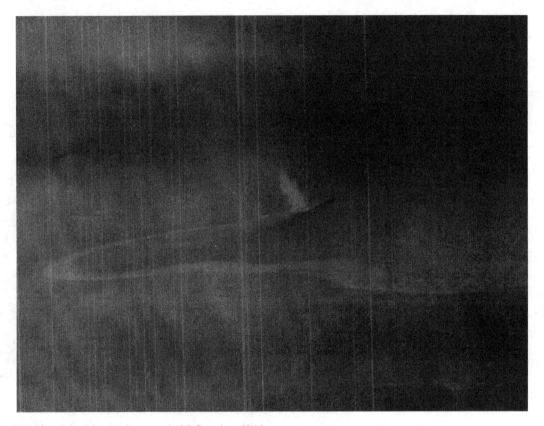

Figure 130: The *Noshiro* under attack 26 October 1944.

The next wave of U.S. aircraft appeared at 1031, and the crippled *Noshiro* opened fire with everything she had left. At 1033, a near-miss bomb exploded alongside; at 1345.5 a torpedo passed her port bow, but a second torpedo hit her abreast turret two at 1039. At 1040, one U.S. aircraft was seen to fall, and three more at 1045, but the *Noshiro* quickly settled by the bow so that by 1100 she was down 10° by the head. Kajiwara understood his ship was sinking, and she only had a few minutes left. He ordered his crew to abandon ship, and at 1106 and her bow slipped beneath the surface. By 1113, she sank, and the destroyers *Hamanami* and the *Akishimo* rescued 328 men; Captain Kajiwara wasn't among them.[628]

---

[627] Ibid.

[628] Ibid.

ON BOARD THE *YAMATO*

Admiral Kurita received word that the *Noshiro* had been attacked again and sunk at 1113. Kurita at the moment didn't realize he had just suffered the last U.S. attack on his force. For him the Battle of Leyte Gulf was now over. Ships that were lagging behind took the brunt of the U.S. air attacks on 26 October. The *Hayashimo* was found south of Mindoro and sunk with a torpedo hit. The destroyer *Fujinami* with the rescued crew of the *Chokai* on board was also sunk off Mindoro. Kurita would send five of his last seven destroyers to refuel at Coron Bay, and his battleships, cruisers, and two destroyers re-entered Brunei Bay on 28 October at 2130.[629]

In an article written after the war, Koyanagi recorded, "On October 26, the air raids against Kurita's force ended around 1100. As on the day before, we expected to be attacked all day long. We had not the least expectation that the enemy would suspend his raids an hour before noon. Perhaps it was because we had pulled out of combat range of the enemy carrier task force.[630]

"Our greatest concern was that the enemy, following up his successes, might pursue us westward through San Bernardino Strait and into the Sibuyan Sea or Sulu Sea and launch annihilating air strikes. American reluctance to give all-out pursuit is perhaps justified by some strategic concept that advocates prudence and step by step procedures; but from the Japanese point of view, the Americans gave up pursuit all too soon. Analyzing the whole course of events of this battle, we see that chance played a definite role in each part of the action and thus influenced the whole. As in all things, so in the field of battle, none can tell when or where the breaks will come. Thus, events and their consequences were often determined by some hairbreadth chance in which the human factor has no control at all. Chance can make the victor of one moment into the vanquished of the next."[631]

---

[629] *Yamato* Detailed Action Report.

[630] Evans, David, *The Japanese Navy in World War II*, pp 355-384.

[631] Ibid.

Figure 131: The *Suwannee* was hit on the bow by a kamikaze from the Yamato Unit out from Cebu at 1240 on 26 October 1944.

Figure 132: The *Suwannee* burning on 26 October 1944.

ON BOARD THE *SANGAMON*

On the morning of 26 October Thomas Sprague received a report from *Hazelwood* that she had sighted a periscope bearing 009° at 0750. He immediately ordered a 90° emergency turn for the entire formation, and the *Hazelwood* attacked the submarine contact. At 0825, a strike of thirteen fighters and five torpedo planes was launched against reported Japanese crippled ships in the Visayan Sea. Then at 0833, *Rowell* reported a submarine sound contact bearing 009° and immediately attacked. *Rowell* sighted a periscope again at 0900 and made a second attack and stayed with the contact. Then at 0910, enemy aircraft were reported over Homonhon Island. *Hazelwood* was ordered to rejoin the formation at 1030. *Rowell* reported sinking a submarine, oil bubbling up; pieces of deck plating were recovered at 1055.[632]

At 1200, local CAP shot down four Zekes, but by 1230 eight to twelve enemy aircraft attacked TU 77.4.1. At 1240 a dive bomber crashed *Suwannee* on forward elevator, setting fire to three or four planes and extensively damaging the flight deck and bridge with fire. Two more aircraft attempted to hit *Sangamon* and *Petrof Bay* but were beaten off by the ships AA guns while the other Japanese aircraft were shot down by the task-units fighters. Thomas Sprague ordered *Coolbaugh* to pick up crewmen from *Suwannee* that had been blown overboard and *Trathen* to stand by the wounded ship while the others recover aircraft. By 1300, *Suwannee* reported she could make five knots, and then by 1318 she reported her fires were out, and she could make eighteen knots. Between 1325 and 1345 there were many air alerts, but landing operations were over, and Thomas Sprague turned the formation onto a course which would return his force to the *Suwannee's* location. Several returning

---

[632] CTU 77.4 Action Report.

aircraft crashed in the water, which required screening destroyers to pick up the pilots. No more air attacks were launched on the Japanese, and no more Japanese attacks were made on Taffy 1.[633]

ON BOARD THE *NATOMA BAY*

Felix Stump's Taffy 2 was farther to the south than its normal operational area as a result of the retirement during the night. He planned to work his way north due to reports of enemy submarines in the current operational area. Strikes were ordered to be launched on the crippled Japanese ships in the Visayan Sea. There were no attacks made on Taffy 2, but Stump was aware that Taffy 1 had come under attack. By the afternoon his destroyers were low on fuel, so Felix Stump retired his force to the northeast.[634]

WITH THE CREW OF *GAMBIER BAY*

At 0900, the survivors of the *Gambier Bay* spotted two U.S. planes approximately five miles to the east. Red and green star-shells were fired, and dye markers thrown in the water, but the planes failed to see any of it and continued on a northerly course. At 0945 two (possibly the same) planes were seen on a southerly course, but all attempts to attract their attention failed. The currents were spreading the groups apart. From time to time several groups would sight each other and closed to within hailing distance. The morning turned to afternoon and then dusk. As night fell, there was still no sign of rescue.[635]

WITH THE CREW OF *HOEL*

The crew of the *Hoel* reported getting the attention of at least three American aircraft while in the water, but no rescue was forthcoming. Forty men died while waiting rescue, and Cdr. Kintberger reported if the men had stayed in the water another twenty-four hours there would've been no survivors.[636]

WITH THE CREW OF *SAMUEL B. ROBERTS*

The crew of the *Samuel B. Roberts* saw two formations of friendly aircraft on the morning of the 26th, but there was no evidence that they sighted the men in the water. The men that were adrift in twos and threes using empty powder cans as floats were missing. Morale was low as the men saw no

---

[633] Ibid.
[634] CTU 77.4.2 Action Report.
[635] *Gambier Bay* Action Report.
[636] *Hoel* Action Report.

attempt to rescue them for a second day as night fell. Cdr. Copeland wasn't hopeful any men would survive if they were not found within the next twenty-four hours.[637]

WITH THE CREW OF *JOHNSTON*

Lt. Hagan saw thirty-five men die within his group awaiting rescue. At one point he fell asleep and drifted away from the raft. Luckily he awoke in time and had enough strength to swim back to the raft. Cdr. Evans at some point disappeared, and he was never rescued. After three days and two nights in the water, the men saw *PC-623* approach; 141 men were saved. William Shaw and Orin Vadnais were saved after four days and three nights in the water, the last *Johnston* crewmen to be rescued.[638]

ON BOARD THE *PC-623*

Lt. Cdr. Baxter didn't arrive at the reported position of the men in the water until 0830 on 26 October. He formed a line abreast formation with one mile between ships and headed north and then south for 25-mile sweeps heading westward with each sweep. Nothing was found all day. The sun went down, but the search continued. Then at 2229, Baxter's ships sighted star-shells eighteen to twenty miles west of their position. They immediately headed for the area and by 0000 on 27 October had found the survivors from the *Gambier Bay*.[639]

Rescue operations immediately commenced, and the small fleet picked up approximately 700 survivors from the *Gambier Bay* by 0430. The men had drifted over thirty miles to the west during the time they were in the water. After survivors from the *Gambier Bay* were picked up, the search continued. At 0745, more rafts were spotted, and the first survivors from the *Samuel B. Roberts* were rescued. By 0845, more rafts were spotted, and men from *Hoel* were discovered. Lastly by 0930, fifteen men from the *Johnston* were sighted, and the first men rescued from this ship. At 1000, Lt. Cdr. Baxter had taken on board his seven ships 1,150 men and headed for San Pedro Bay where he would arrive at 0113 on 28 October to transfer the wounded to hospital ships and transports.[640]

201ST AIR GROUP LOCATED AT MABALACAT NEAR MANILA

Vice Admiral Onishi in command of the First Air Fleet met with Vice Admiral Fukudome in command of the Second Air Fleet for a third time late in the evening of 25 October. Reports for the past two days showed that thirteen aircraft using the kamikaze tactics had sunk two carriers and a

---

[637] Samuel B. Roberts Action Report.

[638] Hagen, "We Asked for the Jap Fleet—and Got It."

[639] CTU 77 Action Report.

[640] Ibid.

cruiser and heavily damaged at least four other carriers,[641] compared to the 250 aircraft using conventional attacks that had sunk only the light carrier *Princeton*. Onishi argued that the evidence was quite conclusive, and that special attacks were their only hope. Fukudome conceded the effectiveness of these tactics but was still reluctant to adopt them. The meeting went through the night, and at 0200 on 26 October Fukudome finally agreed to adopt kamikaze attacks for the Second Air Fleet. The adoption of these tactics shifted Japan's dwindling fuel reserves away from the fleet, so the Battle of Leyte Gulf would be the last time that the Imperial Japanese Navy would sortie in strength. The only other fleet operation would be a suicide mission led by the *Yamato* and the light cruiser *Yahagi* during the Okinawa campaign, which resulted in the loss of both ships on 7 April 1945.[642]

EPILOGUE

The celebration of American fighting spirit at Samar centers on Taffy 3's ability to confront and survive an onslaught by an apparently overwhelming force, but Clifton Sprague's little task unit didn't emerge from the fight looking like a triumphant champion. Taffy 3 had five out of six carriers sunk or so badly damaged they had to withdraw immediately. The *White Plains* and the *Kalinin Bay* would never see combat operations again. The *Fanshaw Bay* would not return until the Okinawa campaign. Only the *Kitkun Bay* remained in the operational theater after the battle. Of the seven escorts, three were sunk, and two so severely damaged as to force their withdrawal, leaving only two destroyer escorts in condition to continue operations.

Taffy 1 also suffered heavily due to land-based air attack. *Suwannee* and *Santee* were forced to withdraw after the battle. Including crash landings and write-offs, the Seventh Fleet lost 128 aircraft during 25-26 October: fifty-one FM-2 fighters, twenty-one F6F fighters, and fifty-six TBM torpedo planes. The Taffies suffered 43 airmen killed and 9 wounded. Of the shipboard crews, Taffy 3 lost 792 men killed or missing and 768 men wounded; Taffy 1 had 283 killed or missing and 136 wounded. Pilots from TG 38.1 suffered 12 killed. Total U.S. losses for the Battle off Samar reached 1,130 killed or missing and 913 wounded. It was known that 116 men were seen in the water alive that were never rescued.[643]

The Japanese side of the ledger is a bit confused since most of the ships lost by Kurita went down either before or after the surface battle of 25 October. Total casualties can only be estimated as some ships' records were lost and some ships went down with their entire crews.

---

[641] The inaccurate number of U.S. ships sunk or damaged came from the Japanese reports given to Vice Admiral Onishi, and this represented his perception at the time he made his argument for Vice Admiral Fukudome to adopt kamikaze tactics.

[642] Inoguchi, Rikihei; Nakajima Tadashi; and Roger Pineau. *The Divine Wind*. Bantam Books, 1958, pp 74-76.

[643] CTU 77 Action Report.

Yamato: 33 killed, 95 wounded

Musashi: 1,023 killed[644]

Nagato: 38 killed, 105 wounded

Kongo: 12 killed, 36 wounded

Haruna: no casualties listed

Atago: 350 killed

Takao: 33 killed

Maya: 336 killed[645]

Chokai: lost with all hands, approximately 773 men

Haguro: 30 killed

Myoko: casualties not listed[646]

Kumano: losses unknown[647]

Suzuya: approximately 230 killed

Tone: 19 killed

Chikuma: lost with all hands, approximately 850 men

Noshiro: approximately 402 killed

Yahagi: reported 80 killed or wounded

Nowaki and *Fujinami*: lost with all hands, approximately 230 men each

Hayashimo: 110 killed

Okinami: 34 killed

The casualties totaled approximately 5,049 men killed or wounded from 23 October to 26 October 1944.[648]

---

[644] The *Musashi* was lost 24 October in the Sibuyan Sea.

[645] *Atago*, *Takao*, and *Maya* were torpedoed at Palawan Passage 23 October by the U.S. submarines *Darter* and *Dace*. *Atago* and *Maya* were sunk. *Takao* was heavily damaged but made it back to Singapore. *Darter* eventually run aground while in pursuit of *Takao* and had to be scuttled.

[646] *Myoko* was torpedoed on 24 October by U.S. aircraft and forced to withdraw. She made it back to Brunei.

[647] *Kumano*'s detailed action report for the Battle off Samar was missing though her final report when she was sunk in November 1944 did come to light.

Circumstances conspired against Kurita. Poor visibility throughout the action severely handicapped Japanese naval gunnery; smoke screens and rain squalls made a sustained rate of fire on any one target impossible. At the same time, the resultant "fog of war" gave Japanese commanders a false perception of events. This played to the advantage of the underdog Americans.

Nevertheless, Japanese battleships played a much greater role off Samar than what is depicted in most battle histories. The *Yamato* contributed to the loss of *Gambier Bay*, *Johnston*, and *Hoel* and inflicted serious damage on the *White Plains*. The *Haruna* damaged *Kalinin Bay* as well as *Gambier Bay*. The *Nagato* contributed to the destruction of the *Hoel*. The *Kongo* played a role in *Heermann*'s damage and the sinking of *Samuel B. Roberts*.

The tactical scoreboard mattered little amid the strategic outcome of the overall Battle of Leyte Gulf. The Americans retained sea control, though the failure in command unity prevented the battle of annihilation Nimitz was hoping for. A significant portion of Japan's battle fleet remained available, but to no purpose; exhausted fuel reserves stole its ability to operate.

In war, mistakes are normal and should be expected. Rarely if ever are the commanders' perceptions completely accurate. Concerning why Kurita broke off his attack on the American carriers, Rear Admiral T. Koyanagi wrote, "After the war I was astonished to learn that our quarry had been only six escort carriers, three destroyers, and four destroyer escorts, and that the maximum speed of these carriers was only eighteen knots. Giving up pursuit when we did amounted to losing a prize already in hand. If we had known the types and number of enemy ships, and their speed, Kurita would never have suspended the pursuit, and we would've annihilated the enemy. Lacking this vital information, we concluded that the enemy had already made good his escape."[649]

In an interview with Masanori Ito, Kurita explained his turn to the north. "At the time I believed it was the best thing to do. In thinking about it since that time, I have concluded that my decision may have been wrong. I had been given orders and, as a military man, I should have carried them out. As I consider it now, my judgment does not seem to have been sound. Then the decision seemed right, but my mind was extremely fatigued. It should probably be called a judgment of exhaustion. I didn't feel tired at the time but under great strain and without sleep for three days and nights, I was exhausted both physically and mentally."[650]

But had Kurita made the wrong choice? Continued pursuit of Taffy 3 would merely have aggravated the destruction of a task unit that was already operationally wrecked, and while it would have tallied more American deaths, it would also have increased Kurita's exposure to subsequent

---

[648] Casualties come from various ships detailed action reports or from crew complement of various ship classes. Unless specifically reported by the detailed action report, the casualties are only estimated.

[649] Evans David, *The Japanese Navy in World War II*, pp 355-384.

[650] Ito, *The End of the Japanese Navy*, pp 165-166.

attacks while offering no prospects for strategic gain. Kurita accepted a gamble by seeking an unspecified enemy, but at least he kept intact the principle of tying a strategic goal to a decisive battle, as his training demanded. His exhausted mind overlooked that the reports of a U.S. task force to the north were unconfirmed, and any such enemy would be difficult if not impossible to locate. He found encouragement in the fact that Vice Admiral Willis Lee, the commander of the U.S. battleline, would also be looking for him. Ironically, Kurita was correct; Halsey and Lee had turned back south to engage him, but the distance separating the two fleets was far greater than Kurita ever imagined.

On the American side, Halsey had his own misperceptions, rooted in overly optimistic reports of the damage his airmen had inflicted on Kurita in the Sibuyan Sea. Despite the approximately 250 aircraft sorties that took place, Kurita's force was almost entirely intact.

After the battle, Vice Admiral Halsey sent message 251317 to Admiral Nimitz concerning his action's and decisions. He said, "That there be no misunderstanding concerning recent operations of the Third Fleet, I inform you as follows: To obtain information of Jap plans and movements became vital on 23 October so three carrier groups were moved into the Philippine coast off Polillo, San Bernardino and Surigao to search as far west as possible. On 24 October the Third Fleet searches revealed Jap forces moving east through the Sibuyan and Sulu Seas and both of those forces were brought under attack by Third Fleet air strikes. The existence of a Jap plan for coordinated attack was apparent but the objective was not sure and the expected carrier force was missing from the picture. Third Fleet carrier searches revealed the presence of the enemy carrier force on the afternoon of 24 October, completing the picture.[651]

"To statically guard San Bernardino Strait until enemy surface and carrier air attacks could be coordinated would have been childish, so three carrier groups were concentrated during the night and started north for a surprise dawn attack on the enemy carrier fleet. I considered that the enemy forces in Sibuyan Sea had been so badly damaged that they constituted no serious threat to Kinkaid and that estimate has been borne out by the events of the 25th off Surigao. The enemy carrier force was caught off guard, there being no air opposition over the target and no air attack against our force. Their air groups were apparently shore based and arrived too late to land on their carriers or get into flight.[652]

"I had projected surface striking units ahead of our carriers in order to coordinate surface and air attacks against the enemy. Commander Seventh Fleet's urgent appeals for help came at a time when the enemy force was heavily damaged and my overwhelming surface striking force was within forty-five miles of the enemy cripples. I had no alternative but to break off my golden opportunity and

---

[651] CTU 38 Action Report.

[652] Ibid.

head south to support Kinkaid although I was convinced that his force was adequate to deal with the enemy force that was badly weakened by our attacks of the twenty-fourth—a conviction justified by later events off Leyte."[653] Halsey never admitted to making any mistake and said that, if he had to do everything again, he would have made the same choices.[654]

Vice Admiral Kinkaid's interpretation of the orders from Nimitz for KING II differed dramatically from Halsey's. In 1960 in an oral interview Kinkaid said, "As Commander of the Seventh Fleet, I was to transport the landing forces to Leyte Gulf beaches, establish them ashore, and see that they were covered and stayed ashore. The Third Fleet under Halsey was to give us protection during the landing and during whatever actions might take place afterwards. His was a strategic cover; mine was a direct cover and the protection of the landing forces. It's a very important point that I have brought out frequently, because I had a mission and Admiral Halsey had a mission. In spite of the fact that we did not have a common superior, I have frequently said that if both Halsey and I had carried out our respective missions correctly there would have been no confusion…. It has always been my opinion … that one commander would not have been better than two where each of us had a mission … very clearly stated."[655]

In a top-secret message to Admiral King dated 28 October 1944, Admiral Nimitz expressed two regrets. The first dealt with the loss of the light carrier *Princeton* on 24 October. Concerning the Battle off Samar, Nimitz said, "My second exception and regret is that the fast battleships were not left in the vicinity of Samar when Task Force 38 started after the striking force reported to be in the north end of the Philippine Sea, and composed of carriers, two battleships, cruisers and destroyers in support. It never occurred to me that Halsey, knowing the composition of the ships in the Sibuyan Sea, would leave San Bernardino Strait unguarded, even though the Jap detachment in the Sibuyan Sea had been reported seriously damaged. That Halsey feels that he is in a defensive position is indicated in his top secret dispatch 251317.[656]

"That the San Bernardino detachment of the Japanese Fleet, which included the *Yamato* and the *Musashi*, did not completely destroy all of the escort carriers and their accompanying screen is nothing short of special dispensation from the Lord Almighty; although it can be accepted that the damage the Japs had received the day before in the Sibuyan Sea undoubtedly affected their ability to steam and shoot when they attacked Sprague's escort carriers."[657]

---

[653] Ibid.

[654] Ibid.

[655] Wheeler, Gerald E. *Kinkaid of the Seventh Fleet*. Naval Institute Press, 1995, p 406.

[656] Potter, E. B. *Nimitz*. Naval Institute Press, 1976, p 344.

[657] Ibid.

The three-word padding left at the end of Nimitz's signal regarding TF 34—"The World Wonders"—was prophetic. The mistakes that prevented Kurita and Halsey from coming to blows denied them and the world the opportunity to see the world's mightiest battleships locked in decisive combat. An account of the Battle off Samar, told as accurately as it can be, still leaves the world wondering what might have been. And this is the way it will always be.

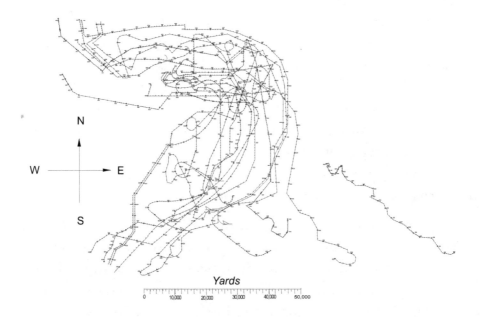

Figure 133: The fog of war. The tangled mass formed by the combined Japanese and American track chart of the Battle off Samar illustrates the confusion confronting the commanders there.

BIBLIOGRAPHY

PRIMARY DOCUMENTATION

Commander Reports:

Third Fleet

Vice Admiral William F. Halsey, CTU 38, Action Report, November 13, RG 38

Rear Admiral Gerald Francis Bogan, CTU 38.2, Action Report, November 8, 1944, RG 38

Rear Admiral Frederick C. Sherman, CTU 38.3, Action Report, November 15, 1944, RG 38

Rear Admiral Ralph Eugene Davison, CTU 38.4, Action Report, November 12, 1944, RG 38

Seventh Fleet

Vice Admiral Thomas Kinkaid, CTU 77 Action Report, January 31, 1945, RG 38

Rear Admiral Jesse Oldendorf, CTU 77.2, Action Report, December 6, 1944, RG 38

Rear Admiral Thomas Sprague, CTU 77.4 Action Report, November 8, 1944, RG 38

Rear Admiral Felix Stump, CTU 77.4.2 Action Report, November 2, 1944, RG 38

Rear Admiral Clifton Sprague, CTU 77.4.3, Action Report, October 29, 1944, RG 38

U.S. Ship Reports:

Dennis Action Report, November 5, 1944, RG 38

Enterprise Action Report, November 3, 1944

Fanshaw Bay Action Report, November 2, 1944, RG 38

Franks Action Report, November 3, 1944, RG 38

Gambier Bay Action Report, November 27, 1944, RG 38

Haggard Action Report, November 3, 1944, RG 38

Hailey Action Report, October 31, 1944, RG 38

Heermann Action Report, November 2, 1944, RG 38

Hoel Action Report, November 15, 1944, RG 38

Iowa, Action Report, November 1, 1944, RG 38

John C Butler Action Report, November 9, 1944, RG 38

Johnston Action Report, November 14, 1944, RG 38

Kadashan Bay, Action Report, October 31, 1944, RG 38

Kalinin Bay Action Report, October 30, 1944, RG 38

Kitkun Bay Action Report, October 28, 1944, RG 38

Lexington, Action Report, November 22, 1944, RG 38

Louisville, Action Report, November 7, 1944, RG 38

Manila Bay Action Report, November 2, 1944, RG 39

Marcus Island Action Report, November 1, 1944 RG 38

Miller, Action Report, October 28, 1944, RG 38

Natoma Bay Action Report, November 1, 1944, RG 38

New Jersey Action Report, November 3, 1944, RG 38

Ommaney Bay Action Report, November 3, 1944, RG 38

Owen, Action Report, October 28, 1944, RG 38

Petrof Bay Action Report, November 28, 1944, RG 38

Raymond Action Report, November 2, 1944, RG 38

Samuel B Roberts Action Report, November 20, 1944, RG 38

Sangamon Action Report, November 4, 1944, RG 38

Santa Fe, Action Report, November 15, 1944, RG 38

Santee Action Report, November 5, 1944, RG 38

Savo Island Action Report, November 3, 1944, RG 38

St. Lo Action Report, November 23, 1944, RG 38

Suwannee Action Report, November 6, 1944, RG 38

Vincennes, Action Report, November 2, 1944, RG 38

Wasatch, Action Report, November 6, 1944, RG 38

White Plains Action Report, October 27, 1944, RG 38

U.S. AIR-GROUP REPORTS

Air Group-19, *Lexington*, Commander T. H. Winters, RG 38

Air Group-26, *Santee*, Lt. Commander H. N. Funk, RG 38

Air Group-37, *Sangamon*, Lt. Commander S. E. Hindman, RG 38

Air Group-60, *Suwannee*, Lt. Commander H. O. Feilbach, RG 38

Composite Squadron VC-3, *Kalinin Bay*, Lt. Commander W. H. Keighley, RG 38

Composite Squadron VC-4, *White Plains*, Lt. E. R. Fickenscher, RG 38

Composite Squadron VC-5, *Kitkun Bay*, Commander R. L. Fowler, RG 38

Composite Squadron VC-10, *Gambier Bay*, Lt. Commander E. J. Huxtable, RG 38

Composite Squadron VC-20, *Kadashan Bay*, Lt. Commander J. R. Dale, RG 38

Composite Squadron VC-21, *Marcus Island*, Lt. Commander T. O. Murray, RG 38

Composite Squadron VC-27, *Savo Island*, Lt. Commander P. W. Jackson, RG 38

Composite Squadron VC-65, *St. Lo*, Lt. Commander R. M. Jones, RG 38

Composite Squadron VC-68, *Fanshaw Bay*, Lt. Commander R. S. Rodgers, RG 38

Composite Squadron VC-75, *Ommaney Bay*, Lt. A. W. Smith, RG 38

Composite Squadron VC-76, *Petrof Bay*, Commander J. W. McCauley, RG 38

Composite Squadron VC-80, *Manila Bay*, Lt. Commander H. K. Stubbs, RG 38

Composite Squadron VC-81, *Natoma Bay*, Lt. Commander R. C. Barnes, RG 38

JAPANESE PRIMARY DOCUMENTATION

Combined Fleet Headquarters Detailed Action Report. _ (17 October to 28 October 1944):

First Battleship Division Detailed Action Report. _ (17 October to 28 October 1944):

Haguro Detailed Action Report. _ (23 October to 26 October 1944):

Haruna Detailed Action Report. _ (24 October to 26 October 1944):

Kishinami Destroyer Division 31 Detailed Action Report. _ (24 October to 26 October 1944):

Kongo Detailed Action Report. _ (22 October to 28 October 1944):

Musashi Detailed Action Report. _ (24 October 1944):

Myoko Detailed Action Report. _ (24 October to 25 October 1944):

Nagato Detailed Action Report. _ (24 October to 26 October 1944):

Noshiro Detailed Action Report. _ (23 October to 26 October 1944):

Suzuya Detailed Action Report. _ (24 October to 25 October 1944):

Tone Detailed Action Report. _ (24 October to 26 October 1944):

Yahagi Detailed Action Report. _ (22 October to 28 October 28 1944):

Yamato Detailed Action Report. _ (17 October to 28 October 1944):

FEDERAL SOURCES

Captain W. V. R. Vieweg's transcript of the Battle of Samar, taken December 18, 1944, Office of Naval Records and Library.

Dictionary of American Naval Fighting Ships, Navy Department, Office of the Chief of Naval Operations, Naval History Division, Washington DC 1959

Bureau of Ships, Navy Department, War Damage Report No. 51, Section IV, Loss of the *Johnston,* January 25, 1947

Bureau of Ordnance OP 1667, JAPANESE EXPLOSIVE ORDNANCE

United States Strategic Bombing Survey (Pacific) *The Campaigns of the Pacific War* Naval Analysis Division, 1946, *XII Philippine Campaign*, pages 280-323

United States Strategic Bombing Survey (Pacific). *Interrogations of Japanese Officials.* OPNAV-P-03-100. Naval Analysis Division.

- Fukudome, Shigeru, Vice Admiral IJN, Interrogation Nav. No. 115, USSBS No. 583
- Koyanagi, Tomiji, Rear Admiral IJN, , Interrogation Nav. No. 35 USSBS No. 149
- Kurita, Takeo, Vice Admiral IJN, Interrogation Nav. No. 9, USSBS No. 47
- Otani, Tonosuke, Commander IJN, Interrogation Nav. No 41, USSBS No. 170
- Toyoda Soemu, Admiral IJN, Interrogation Nav. No. 75 USSBS No. 378

Combat Narratives of specific naval campaigns produced by the Publications Branch of the Office of Naval Intelligence during World War II.

- Naval Battle of Leyte Gulf

- Lessons Learned From the Naval Battle of Leyte Gulf

Technical Mission to Japan, Index No. S-06-3 Ships and related targets, Reports of damage to Japanese warships, Japanese records of major warship losses.

PUBLISHED SOURCES

Asada, Sadao. From Mahan to Pearl Harbor: The Imperial Japanese Navy and the United States. Naval Institute Press, 2006.

Campbell, John. *Naval Weapons of World War Two.* Conway Maritime Press, 1985.

Corbett, Julian S., *Principles of Maritime Strategy*, London, 1911

Drea, Edward J., *In the Service of the Emperor*, University of Nebraska Press, 1998

Dull, Paul S. A Battle History of the Imperial Japanese Navy 1941-1945. Naval Institute Press, 1978.

Evans, David C. (ed.). *The Japanese Navy in World War II.* Naval Institute Press, 1986.

Fukudome Shigeru pages 334-354

Koyanagi, Tomji pages 355-384

Inoguchi, Rikihei pages 415 to 439

Nakajima, Tadashi pages 415 to 439

Nomura, Minoru pages 278 to 333

———————— and Mark R. Peattie. *Kaigun.* Naval Institute Press, 1997.

Field, James A. *The Japanese at Leyte Gulf*, Princeton University Press, 1947

Fuller, Richard, *Japanese Admirals*, Schiffer LTD. 2011

Goldstein, Donald M. and Katherine V. Dillon (eds.) *The Pacific War Papers: Japanese Documents of World War II.* Potomac Books Inc., 2004.

Hoyt, Edwin P. The Battle of Leyte Gulf: The Death Knell of the Japanese Fleet. Weybright and Talley, 1972.

———————, *The Men of the Gambier Bay*, The Lyons Press, 1979

Inoguchi, Rikihei, Nakajima Tadashi and Rodger Pineau, *The Divine Wind*, Bantam Books, 1958

Ito, Masanori, *The End of the Japanese Navy*, W. W. Norton & Company INC. 1956

Lacroix, Eric and Linton Wells II. *Japanese Cruisers of the Pacific War.* Naval Institute Press, 1997.

Mahan, Alfred T., *The Influence of Sea Power upon History 1660-1783*, Little Brown, and Company, Boston, 1890

_____., *Sea power in its relations to the war of 1812*, Little Brown, and Company, Boston, 1919 Volume 1

Marder, Arthur, J. *Old Friends and New Enemies*, Clarendon Press, Oxford, 1981

Morison, Samuel Eliot, *Leyte June 1944-January 1945*, University of Illinois Press, 1958

_____, *The Two Ocean War*, Atlantic Monthly Press , 1963

Potter, E. B., *Bull Halsey*, Naval Institute Press, 1985

_____., *Nimitz*, Naval Institute Press, 1976

Raven, Alan, *Fletcher-Class Destroyers*, Naval Institute Press, 1986

Ross, Al, *The Escort Carrier Gambier Bay*, Anatomy of the ship series, Naval Institute Press, 1993

Ugaki, Matome. *Fading Victory: The Diary of Admiral Matome Ugaki 1941-1945*. University of Pittsburgh Press, 1991.

Vego, Milan, *The Battle for Leyte, 1944*, Naval Institute Press, 2006

Wheeler, Gerald E., *Kinkaid of the Seventh Fleet*, Naval Institute Press, 1995

Kaigun Hôjutsu-shi [The History of Naval Gunnery]. Kaigun Hôjutsu-shi Kankôkai, 1975.

ARTICLES

Bates, Richard W., The Battle for Leyte Gulf, Preliminary Operations until Oct 17th, Strategic and Tactical Analysis, Vol. I, Naval War College, 1953.

_____, The Battle for Leyte Gulf, October 17th to October 20th Strategic and Tactical Analysis, Vol. II, Naval War College, 1955.

_____, The Battle for Leyte Gulf, October 20th to October 23rd Strategic and Tactical Analysis, Vol. III, Naval War College, 1957.

_____, The Battle for Leyte Gulf, October 24th to October 25th Strategic and Tactical Analysis, Vol. V, Naval War College, 1958.

Hagen, Robert C. We Asked For the Jap Fleet – and Got It, The Saturday Evening Post, May 26, 1945.

Hathaway A.T., The Story of the Heermann, The American Magazine, April 1945.

Hone, Trent, U.S. Navy Surface Battle Doctrine and Victory in the Pacific, Naval War College Review, Winter 2009, Vol. 62, No. 1.

Keil, A. H. The Response of Ships to Underwater Explosions, Department of the Navy, David Taylor Model Basin, 1961.

Montman, James H., Major, The Military Strategies of Spruance and Halsey, Air Command and Staff College, Air University, Maxwell AFB, 1947.

Ried, Warren D. The Response of Surface Ships to Underwater Explosions, Department Of Defense, 1996.

Robertson, D. C. Lt. Commander USN, Operational Analysis For The Battle of Leyte Gulf, Naval War College, Newport, Rhode Island, March 10, 1993.

Sprague, Clifton, They Had Us on the Ropes, American Magazine, April 1945.

Kaigun Hôjutsu-shi [The History of Naval Gunnery]. Kaigun Hôjutsu-shi Kankôkai, 1975.

SHIP PLANS

BuShips, Booklet of General Plans, CVE 90

BuShips, Booklet of General Plans, Destroyer No. 502

BuShips, Booklet of General Plans, Destroyer Escort No. 339

INDEX

A

Abercrombie, 6

Akishimo, 8, 261

Altman R.G., 52, 95

Anderson R., 50

Aoba, 127

Archer E.L., 52, 53, 96

Arkansas, 19

Atago, 173, 199, 267

B

Badger, 248, 253

Barbey Daniel, 4, 250

Bassett H.B., 58, 80, 81

Baxter J.A., 250, 265

Bennett P.A., 58, 59, 60

Beyer, 89, 123, 124, 160, 245

Bogan Gerald, 7, 273

Botzer W.H., 50

Brady, 151, 204

Brooks William, 21, 22, 54

Bunyon J.B.L., 129

Buzbee, 215

C

California, 19, 22

Capano Patsy, 52, 95

Carney Mick, 210

Chikuma, 8, 17, 62, 82, 90, 122, 127, 142, 154, 168, 171, 194, 195, 198, 199, 200, 212, 251, 254, 267

Chokai, 8, 17, 82, 85, 86, 87, 90, 154, 159, 168, 177, 193, 212, 251, 262, 267

Clifton Sprague, 6, 15, 21, 22, 47, 48, 49, 51, 64, 65, 66, 67, 68, 69, 70, 71, 88, 89, 90, 91, 92, 94, 96, 98, 100, 112, 114, 150, 151, 153, 156, 160, 164, 167, 187, 189, 190, 191, 202, 205, 209, 215, 216, 217, 221, 232, 239, 241, 243, 245, 250, 266, 273

Colorado, 19

Coolbaugh, 6, 246, 247, 250, 263

Copeland, 65, 66, 88, 127, 150, 265

Crocker R.L., 58, 62, 81, 98, 99, 103

Crockett W.D., 52, 53, 95, 96

D

Davison Ralph, 7, 273

Dennis, 6, 47, 67, 68, 90, 91, 114, 124, 125, 126, 147, 156, 157, 158, 159, 160, 191, 200, 201, 216, 217, 243, 244, 273

Dillard, 58, 59

E

Ekstrom, 197

Ellwood C.R., 58

Ens. Bankston, 199, 200

Ens. Brown, 103

Ens. Curtright, 103

Ens. Gallagher, 98, 99, 131

Ens. Loverin, 103

Ens. Robinson, 50

Ens. Walker, 199, 200

Ens. Wand, 198

Enterprise, 220, 273

Evans Ernest, 20, 60, 61, 75, 77, 148, 149, 167, 168, 178, 179, 180, 223, 252, 262, 265, 268, 278

Eversole, 6, 247, 249, 251

F

Fanshaw Bay, 6, 15, 16, 21, 22, 24, 33, 36, 41, 47, 48, 49, 50, 53, 59, 61, 65, 67, 68, 91, 92, 93, 94, 98, 108, 111, 113, 114, 129, 130, 138, 139, 142, 148, 151, 153, 154, 157, 160, 187, 189, 190, 194, 196, 202, 215, 216, 231, 232, 244, 250, 266, 273, 275

Farmer, 103, 104, 105

Fields, 55, 56

Fowler R.L., 51, 97, 155, 156, 176, 177, 196, 275

Franks, 6, 132, 134, 151, 152, 204, 205, 273

Fujinami, 8, 212, 261, 267

Fukudome Shigeru, 8, 265, 266, 277, 278

Fukuoka Tokujiro, 63, 83, 125, 162, 177

Fuso, 14, 58, 80, 99, 177

G

Gambier Bay, 6, 38, 47, 57, 58, 59, 60, 62, 80, 81, 94, 97, 98, 99, 107, 108, 130, 132, 133, 138, 139, 140, 142, 143, 144, 145, 146, 148, 149, 151, 152, 153, 155, 156, 158, 159, 160, 162, 167, 169, 170, 180, 182, 191, 196, 249, 251, 264, 265, 268, 274, 275

Garrison Paul, 196

Gore J.H., 56

Green E. J., 52

Gringeri, 215

H

Hagen R., 75, 76, 148, 149, 150, 179, 180, 214, 215, 252, 265, 279

Haggard, 6, 71, 100, 132, 134, 151, 204, 274

Haguro, 8, 12, 17, 18, 23, 42, 62, 74, 82, 84, 85, 110, 121, 127, 128, 129, 130, 142, 144, 154, 182, 193, 194, 195, 213, 214, 229, 259, 267, 276

Hailey, 6, 132, 134, 151, 152, 204, 274

Hale, 247, 250

Halsey William F., 2, 4, 5, 6, 7, 14, 19, 22, 71, 92, 105, 106, 163, 164, 206, 207, 208, 209, 210, 211, 212, 217, 254, 269, 270, 271

Hamakaze, 8

Hamanami, 8, 255, 260, 261

Hamman J.A., 182

Hammett W.E., 182

Hansen, 67, 90, 124, 158, 244

Harris, 71, 100, 134, 151, 204

Haruna, 8, 12, 17, 18, 20, 23, 24, 49, 53, 61, 62, 67, 78, 79, 80, 87, 93, 104, 107, 108, 110, 111, 115, 116, 118, 119, 120, 121, 127, 130, 138, 139, 147, 151, 152, 153, 166, 167, 171, 175, 176, 203, 228, 229, 257, 258, 267, 268, 276

Hathaway, 65, 88, 121, 125, 173, 174, 175, 216, 241, 243, 279

Hayakawa Mikio, 255, 260

Hayashimo, 8, 261, 267

Hazelwood, 6, 263

Heermann, 6, 47, 65, 88, 89, 115, 120, 121, 122, 125, 126, 127, 128, 138, 144, 147, 148, 149, 150, 151, 153, 159, 169, 172, 173, 174, 175, 178, 203, 216, 234, 241, 242, 243, 244, 245, 268, 274

Himelright, 215

Hoel, 6, 47, 64, 67, 73, 74, 79, 83, 84, 85, 86, 88, 115, 116, 117, 118, 120, 121, 125, 156, 159, 161, 162, 168, 174, 177, 178, 203, 251, 264, 265, 268, 274

Hunting, 58, 99

Huxtable E.J., 57, 58, 59, 80, 81, 196, 275

I

I-26, 99, 131, 133

Iowa, 19, 49, 248, 253, 274

Isokaze, 8

J

Jensen Hans, 20, 21

John C. Butler, 6, 47, 50, 69, 90, 91, 114, 125, 147, 156, 157, 158, 159, 160, 201, 202, 217, 243, 244, 245

Johnston, 6, 27, 33, 41, 47, 60, 61, 62, 63, 64, 65, 66, 73, 74, 75, 76, 78, 79, 80, 82, 83, 85, 88, 120, 130, 144, 148, 149, 150, 168, 174, 177, 178, 179, 180, 181, 186, 187, 188, 214, 215, 252, 265, 268, 274, 277

Jones B, 254

Jones B., 253

Jones R. M., 56, 253, 254, 275

K

Kadashan Bay, 6, 21, 274, 275

Kajiwara, 63, 82, 87, 124, 161, 177, 214, 230, 231, 260, 261

Kalinin Bay, 6, 25, 32, 33, 47, 50, 51, 52, 53, 87, 92, 93, 94, 95, 96, 107, 108, 109, 110, 111, 130, 138, 139, 140, 142, 145, 146, 147, 148, 154, 155, 157, 158, 159, 160, 180, 181, 182, 183, 184, 185, 186, 187, 188, 194, 216, 231, 232, 235, 236, 237, 250, 266, 268, 274, 275

Kash, 56

Keighley, 52, 94, 95, 275

King, 4, 59, 270

Kinkaid, Thomas, 3, 4, 5, 14, 15, 70, 71, 105, 106, 114, 135, 152, 163, 164, 206, 207, 208, 209, 211, 218, 219, 221, 223, 245, 246, 247, 250, 270, 273, 279

Kintberger, 64, 83, 84, 116, 118, 168, 251, 264

Kishinami, 8, 63, 83, 125, 162, 177, 276

Kitkun Bay, 6, 31, 33, 36, 41, 47, 50, 51, 65, 69, 90, 94, 97, 107, 108, 142, 155, 176, 177, 191, 196, 216, 232, 237, 238, 239, 266, 274, 275

Kiyoshimo, 8

Kobe Yuji, 11, 24, 28, 30, 60, 79, 86, 119, 161, 169, 171, 213, 224, 225, 256, 257

Kongo, 8, 12, 17, 18, 20, 21, 23, 24, 25, 49, 53, 61, 64, 67, 76, 84, 85, 86, 87, 94, 95, 104, 120, 126, 130, 138, 139, 140, 142, 153, 169, 171, 172, 173, 174, 197, 202, 203, 205, 213, 227, 251, 257, 258, 267, 268, 276

Koyanagi Tomji, 20, 166, 167, 223, 256, 262, 268, 277, 278

Koyanagi, Tomiji, 277

Kumano, 8, 17, 61, 62, 82, 86, 119, 212, 230, 259, 267

Kurita Takeo, v, 1, 2, 7, 10, 11, 13, 14, 16, 17, 19, 20, 23, 27, 30, 42, 43, 60, 73, 74, 75, 86, 101, 130, 138, 166, 167, 168, 212, 220, 221, 222, 223, 224, 248, 249, 255, 261, 262, 268, 269, 271, 277

L

Le Ray Wilson, 6

Lee Willis, 16, 105, 206, 207, 208, 221, 222, 248, 269

Lehman D.G., 20

Lexington, 16, 274, 275

Lischer J.F., 58, 59, 196

Lodhole R.P., 103, 104, 105

Louisville, 105, 274

Lt Henry, 197

Lt. (jg) Allen, 94

Lt. (jg) Calan, 21

Lt. (jg) Evans, 94

Lt. (jg) Nathan, 198

Lt. (jg) Yeaman, 198

Lt. Bitting, 198

Lt. Fields, 21

Lt. Forsythe, 103

Lt. Henry, 197, 198

Lt. Jackson, 99

Lt. Johnston, 129

Lt. MacBride, 21

Lt. Marke, 103

Lt. R. Anderson, 50

Lt. Van Brunt, 21, 54

Lt. W. H. Botzer, 50

M

MacArthur Douglas, 4, 222, 246

MacBride, 55

Maino C.K., 182

Manila Bay, 6, 274, 276

Marcus Island, 6, 54, 197, 199, 200, 274, 275

Maya, 173, 267

Mayuzumi Haruo, 122, 142, 153, 194, 195, 230

McCain John, 6, 206

McCord, 6

McGraw J.D., 58, 99

McKenna, 53, 96, 97, 157, 181, 216, 233, 234, 241

Merchant J.E., 52, 95

Miller, 253, 254, 274

Mitscher Marc, 3, 6, 16, 217

Mogami, 14, 21, 49, 59, 80, 81, 99, 152, 176, 196, 197

Morishita Nobuei, 10, 212, 213, 219, 223, 224, 255

Musashi, 1, 13, 221, 267, 271, 276

Myoko, 2, 267, 276

N

Nachi, 49, 94, 95, 109, 154, 190, 191, 202, 238

Naganami, 8

Nagato, 7, 11, 12, 13, 17, 18, 23, 24, 28, 29, 30, 31, 33, 41, 42, 45, 49, 56, 58, 60, 79, 83, 86, 87, 94, 95, 99, 104, 105, 119, 120, 138, 139, 161, 167, 169, 171, 213, 221, 224, 225, 226, 227, 256, 257, 267, 268, 276

Nashville, 135

Natoma Bay, 6, 70, 100, 134, 152, 205, 217, 218, 264, 274, 276

Nevada, 19

New Jersey, 2, 6, 16, 19, 164, 206, 209, 217, 248, 254, 274

New Mexico, 19

Niemann W.E., 103, 104

Nimitz Chester, 4, 164, 207, 208, 209, 210, 212, 268, 269, 270, 271, 278

Nishimura Shoji, 2, 7, 10, 13, 14, 27, 222

North Carolina, 19

Noshiro, 8, 12, 17, 18, 23, 42, 63, 82, 83, 87, 90, 124, 125, 161, 162, 177, 203, 214, 230, 231, 255, 260, 261, 267, 276

Nowaki, 8, 200, 212, 254, 267

O

O'Gorek J., 215

Oberrender, 6

Okinami, 8, 230, 259, 268

Oldendorf Jesse, 5, 14, 105, 135, 163, 211, 246, 273

Ommaney Bay, 6, 56, 105, 274, 276

Onishi Takijiro, 8, 101, 265, 266

Osterkorn, 58, 59

Otani, Tonosuke, 166, 277

Owens, 253, 254

Ozawa Jisaburo, 1, 3, 7, 12, 13, 14, 16, 166

P

Pace, 69, 90, 125, 245

PC-1119, 251

PC-623, 251, 265

Pennsylvania, 15, 19

Perrell Jr. J.J., 52, 95

Petrof Bay, 6, 101, 102, 103, 104, 105, 131, 206, 246, 247, 249, 250, 263, 274, 276

Phillips, 58

Picking, 247, 250

Powell, 215

Princeton, 266, 270

R

Ranger, 143

Raymond, 6, 47, 52, 55, 88, 89, 90, 115, 123, 124, 127, 160, 161, 192, 200, 243, 244, 245, 274

Reynolds, 134

Richard M. Rowell, 6, 246, 247

Richard S. Bull, 6, 246, 247, 249, 251

Richard W. Suesens, 6

Riley J.T., 182

Robinson, 50

Roby R.W., 58, 59

Rodgers R.S., 50, 275

Rowell, 211, 247, 263

S

Samuel B. Roberts, 6, 25, 31, 33, 36, 45, 47, 64, 65, 66, 88, 89, 124, 127, 128, 130, 150, 174, 177, 202, 203, 251, 252, 264, 265, 268

Sangamon, 6, 15, 70, 101, 133, 164, 206, 211, 246, 249, 263, 274, 275

Santee, 6, 101, 102, 105, 131, 132, 133, 135, 164, 211, 247, 249, 266, 274, 275

Savo, 6, 196, 197, 199, 274, 275

Sawyer E.B., 103, 104, 105

Schwarzwalder A E, 103, 104

Seitz E.W., 58

Sherman Frederick, 7, 273

Shigenaga, 24, 61, 79, 87, 107, 119, 130, 151, 175, 176, 203, 228, 229, 258

Shima Kiyohide, 2, 7, 10, 14, 222

Shimakaze, 8

Shimazaki, 24, 61, 85, 86, 139, 171, 202, 213, 227, 228, 257

Shroyer W.C., 58, 81, 196

Slone W.J., 93, 94

Smith G.N., 52, 53, 96, 276

Soter K.M., 21

South Dakota, 19

Sproston, 247, 250

St. Lo, 6, 21, 47, 52, 53, 54, 55, 56, 92, 94, 96, 97, 108, 138, 139, 142, 154, 156, 157, 158, 159, 160, 181, 182, 186, 190, 216, 231, 232, 233, 234, 235, 240, 241, 243, 244, 245, 249, 275

Stephan, 152, 204

Stump Felix, 6, 15, 70, 71, 100, 105, 130, 134, 151, 152, 205, 217, 218, 219, 246, 264, 273

Sugiura, 62, 82, 84, 110, 121, 128, 129, 144, 193, 213, 214, 229, 259

Sullivan C.J., 25, 26, 29, 32, 35, 36, 39, 99, 240

Suwannee, 6, 133, 134, 135, 136, 164, 211, 246, 247, 262, 263, 266, 275

Suzuya, 8, 17, 18, 23, 61, 62, 63, 82, 86, 214, 229, 230, 259, 267, 276

T

Takao, 267

Tennessee, 19

Teraoka Masao, 62, 63, 82, 229, 230

Terutsuki, 158, 179, 190

Texas, 19

Thomas Sprague, 5, 15, 70, 71, 101, 105, 133, 152, 164, 206, 211, 219, 246, 247, 249, 250, 263, 273

Thomas W.D., 3, 4, 5, 15, 70, 71, 88, 91, 101, 105, 152, 164, 249, 263, 273

Thompson G.D., 93, 215

Tone, 8, 12, 17, 18, 23, 49, 62, 82, 86, 94, 95, 96, 99, 109, 121, 122, 127, 129, 142, 143, 144, 146, 150, 153, 154, 173, 182, 190, 192, 193, 194, 195, 196, 197, 198, 230, 238, 243, 267, 276

Toyoda Soemu, 277

Tracy R.F., 103, 104

Trathen, 6, 133, 263

U

Ugaki Matome, 13, 20, 27, 30, 43, 74, 116, 169, 171, 279

Urakaze,, 8

V

Vieweg W.V.R., 57, 97, 98, 130, 131, 132, 169, 170, 276

Vincennes, 253, 275

W

Waldrop L.E., 56, 181, 182

Walter C. Wann, 6

Wasatch, 5, 14, 71, 105, 135, 163, 211, 245, 250, 275

Weatherholt R.E., 98

West Virginia, 105

White Plains, 6, 24, 25, 28, 29, 31, 32, 33, 34, 35, 36, 37, 38, 39, 40, 41, 42, 43, 45, 47, 48, 49, 53, 58, 65, 66, 89, 92, 93, 94, 98, 99, 100, 107, 108, 110, 114, 154, 157, 191, 192, 193, 194, 195, 216, 235, 240, 242, 243, 266, 268, 275

Whiting Maynard, 253

Whitney J.P., 51, 97, 155

Wilkinson Theodore, 4

Williamson, 51, 94, 107, 109

Y

Yahagi, 8, 12, 17, 18, 23, 42, 64, 87, 88, 116, 119, 120, 150, 154, 158, 178, 179, 181, 182, 186, 187, 190, 214, 220, 266, 267, 276

Yamato, ix, 2, 5, 7, 10, 11, 12, 13, 14, 16, 17, 18, 19, 20, 23, 24, 25, 26, 27, 28, 29, 30, 31, 33, 34, 36, 38, 41, 42, 43, 44, 49, 50, 60, 62, 63, 64, 73, 74, 75, 76, 77, 79, 83, 84, 85, 86, 87, 104, 107, 115, 116, 117, 119, 120, 121, 129, 138, 139, 140, 142, 144, 153, 161, 162, 166,

167, 168, 169, 171, 172, 175, 177, 194, 202, 203, 212, 213, 214, 219, 220, 221, 222, 223, 224, 225, 227, 229, 231, 248, 249, 251, 255, 256, 257, 261, 262, 266, 267, 268, 271, 276

Yoshimura Masatake, 64, 87, 88, 120, 150, 178, 214

Yukikaze, 8

Z

Zeitvogel J.R., 52, 53

CPSIA information can be obtained
at www.ICGtesting.com
Printed in the USA
LVHW061023010419
612527LV00003B/4/P

9 781608 880461